The Bedside
Guardian 2017

The Bedside
Guardian 2017

EDITED BY GARY YOUNGE

guardianbooks

Published by Guardian Books 2017

2 4 6 8 10 9 7 5 3 1

Copyright © Guardian News and Media Ltd 2017

First published in Great Britain in 2017 by
Guardian Books
Kings Place, 90 York Way
London N1 9GU

www.guardianbooks.co.uk

A CIP catalogue record for this book is available from the British Library

ISBN 978-1783-56125-4

Cover design by Two Associates
Typeset by seagulls.net

Printed and bound in Great Britain by
CPI Group (UK) Ltd, Croydon CR0 4YY

Contents

SPRING

SUMMER

Foreword

SADIQ KHAN

For 66 years, the *Guardian* has published this annual compendium of its journalism.

Over this period, it has covered the changing attitudes, fashions and personalities of Britain, as well as the defining moments and events in modern British history that changed our country for ever. The end of the British empire. The establishment of the NHS. The Suez Canal crisis. The rise of Thatcherism. The miners' strike. The first ever three-term Labour government. The Iraq war. And the global financial crash.

It's rare that you can say this in the present tense, but we can be certain that the period we are living through now will come to be seen as another one of these defining moments in our history. The result of the EU referendum has changed everything. The future direction of British politics is becoming ever more unpredictable. And we are seeing populism on the rise around the world. There is a palpable sense that we are in an unprecedented state of flux as uncertainty rules.

With Brexit, the one thing we can say for sure at this stage is that we are set for massive change. Although the ship has left the harbour, the nature of the waters during the journey ahead, and the final destination, are far from certain. It is during these moments – with decisions being taken that could have a profound impact on the future direction for decades to come – that journalism and national debate are at their most significant.

This value of the fourth estate has been exemplified by the quality of journalism in the *Guardian*. Holding those in power to account. Explaining to the public the potential ramifications of different courses of action. And continually informing and inspiring the national debate, while using humour to highlight hypocrisy, incompetence and foolishness.

But, as well as raising questions about our direction and future place in the world, the result of the EU referendum has uncovered deeper issues that have remained hidden under the surface of our society for some time.

Larry Elliott's contribution to this book looks at the rise of populism, and Polly Toynbee writes about how Brexit exposed a divide between younger and older generations. Both these pieces point to a wider fact that too many people feel left behind or sidelined by the rapid economic and technological change they have experienced in recent decades.

Significant numbers of British people have missed out on the fruits of globalisation. At the same time, the lack of social integration in many parts of the country – including London – means that it has become harder for people from different backgrounds truly to know and understand one another – fuelling the politics of division. This is something we know from recent history not only to be dangerous, but it also has the capacity to spiral quickly in the wrong direction if left to fester.

One of the most crucial tasks for us now is to take proactive steps to build fairer, stronger and more integrated cities and communities, and to ensure that everyone benefits from globalisation. This will be the defining challenge ahead – not only in the short term, but for the rest of this century. That's why it's vital that, while so many minds in Westminster are preoccupied with Brexit, we don't forget about the myriad of economic and social issues that contributed to millions of people voting for Brexit in the first place.

As you will see from the wide mix of articles in this book – as well as the journalism you experience every day – the *Guardian* is rising to the occasion, unbound by vested interests and as determined as ever to be a beacon for liberal, open and social democratic values.

In London, I'm focusing on creating a fairer, safer and healthier city – one where everyone has the opportunity to reach their full potential. As part of this work, I am ensuring more genuinely affordable houses for Londoners get built; tackling air pollution, which has become a true public health emergency; ensuring young people have the skills they need for the jobs of tomorrow; making our transport network greener and more affordable; increasing access to culture; fighting for equality; and trying to build more socially integrated communities. It's great to have the *Guardian* alongside as a champion for creating a fairer, greener and healthier capital city – one that the whole country can be inspired by, benefit from and look to with pride.

Unsurprisingly, another recurring theme throughout this book is Donald Trump and the rise of a new kind of nationalist politics on the other side of the Atlantic. Over the past year, I've had more than my fair share of run-ins with the new president. So, tempting as it may be, I think I'll avoid fuelling the flames here and let the words of the excellent *Guardian* contributors speak for themselves!

Finally, this book, quite rightly, is also punctuated with reminders of some of our darkest times over the past year – with articles about the terrorist attacks in London and Manchester as well as the horrific Grenfell Tower fire. As the mayor of London, these pieces are particularly poignant for me. We are all still mourning the victims, thinking of their families and working to do everything possible to prevent similar events from happening again. But whenever I talk about the great sorrow and anger we still feel at the unnecessary loss of innocent life, it is important to highlight the great resolve and kindness that has been shown by Londoners and people right across the country – and how we remain optimistic about our future.

In our response to these tragedies, we have seen people at their best. Whether it's the heroism of the emergency services running towards danger, the bystanders who fought off the terrorists or the generosity of Londoners who reached out to help the Grenfell Tower residents, there are countless examples that give us hope that we can stay united, navigate these uncertain times and work together to meet the major challenges ahead.

September 2017

Introduction

GARY YOUNGE

At 1.24am on 9 November 2016, the *Guardian* liveblog reported that pundits were predicting a tipping point in the US election: Donald Trump was vulnerable in Florida, which was leaning positively towards Hillary Clinton. Seven months later, just 10 minutes before the polls closed in Britain, our liveblog quoted Piers Morgan predicting a 90 100 Conservative majority while the deputy political editor of the *Sun* heard rumours that 'Tories could be looking at 400 seats'.

Trump won Florida, and the nation; the Conservatives lost their majority, taking just 318 seats. It's been that kind of year. And the *Bedside Guardian* (which runs from October to October) set out to capture it.

As a news organisation we are driven by events. It's what we do; it's why we're here. And yet somehow the scale and pace of them have at times this year seemed overwhelming. Trump's election and the protests that came with it; the UK election and the instability that followed; terror attacks one after another; hurricanes one after another; the tragedy of Grenfell; neo-Nazis marching; credible threats of nuclear war; and throughout it all, Britain marching, fully conscious, but somehow neither fully aware nor remotely prepared, towards Brexit.

To those head-spinning happenings one must add the perennial challenge of editing this collection – immersing oneself in the wonderful work of colleagues only to then emerge with a fraction of what they have produced. Online we have unlimited space: print demands more discipline. And where there is discipline there will be casualties. Brilliant writers and brilliant writing fall foul to the constraints of space, theme and range. (Why slash a well-crafted piece in half so it can fit into a book when it has a perfectly fine life online in its full, original form? How many pieces on Trump is it reasonable to subject a reader to, particularly at Christmas?) There's not a single editor, in any given year, who hasn't surveyed the contents page as they go through the proofs with a twinge of regret for a piece or person not included.

It is the matching of those two challenges, the perennial pruning and a feverish news agenda, that has made this year's *Bedside* what it is: the best writing we produce – be it commentary, reportage, interviews, obituaries, reviews or investigations – framed (though not wholly determined) by the narrative of the year's main events.

In a year that produced both Donald Trump and a snap UK election with a surprise result, this particular *Bedside Guardian* is both more transatlantic and less global than usual and perhaps more driven by the news agenda than in other years. That doesn't compromise the quality of what you'll read. But it has informed the mix.

These are extraordinary times. Both volatile and replete with crises, they pose a particular professional challenge to journalism, which has proven itself far more effective when descriptive than predictive. Daniel Taylor's ground-breaking investigation into sexual abuse in football, Melissa Denes' in-depth look inside rape trials or Ian Cobain's portrait of the struggling education system in his native borough of Knowsley illustrate what journalism can do when it sets itself the task of holding up a mirror so we can see who or what we've become and why.

There have been times, though, when it has felt like a distorting fairground mirror, reflecting a world we don't fully recognise. The rise of populism, the erosion of traditional electoral allegiances, the aftershocks of terror, war, austerity and neoliberal globalisation engender considerable instability. I chose the liveblog for the election nights in both the US and the UK because with both you see the unravelling of certainties in real time. Read Larry Elliott or Naomi Klein on the economic roots of populism or John Harris on Corbyn and you get a sense of where this is all coming from and why. Read Polly Toynbee and Amelia Gentleman on Grenfell, Aditya Chakrabortty on those 'just about managing' in Pontypool or Philip Oltermann travelling down the Elbe talking to voters either side of the old East/West German divide and one gets a sense of how this moment is lived by many in the west.

And yet life goes on. This is the year Alys Fowler came out, Lindy West came off the internet, Steven Thrasher turned 40, Deborah Orr took her first anti-depressant and Tim Dowling moved house. Despite the dark times – or maybe even thanks to them – Marina Hyde and Jonathan Crace are still funny while the likes of Owen Jones and George Monbiot remain engaged and enthused and, occasionally, enraged.

It is this mix – of light and shade, analysis and reporting, personal and political – that makes the *Guardian* such a delightful organisation to write for. It is the same mix that, I hope, makes this an enjoyable book to read.

Acknowledgements

During a visit to NASA in 1962, the US President, John F. Kennedy, met a janitor carrying a broom. 'Hi, I'm Jack Kennedy,' the president said. 'What are you doing?'

'Well, Mr President,' the janitor replied. 'I'm helping put a man on the moon.'

In that spirit, the first people I want to acknowledge here are those generally paid the least, whose primary task is not journalism, but without whom *Guardian* journalism would not be possible: the administrative staff, cleaners and canteen workers who are key to our functioning. Behind the scenes, journalistically, are the sub-editors, desk editors, technicians, community teams, researchers and data teams. Ideas often start with them, are informed by them or pass through through their hands. The liveblog in particular, is an impressive collective effort stewarded by some of the keenest minds and fastest writers we have, to which many contribute.

With this book specifically I would like to thank Jonathan Baker for the design, Sophie Lazar for copy-editing, Lorraine Jerram for proofreading and Andy at MFE for the index. I am grateful to Claire Armitstead, for her generosity in passing on her wisdom from editing the collection last year. Fiona Shields, the picture editor, could not have been kinder or more professional when I approached her at the 11th hour asking the unreasonable if not the impossible. But most of all I would have been lost without the firm guiding hand of Lindsay Davies. Having ushered the book through the process many times it is her institutional memory and publishing nous that kept the show on the road and made sure it was a show worth seeing.

Autumn

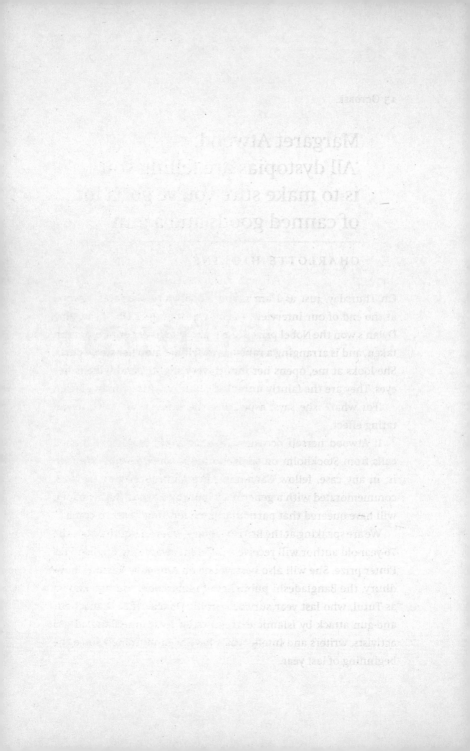

Margaret Atwood: 'All dystopias are telling you is to make sure you've got a lot of canned goods and a gun'

CHARLOTTE HIGGINS

On Thursday, just as I am saying goodbye to Margaret Atwood at the end of our interview, I get a text message. 'Oh,' I say. 'Bob Dylan's won the Nobel prize.' She is about to have her photograph taken, and is arranging a rakish grey felt hat atop her steely curls. She looks at me, opens her mouth very slightly, and widens her eyes. They are the faintly unrealistic blue of a Patagonian glacier.

'For what?' she says, aspirating the word 'what' with devastating effect.

If Atwood herself occasionally checks her phone for missed calls from Stockholm on such mornings, she does not admit to it; in any case, fellow Canadian Alice Munro's victory in 2013, commemorated with a generous tribute by Atwood in this paper, will have queered that particular pitch for some years to come.

We are speaking at the British Library, where, later that day, the 76-year-old author will receive a different award: the English PEN Pinter prize. She will also bestow one on Ahmedur Rashid Chowdhury, the Bangladeshi publisher of remarkable courage known as Tutul, who last year survived, in his Dhaka office, a machete-and-gun attack by Islamic extremists. At least nine Bangladeshi activists, writers and intellectuals have been murdered since the beginning of last year.

Atwood's PEN Pinter prize lecture, titled *An Improvisation on the Theme of Rights*, which she also delivered on Thursday, ends with a reflection on the dystopias of her fiction: that of *The Handmaid's Tale* (1985) and of her recent *MaddAddam* trilogy. The first describes an America transformed into a theocracy that treats women as mere childbearing chattels – after a state of emergency is declared following an assassination. ('They blamed it on the Islamic fanatics at the time', the novel's narrator explains.) The second deals with a world in which the planet's resources are severely depleted. A situation, she explained in the lecture, that leads to civil chaos. 'Then ... warlords and demagogues take over, some people forget that all people are people, enemies are created, vilified and dehumanised, minorities are persecuted, and human rights as such are shoved to the wall.' Not so much a distant and frightening future, she said, as 'the cusp of where we are living right now'.

Readers of *The Handmaid's Tale* have indeed found elements of its story looming alarmingly close in recent weeks. See Donald Trump's remarks about women; see the virulently anti-choice Republican vice-presidential candidate Mike Pence. See, even, Trump's Republican detractors, such as Mitt Romney, decrying his remarks on groping because they 'demean our wives and daughters'. Are we in Gilead – the America of *The Handmaid's Tale*? 'Close, yes. For sure.' And everything in it, she says, was based on things that had actually happened. 'Including everyone tugging on a rope during hangings so that no one is guilty: that's from English history,' she says. 'Ceaușescu in Romania forcing women to have children – quotas for childbirth. The fact that, in the United States, teaching a slave to read was against the law. And then sumptuary laws – who can wear what. Who can cover up what, who has to, and can, cover up what part of which bodies – that's been a part of human culture for a very long time.'

She mentions an article that famously accurate US psephologist Nate Silver published on his website, fivethirtyeight.com. (His one famous failure was in not predicting Trump's victory in the Republican primaries.) Silver's article includes a pair of maps. One shows how the US would look if only men voted: almost entirely red. The other shows how the US would look if only women voted: almost entirely blue. 'It spawned a hashtag', says Atwood (who is a frequent poster on Twitter), 'called #Repealthe19th. The 19th Amendment is what gave women the vote. So there are Trump supporters who want to take the vote away from women. *The Handmaid's Tale*, unfolding in front of your very eyes.' (In fact, the *Washington Post* pointed out that #Repealthe19th spiked as a social media topic not only through the enthusiasm of Trump supporters, but through its being heartily condemned by his detractors; but still, there it was as a notion, red and bleeding and out there.)

Her whistle-stop tour through feminism goes like this: 'First wave, the vote. Second wave, the image. Now it's about violence and rape and death: we've got down to the nitty-gritty.' Earlier this month, when she spoke at the Southbank literature festival in London, she talked about 'the most amazingly vicious online abuse' of women. 'What century are we in?' she asked. 'Apparently, the 12th.'

When *The Handmaid's Tale* was published, she says, the novel was reviewed by British critics as an enjoyable fantasy, and by the Canadians with a certain anxiety ('Could it happen here?'). In America, though, there was a sense of: 'How long have we got?' She sighs. 'Apparently, not as long as I thought ... With any cultural change there is a push and a pushback. Trump has brought out a huge pushback that was originally against immigrants. Now it has shifted to being very misogynistic, partly because of Hillary Clinton. You have not seen anything like this since the 17th-century witch-hunts, quite frankly.'

Can you understand the appeal of Trump, I ask? 'He brings out the temper tantrum-throwing wilful brat in all of us. "Why can't I do what I want? Why can't I have what I want? Those other people are stopping me. Those other people have a bigger lollipop than I do, I'm going to take their lollipop away from them." But on the other hand, he couples that with the most amazing whining.' She mentions the complaint by Trump that his microphone malfunctioned during the first televised presidential debate. ('Rubbish.')

'I tell you this,' she continues. 'Hillary Clinton is a better man than Trump. She has more connection to the traditional male virtues. She has comported herself in a much more manly fashion. Ask any real alpha males that you know and they'll say of Trump, "This is the guy we didn't like at school because he was a bully, but as soon as anyone pushed back at him he started to whine."'

What does she think, then, of Clinton's campaign? 'Well, it's more of a campaign. Trump has taken about 10 different positions on everything, so there is no way of knowing what he really thinks. You actually just don't know. He will adopt a position depending on what reaction is mirrored back to him. Basically, it's very close to being a manifestation of a mob: burn them at the stake, screaming and yelling.'

Like the Salem witch trials, then? She proceeds to talk about them: Atwood likes to take a long historical sweep. Her heroes of this tragic episode, dramatised by Arthur Miller in *The Crucible*, are Rebecca Nurse, who refused to admit that she was a witch and declined to accuse others, meaning she was hanged; and Giles Corey, who refused to plead at his trial, meaning that he was pressed – that is, crushed by heavy stones until his lungs collapsed and he died. By sacrificing himself thus, and not allowing his case to be tried, his family inherited his property, which otherwise would have been confiscated.

However, she says, after a fairly long disquisition on the legal history of 17th-century Massachusetts, this is not at all what the Trump situation is like. 'Salem was much more dignified ... Salem at least had rules for the trials.' She hunts around for a better comparison. It's like *Night of the Hunter*, she says. 'Robert Mitchum. Directed by Charles Laughton. Just a great film. At the end they catch this guy who's been murdering women and has been trying to get hold of some children to kill them too. He is seen off by Lillian Gish playing an old lady in a rocking chair with a shotgun.' (A sudden vision arrives, unbidden, of Atwood in a rocking chair with a shotgun.) 'She peppers him with shot, he gets caught and put in jail and there's a mob outside who want to lynch him. So the very same Christian, righteous people who have played the virtuous townspeople are now screaming for his blood. This is what it's like. Those mob scenes at Trump rallies: burn her, lock her up, kill her. They think they are at the wrestling, but let those people out, and you have a lynch mob.'

We turn to the scenarios she sketched in the *MaddAddam* trilogy: a world of internet insecurity, pig-human hybrids, environmental devastation, oil fetishists and complete corporate takeover of states. Do dystopian novels, I wonder, actually do anything? Can they change behaviour? They are, she says, more like weather vanes than guides on averting disaster. 'All dystopian novels are telling you to do is make sure you've got a lot of canned goods and a gun.' Do you have canned goods and a gun in Toronto? 'I'm too freaking old. I'm probably not going to make it through the zombie apocalypse anyway.'

The literary news, as we speak, has been recently all about the 'unmasking' by an Italian investigative journalist of the real identity of Elena Ferrante, the pseudonymous author of the hugely popular Neapolitan novels. 'She probably went too far in putting out a fake autobiography. Which is like an invitation: expose me,' says Atwood. (She is referring to *Frantumaglia*, which is about to be published in English – not an autobiography as such, but a collection of letters, essays, interviews and the like.) 'But she's not committed a crime. Nor do I feel that she was a bad person to write under a pseudonym. She did what she wanted to do. It worked spectacularly well, and then there are the books. People will read them a bit differently, that's inevitable. But it doesn't make them bad books.'

Atwood herself published pseudonymously a bit, when she was young – in the student magazine, to fill the pages. And she wrote a comic strip under another name in the 1970s. Then there was a skittish review of one of her own books she wrote once, under the not-very-veiled byline of Margarets Atwood, which referred to certain anagrammatic figures: ethnologist Gwaemot R Dratora, the architect Wode M Gratataro, and the profile-writer Greta Warmodota. Invisibility is not her thing: especially when she, and fellow Canadian writers, worked so hard in the 1970s to improve their own visibility. 'I don't think I'm entitled to whinge too much, because it's my fault. I used to go on the Greyhound bus with copies of my books in a cardboard box, and give readings in school gymnasiums. I'd sell my own books and collect the money, put it in a brown paper envelope and take it back to the publisher.' She looks at me with wide eyes. 'What sort of a wimp are you? Have you never tramped through the snow with your books in a cardboard box – on a sled?'

The latest book that she is, metaphorically at least, carrying around with her on a sled is neither dystopian nor utopian, but a story based on *The Tempest*, called *Hag-Seed* – part of a series of Shakespearean reworkings commissioned from writers including Jeanette Winterson and Anne Tyler. In her deft story, Prospero is a director called Felix, deposed from his position as artistic director of an important theatre. Bent on revenge, he stages a version of *The Tempest* in a prison, and plots his payback. I worry, though, that Prospero is a part often taken on by actors reaching the end of their careers. I hope there's to be no talk of Atwood's abjuring magic, or any nonsense like that. No, she tells me. No need to fear. 'The last part actors usually take is Lear. That really makes people cry.'

This is very Atwood: nearly everything she says is delivered precisely, and lightly iced with irony, whether she's being immensely warm, or plunging her dagger into some unfortunate victim.

8 NOVEMBER

Theresa struggles to take back control – from her own Maybot

JOHN CRACE

About halfway through a rather soporific appearance before the public administration and constitutional affairs select committee, the former head of the civil service, Gus O'Donnell, thought it worth reminding everyone that civil servants were more like humans than robots. Which could be just as well, as the prime minister is increasingly acting like someone who is more robot than human. Sometime between July, when she looked like the safest pair of hands amid a sea of idiots, and now, Theresa May's brain appears to have been hacked. Ask her a sensible question and you're now guaranteed a senseless answer.

'Have you made any plans for a Brexit transitional deal?' inquired a Sky News reporter, at the end of the prime minister's near-pointless jolly to India.

Whirr. Clunk. Clang. The Maybot's eyes rotated into life. 'I'm focusing on delivering article 50,' she replied, unable to prevent herself from answering an entirely different question.

'Will you be able to deliver on the £350m that was promised to the NHS?' the reporter persevered.

'When the people. Whirr. Voted in the referendum. Clunk. They wanted. Clang. A number of different things,' said the Maybot, struggling with her circuit board.

'Was the referendum dishonest ... ?'

Inside the Maybot, the last shards of the real Theresa were fighting to get out. She was not a number. Especially not 350 million. She was a person in her own right. She did still have a mind of her own. Then the malware took over again.

'Whirr. The referendum took. Clunk. Place. I'm focusing ...' She wasn't. She really wasn't.

'You weren't part of the Vote Leave campaign, you weren't prime minister at the time of the referendum and you have no mandate,' observed the reporter sharply.

'I'm. Whirr. Determined ...'

'Stephen Phillips, the MP who resigned last week, said that the Conservative party is becoming more like Ukip. How do you feel about that?'

'I'm. Whirr. Determined,' the Maybot clunked.

'You're determined to be what ...?'

'I'm. Whirr. Determined. To be. Clunk. Determined to focus on the. Clang. Things that the British public determined ...'

At this point the Sky reporter cut his losses and left. There was no point in trying to deal with a severe Maybot malfunction.

With the Maybot temporarily on idle, Theresa frantically hammered at the control-alt-delete keys to crash herself, in a last-ditch attempt to return to her factory settings.

'Please ask me about my holiday in India,' she begged.

'Er, no,' said a BBC reporter. 'The Institute for Fiscal Studies is forecasting a £25bn slowdown. Is that a price worth paying for greater controls of immigration?'

'I'm. Whirr. Determined,' the Maybot laughed, thrilled to have survived the reboot. 'Brexit offers a. Clunk. World of opportunities. I'm determined to be here in India determinedly delivering. Clang. On a determined global Britain through some determined trade deals. Whirr ...'

'Is an economic slowdown a Brexit price worth paying?' the reporter repeated, generously giving the prime minister the benefit of the doubt that she had not heard the question properly first time round.

'Do you want to see my snaps?' the Maybot whirred. 'There's a great one of me in the hotel lobby with Geoffrey Boycott. Such a sweet man. I've always been a huge fan of his. Who is he again?'

'Thank you, prime minister ...'

'India is a lovely place. Whirr. And we've been determined to do some. Clunk. Good deals that are not worth the determined paper they are. Clang. Written on as nothing can be determined Clunk. Before we determine how determined we are to be in a determined customs union ...'

'What about the slowdown?'

'I'm determined to be. Whirr. Determined ...'

Theresa knew she was determined. But what about? Slowly it came back to her. Whirr. She was determined to take back control. And she would start by taking back control of her own brain. The Maybot laughed. Some hope.

8–9 NOVEMBER

US election:
A night to remember (I)

LIVEBLOG

22.52 Preliminary exit polling data is out and some of it rein-
forces the information we already had. If current polling
predictions hold true and turnout rates remain relatively
consistent, that could work in Clinton's favour.

We add this caveat: exit polling is notoriously inexact,
and should not be mistaken for actual results.

00.18 Florida results in the 2016 presidential race are starting
to come in. There continues to be solid news in the state
for Clinton.

00.24 Vigo County, Indiana, which has voted for the winner of
every presidential election since Eisenhower, has gone for
Trump. Is Vigo's streak ending? Or ...

00.44 Very hard to see how Trump lays a finger on Virginia based
on the exit polls.

00.45 A mariachi band called 'Sol Mixteco' just arrived outside
Trump Tower and started playing.

01.24 And we're almost at the tipping point already. Florida is
looking very vulnerable for Trump. A must-win for the
GOP, Florida is leaning positively towards Clinton.

01.51 According to Florida's board of elections, Trump is leading
by just over one percentage point. All eyes are on this state.

02.05 Donald Trump is ahead in Virginia – that is surprising,
and for Democrats a worrying sign. Polls had forecast
that Clinton would win the state by a comfortable five-
point margin.

03.01　It's still early in the night but it looks like Trump has over-performed against the polls.

03.07　Where's Michigan at? Not looking dire for Clinton, so far. She needs those 16 electoral votes.

03.31　Traders are reacting to the tightening presidential race in the US – racing to gold, while Asian shares plummet and the peso crashes against the dollar.

03.40　Donald Trump has won Ohio. That's a big win for him, where he led in the polls all along but where Democrats made much in the final weeks of a possible victory.

03.44　Hillary Clinton has won Virginia. That took a while.

03.46　Clinton has won Colorado.

03.53　Donald Trump has taken Florida's 29 electoral votes. That is a huge win for him. It means that Clinton is pushed back as tightly as possible against her needed wins in Michigan and Pennsylvania. She's got no other way now.

　　　　And it's just plainly a stunning win for Trump, in a state where he mostly lagged in the polls, had no campaign ground game to speak of, looked bad in early voting, etc. etc.

03.56　The fear at the Javits Center in New York, where Hillary Clinton is due to greet the results later tonight, is palpable. This was not how the night was supposed to go. Ten o'clock has come and gone with little good news for Clinton. Trump has won Ohio and Florida, he's up in Michigan, and in states like North Carolina where Clinton has enjoyed a small but steady lead, she's been fighting for her life. None of the polls predicted this. Until as recently as a few weeks ago, pundits were predicting she could win this election by historic margins, and even after FBI Director James Comey's recent flap, her margins looked solid, if modest.

04.11 The big picture right now is simple and clear: Hillary Clinton is in trouble. The states to focus on are Pennsylvania (20 electoral votes), Michigan (16) and Wisconsin (10). If Clinton loses either of the larger states, she's finished. She has a path to a 269–269 electoral tie if she loses Wisconsin – but she would have to win New Hampshire, which hasn't been called yet.

It's a very tight race.

04.16 North Carolina awards its 15 electoral votes to Trump. This is a difficult blow to team Clinton.

04.23 Canada's immigration website has crashed multiple times, according to news reports (it was very slow for this reporter).

04.30 Nigel Farage, the leader of Britain's anti-EU UK Independence party, is once again drawing links between the Trump campaign and Brexit.

05.06 Trump has scooped up Iowa's six electoral votes, as it looked he would. There aren't many electoral votes left to scoop.

05.08 A couple embraced outside the Javits Center in New York where Hillary Clinton is due to speak later. The woman wiped a tear from her face and the man stroked her hair.

05.24 Hillary Clinton has won Nevada, and its six electoral votes. There was a strong Hispanic turnout in early voting in the state, enough to sustain her.

05.27 The Republicans will solidly hold onto the House of Representatives.

05.46 The Huffington Post will no longer sign off all articles about Donald Trump with a reminder to readers of his flaws. His potential victory tonight calls for a 'clean slate', according to Ryan Grim, the site's Washington bureau chief.

06.03 Trump is turning in strong numbers across Pennsylvania, compared with Mitt Romney four years ago.

06.13   Donald Trump may win the White House in the electoral college but lose the popular vote.

06.39   Donald Trump has won Pennsylvania and its 20 electoral votes, rocketing him towards the White House. He's at 264 electoral votes and ahead in counting in Wisconsin, Michigan and Arizona, any of which makes him president.

06.55   The first political reaction in France came from the far-right Front National's Marine Le Pen, who is running for president next spring. Le Pen, who has long said Trump's politics were in French interests, congratulated the 'free' American people. Le Pen's most senior strategist, Florian Philippot, tweeted: 'Their world is collapsing. Ours is being built.'

07.05   John Podesta, the Clinton campaign chairman, tells the Javits Center to go home.

07.31   Donald Trump has won the state of Wisconsin.

07.32   Trump is president-elect.

07.40   Both CNN and NBC have reported that Hillary Clinton called Donald Trump to concede the race.

07.52   The crowd won't let Trump speak, chanting: 'USA!'
        'Sorry to keep you waiting, complicated business,' Trump says. 'Thank you very much.'

08.49   Protests against Trump have broken out in cities across the US, including marches in Oakland, Los Angeles, Portland and New York City.

9 NOVEMBER

It was the Democrats' embrace of neoliberalism that won it for Trump

NAOMI KLEIN

They will blame James Comey and the FBI. They will blame voter suppression and racism. They will blame Bernie or bust and misogyny. They will blame third parties and independent candidates. They will blame the corporate media for giving him the platform, social media for being a bullhorn, and WikiLeaks for airing the laundry.

But this leaves out the force most responsible for creating the nightmare in which we now find ourselves wide awake: neoliberalism. That worldview – fully embodied by Hillary Clinton and her machine – is no match for Trump-style extremism. The decision to run one against the other is what sealed our fate. If we learn nothing else, can we please learn from that mistake?

Here is what we need to understand: a hell of a lot of people are in pain. Under neoliberal policies of deregulation, privatisation, austerity and corporate trade, their living standards have declined precipitously. They have lost jobs. They have lost pensions. They have lost much of the safety net that used to make these losses less frightening. They see a future for their kids even worse than their precarious present.

At the same time, they have witnessed the rise of the Davos class, a hyper-connected network of banking and tech billionaires, elected leaders who are awfully cosy with those interests, and Hollywood celebrities who make the whole thing seem unbearably glamorous. Success is a party to which they were not invited, and they know in their hearts that this rising wealth and power is somehow directly connected to their growing debts and powerlessness.

For the people who saw security and status as their birthright – and that means white men most of all – these losses are unbearable.

Donald Trump speaks directly to that pain. The Brexit campaign spoke to that pain. So do all of the rising far-right parties in Europe. They answer it with nostalgic nationalism and anger at remote economic bureaucracies – whether Washington, the North American free trade agreement, the World Trade Organisation or the EU. And, of course, they answer it by bashing immigrants and people of colour, vilifying Muslims, and degrading women. Elite neoliberalism has nothing to offer that pain, because neoliberalism unleashed the Davos class. People such as Hillary and Bill Clinton are the toast of the Davos party. In truth, they threw the party.

Trump's message was: 'All is hell.' Clinton answered: 'All is well.' But it's not well – far from it.

Neo-fascist responses to rampant insecurity and inequality are not going to go away. But what we know from the 1930s is that what it takes to do battle with fascism is a real left. A good chunk of Trump's support could be peeled away if there were a genuine redistributive agenda on the table. An agenda to take on the billionaire class with more than rhetoric, and use the money for a green new deal. Such a plan could create a tidal wave of well-paying unionised jobs, bring badly needed resources and opportunities to communities of colour, and insist that polluters should pay for workers to be retrained and fully included in this future.

It could fashion policies that fight institutionalised racism, economic inequality and climate change at the same time. It could take on bad trade deals and police violence, and honour indigenous people as the original protectors of the land, water and air.

People have a right to be angry, and a powerful, intersectional left agenda can direct that anger where it belongs, while fighting for holistic solutions that will bring a frayed society together.

Such a coalition is possible. In Canada, we have begun to cobble it together under the banner of a people's agenda called The Leap Manifesto, endorsed by more than 220 organisations from Greenpeace Canada to Black Lives Matter Toronto, and some of our largest trade unions.

Bernie Sanders' amazing campaign went a long way towards building this sort of coalition, and demonstrated that the appetite for democratic socialism is out there. But early on, there was a failure in the campaign to connect with older black and Latino voters, who are the demographic most abused by our current economic model. That failure prevented the campaign from reaching its full potential. Those mistakes can be corrected and a bold, transformative coalition is there to be built on.

That is the task ahead. The Democratic party needs to be either decisively wrested from pro-corporate neoliberals, or it needs to be abandoned. From Elizabeth Warren to Nina Turner, to the Occupy alumni who took the Bernie campaign supernova, there is a stronger field of coalition-inspiring progressive leaders out there than at any point in my lifetime. We are 'leaderful', as many in the Movement for Black Lives say.

So let's get out of shock as fast as we can and build the kind of radical movement that has a genuine answer to the hate and fear represented by the Trumps of this world. Let's set aside whatever is keeping us apart and start right now.

11 NOVEMBER

The *Guardian* view on Leonard Cohen: art lasts; life doesn't

EDITORIAL

Leonard Cohen once called himself 'a ninth-rate practitioner in a great tradition' but he'll be remembered as more than that. His best lines will remain, subtle and tough like a poacher's snares to pull tight the knot of pleasure and apprehension around readers who stumble into them long after his obituaries are forgotten. That is something of what it means to be part of a tradition: to strike up new conversations even when you're dead. Memory and poetry are closely entwined. Poems live in memory or not at all and, while they do, they help to shape the people who remember them.

This has been a year, indeed a week, that will be grimly remembered for decades, but it is also a year in which we remember many horrors of the past. The slaughter at the Bataclan nightclub in Paris was exactly a year ago. A concert by Sting will commemorate this and at the same time try to change its meaning and show that music can't be permanently silenced with gunfire.

The incomparably greater slaughter of the first world war (or 'the war to end all wars', as the optimists named it) was commemorated today. Many of the British memories of that war now come through poetry and especially the fierce and bitter eloquence of Wilfred Owen. If any 10 words could be said to have changed the way the British think about war and patriotism, they would be Owen's: 'The old lie: Dulce et decorum est pro patria mori.'

This was a first-rate operator at work in a great tradition, taking the ennobling sentiment of the Latin poet Horace and jamming it into the mouth of a man dying from poison gas so that no one who read it could ever think so lightly that it was 'the sweet and right thing' to die for their country. The sweetness, at least, would never taste the same.

Horace can argue back, in the mouths of his later admirers. That's what tradition means: it is an endless conversational argument with the dead, to which both parties bring only the things they have worth saying. Leonard Cohen argued with dead monks, with Jesus, and with his own ancestors, as well as with all the poets he had read. The disciplines he accepted were moral as well as aesthetic.

Ernest Hemingway described courage as grace under pressure, but this is also the condition of language when it's compressed into poetry. Poetry will do more than almost any other art to strengthen and console us in the face of catastrophe, not with uplift, nor with rhetoric, but with honesty and courage, and with the knowledge that others before us have faced terrible futures with grace.

11 NOVEMBER

Prince Harry is right – millennials must take on the trolls

GABY HINSLIFF

Once upon a time, there was a handsome prince who went in search of a bride. And lo, when he found someone who might eventually fit the glass slipper there was rejoicing throughout the land, but also some rather disturbing undercurrents. So here endeth the fairytale abruptly, with apologies in advance for the language.

'F that hole!' advised one *Daily Mail* online commenter who doesn't sound as if he's in this for a royal wedding souvenir plate, beneath some pictures of Prince Harry's new girlfriend, Meghan Markle, cobbled together into an otherwise inoffensive non-story.

But do remember not to 'knock her up lol', wrote a *Daily Mirror* reader, commenting under a story about (perfectly mainstream) images of the actress being posted on porn sites – noting helpfully that 'not every girl has to be able to do prim and proper to be worth it'. The *Sun* seemingly deleted its online version of the porn story because the reader comments were too grim, but the stuff beneath a *Mail* spread on Markle's clothing line sets the tone: 'Looks like used goods to me. Frequently used.' 'I hope Prince Harry is wearing her out!! HOT.' 'Blac Pippa.'

And that's the context to Prince Harry's statement this week, not just asking the tabloids to leave his girlfriend alone (fat chance) but attacking what Kensington Palace called 'the outright racist and sexist comments of social media trolls and web article comments'.

Lost in the predictable row about press regulation is that Harry wasn't just having a go at the papers. He was having a direct crack at their readers too, and at prejudice more broadly, and that's a matter not of law but of how social norms are set and broken in a digital age. How ironic that in the week America elected Donald Trump, the fifth in line to the stuffy old British throne seems to be discovering his inner liberal feminist.

The idea of Prince Harry, who once famously went as a Nazi to a fancy dress party, undergoing a Damascene conversion after scrolling sadly through his Twitter mentions will be a stretch for some. A cynic might suggest this is just smart PR, spinning an otherwise standard swipe at the tabloids – which might otherwise elicit the standard response that intrusion is the price paid for privilege – as something deeper. But it's part of an interesting pattern for the younger royals, increasingly starting to look like products of their millennial generation and not just of their backgrounds.

Take the Duke and Duchess of Cambridge's campaign, alongside Harry, against the stigma surrounding mental health. Their stress on the importance of talking openly about feelings of depression and anxiety is a big leap from the stiff upper lip favoured by the Queen, and clearly makes some older men faintly uncomfortable, with Prince William criticised in parts of the press for too much sappy emoting.

But that too is arguably a generational thing. Young men generally do talk more readily about their feelings than their grandparents did, and regard it as polite to let others do so. What older people might perceive as a deliberate political choice – a liberal resolve not to sound racist, sexist or otherwise insensitive – just seems unthinkingly normal to professional men of William and Harry's age, more a question of good manners than anything else.

The stereotype can be overdone, but millennials do seem broadly more anxious not to give offence, and more confident in challenging things that offend them, than their elders. So imagine the shock of discovering, as American millennials did this week, that the kindly social norms they take for granted don't seem to be norms any more.

And outside presidential elections, the place that's most obvious is on social media. When Kensington Palace tweeted Harry's statement, the response was largely supportive – unsurprisingly, given most of its followers will be flag-waving monarchists – but nonetheless there were accusations of 'playing the race card' and one 'Yay, HRH Mudshark' (a derogatory term for mixed-race couples). Twitter and Facebook both have deserved reputations as echo chambers but the idea of social media as just one big bubble, somewhere people go to avoid ever meeting an idea they won't like, is simplistic and outdated.

The demographics of Twitter are changing, with an increasingly aggressive minority – some on the right, some on the left, some not obviously political at all – actively looking for a fight. In real life, ironically, they might never have met but here they're thrown together, and the resulting friction fuels the aggression and attracts cranks. The upshot is that death or rape threats are becoming a professional hazard of public life, while for everyone else the spite is a constant low buzz in the background, like an angry bee trapped behind a window. You get used to it eventually.

But perhaps, on reflection, that's part of the problem. Cosy liberal values had become so normalised in real life that we failed to see their opposites were being normalised online. Men too terrified to approach a woman like Markle in the flesh were discovering they could say whatever they liked to her online.

People who'd be ostracised for saying what they really thought at work or over dinner tables were finding each other gratefully in forums, because by instantly connecting billions of people, the net ensured that however extreme the view, there would be someone somewhere who shared it. And like broken windows in a vacant building, creating a subliminal impression that anything goes, each small breach in social norms is quickly followed by another. What had become unsayable in polite company remained eminently sayable online and then it's only a short step to saying it aloud.

Clearly, the idea that Harry can stop any of that is whistling in a hurricane. For every newspaper restricting online comment for fear of reputational damage, there will always be some other platform happy to host whatever punters want to spew. It's hard to see how the prince can realistically protect even his own girlfriend, never mind stuff the genie back in its bottle.

But if we're going to have a constitutional monarchy, then there are worse things for it to do than hold the moral compass steady. Prince Harry's fellow millennials, meanwhile, need to understand that the values they take for granted need defending – and that, as in fairy stories, sometimes things that look dead are really only sleeping, waiting for the magic signal to awake.

15 NOVEMBER

The mansplaining hotline

PASS NOTES

Name: The mansplaining hotline.

Age: Brand new.

Purpose: Allowing female workers to report their patronising male colleagues.

I think you'll find 'condescending' is a more appropriate term. That's exactly what I'm talking about. This sense of superiority is inherent workplace sexism in action.

Hey, don't get mad, I'm just trying to help. No, you're not. You're subtly putting me in my place just because you've been conditioned to adhere to outdated gender stereotypes. You're mansplaining.

Have you heard of mansplaining? It's when men feel the need to ... Stop it! I know what mansplaining is. I just accused you of it. No wonder there's a hotline for this.

Tell me about this hotline. It's a Swedish initiative set up by trade union Unionen, which represents more than half a million workers. Whenever someone feels suppressed at work, they can call the number and seek help.

From whom? From Swedish scientists, comedians and politicians eager to get a hold of this minor yet pervasive annoyance.

Why bother? I could tell you anything about mansplaining you would ever need to know. I don't doubt that for a moment. However, Unionen quotes an American Psychological Association study that claims men 'tend to overestimate their intelligence to a much greater extent than women'.

Isn't this extremely sexist? Well, the issue is being thrashed out on social media at the moment. Some, inevitably, are claiming that the hotline is contributing to an increasingly polarised culture where everyone is either a victim or an aggressor.

That sounds about right. However, it could also be argued that this reaction is exactly what Unionen wanted. The hotline is a stunt designed to provoke debate, which might make some men more aware of their behaviour.

Or everyone will just shout at each other on Twitter about it until they all die alone and unhappy. Well, yes, that is what tends to happen with these things. But, hey, worth a shot, right?

Have you heard of the filter bubble? It's a social media phenomenon where ... Yes, I've heard of the filter bubble, you sexist pig.

Do say: 'Don't delay, call the mansplaining hotline today.'

Don't say: 'Let me explain what a hotline is.'

16 NOVEMBER

Andy Woodward: 'It was the softer, weaker boys he targeted'

DANIEL TAYLOR

It isn't easy sitting opposite Andy Woodward and hearing, close up, the unspeakable horrors of his childhood and the reasons why, at the age of 43, he finally feels able to tell his story and free himself from the secret – 'the massive, horrible burden' – that has shaped his life.

It has been there since the age of 11 when a football-daft kid from a family of Manchester United supporters first came to the attention of the coach, scout and serial paedophile Barry Bennell. It is difficult even to contemplate how much Woodward suffered before reaching this point, where he has offered to waive his anonymity and speak publicly about it for the first time.

He is doing so in the belief there are many others – potentially hundreds, he says – who are living with their own secrets, given Bennell's employment at Crewe Alexandra in the 1980s and 1990s and close association in the past with Stoke City and Manchester City, as well as junior teams in Derbyshire, Staffordshire, Cheshire and Greater Manchester.

Bennell was sentenced to nine years in prison in 1998 after admitting 23 specimen charges of sexual offences against six boys aged nine to 15. Woodward was among the victims at Crewe and knows of other former pros who were targeted. Many more, he suspects, never made it as professional footballers, whereas his own career, also featuring spells at Bury, Sheffield United and Scunthorpe United, ended at the age of 29 because he was unable to cope with the horrendous after-effects of what he'd had to endure.

Woodward had to fake an injury during one game because he was having the kind of panic attack that became a regular feature in his career. He has been suicidal 'on probably 10 occasions'. He has spent his professional life battling depression and anxiety, and is haunted by what a man who described himself in legal proceedings as a 'monster' told him about some of the other victims.

'My life has been ruined until the age of 43,' Woodward says. 'But how many others are there? I'm talking about hundreds of children who Barry Bennell cherry-picked for various football teams and who now, as adults, might still be living with that awful fear.

'We've seen with the Jimmy Savile case how people have had the courage, yet I'd say within the football world it's even harder to speak out. Only now, at the age of 43, I feel I can actually live without that secret and that massive, horrible burden. I want to get it out and give other people an opportunity to do the same. I want to give people strength. I survived it. I lost my career, which was a massive thing for me, but I'm still here. I came through the other side. Other people can have that strength.'

Woodward's ordeal began when he was playing for Stockport Boys and Bennell invited him to train with one of his teams on Manchester City's pitches at Platt Lane. Bennell talent-spotted boys, aged nine to 14, around the north-west and Midlands over three decades and Woodward was talented enough to be directed towards Crewe's youth setup. 'I just wanted to play football. My mum and dad will say that I always had a football in my hands, wherever I went. I saw Crewe as the start of that dream. But I was soft-natured, too, and it was the softer, weaker boys Bennell targeted.'

Bennell arranged for him to stay at his house on the edge of the Peak District. 'It was like a treasure trove, a child's dream,' Woodward says. 'When you walked through the door there were three fruit machines. He had a pool table. There was a little monkey upstairs in a cage who would sit on your shoulder. He had two Pyrenean mountain dogs. He even kept a wild cat. It was my dream, remember, to be a footballer and it was like he was dropping little sweets towards me: "You can stay with me and this is what I can do for you." Plus he had a reputation as the best youth coach in the country. So I'd stay at weekends and summer holidays and even take time out of school sometimes. I'd go to all the Crewe matches with him. He liked dark-haired boys. I was a kid, I trusted him to begin with.'

When the abuse started, Bennell used threats and blackmail to make sure his victims did not go against him. 'What he'd do sometimes, to show the fear factor and make sure I never told anyone, was get out some nunchucks,' Woodward says. 'He was a master with them. He'd tell me to hold out a piece of paper. I'd be physically shaking. Then he'd hit it with enough force to split it in half and make a little comment: "You see what I can do, you see how powerful I am?"

'It was either threats of violence or he'd use football to manipulate control. If I upset him in any way, he'd drop me from the team. "At any point," he'd tell me, "you will go, you will disappear and that dream won't happen." It was emotional blackmail, all the time.'

The young Woodward became 'very introverted, I didn't lead a normal teenage life'. Yet there are other parts of this story that make it even more chilling. When Woodward was 14, Bennell started having a relationship with his victim's 16-year-old sister. 'He was so much older he didn't want people to know at first and told me I would never play football again if I breathed a word of it,' Woodward says. 'I was frightened to death because he had complete power over me by that stage. It was like a double whammy and he would try to abuse me sometimes even with my sister in the same house. Later, when their relationship became public, he would come round for Sunday dinner every weekend, sitting with my mum and dad and my family, laughing and joking. I was so frightened of him I just had to suffer in silence.'

The wedding took place in 1991 and Woodward, at 18, had to go through the hellish ordeal of seeing the man who had exploited, controlled and abused him for years become his brother-in-law. 'I had to live with that on top of everything else,' he says. 'I had to attend that wedding, standing in the church when I really wanted to rip his throat out. It was torture – that's the only word to describe it.'

Despite everything, Woodward progressed through the ranks at Crewe and made his first-team debut a year later. Mentally, however, he could not cope. 'From the age of 11 I had lived with a secret. And living with a secret is probably one of the hardest things you can ever live with. If you look at my career you will see I was plagued with quite a few injuries. A lot of those injuries were actually mental injuries.

'I had desperately wanted to be a footballer. It's all I lived for. Yet there was so much anger and hurt within me that it was actually football, this game I loved, that took away my life as a child. It felt like I was in two worlds. I'd be training when I just wanted to burst into tears. A coach might be screaming and shouting and all I wanted to do is punch him in the face because "you've no idea what you coaches have done to me". There have been lots of dips.'

He signed for Bury in 1995 and after a productive first season at Gigg Lane everything started to unravel again. 'At one point during the police investigation I went to see [the manager] Stan

Ternent in his office and explained what had happened to me. It was hard because us footballers are supposed to be butch and strong, aren't we? It's all banter and changing-room jokes, supposedly. But I'd been having a mental breakdown. I'd lost a couple of years and I felt I had to tell him.'

One of Bennell's victims had reported him and the Cheshire, Derbyshire and North Wales police forces began an investigation that also involved allegations of him preying on boys on football courses in Spain and the United States, as well as at the Butlin's in Pwllheli. The judge talked of Bennell exploiting the power he had to 'point young boys in the right direction and help them with their careers and wishes to become successful footballers. They were prepared to do almost anything you asked.'

The hearing at Chester crown court was told one of Bennell's offences took place on one of Crewe's training pitches. Another occurred at the home of Dario Gradi, the club's manager, though the court heard Gradi did not know about it. One of Bennell's tricks was to encourage boys to stay in his bedroom by frightening them with horror films or ghost stories. He was initially charged with 45 offences, including buggery and attempted buggery, but 22 were allowed to lie on file.

Woodward was 24 when Bennell was jailed. 'For the next two seasons I played some of the best football of my career. Maybe I felt I had got it off my chest and I could finally get on with my life. I was kidding myself but for a while I had loads of positive energy. Neil Warnock had taken over as manager and in November 1999 he told me he was going to Sheffield United. "I'm going to take you and [the goalkeeper] Paddy Kenny," he said, "you're the only ones I want, my best two players." It was a chance for me to play for a bigger club, even though I loved it at Bury. I went shopping at Tesco that Sunday night and – boom – I don't know what hit me. I genuinely thought I was going to collapse and die. My heart was racing. All the adrenaline had rushed to my head. I managed to get home, called an ambulance and went to hospital and they explained it was a panic attack.'

The following week, Bury played at Gillingham and it hit him again. 'The match reports will say I pulled my hamstring but that was just the excuse I used. I'd actually had another full-blown panic attack. We were midway through the first half. I went down to my knees and I just knew I had to get off the pitch. I went to the dressing room and started crying my eyes out, thinking my whole life was ending.'

He did confide in Warnock and, as with Ternent, will always be grateful for his manager's support. Yet the player did not feel able to tell his team-mates. 'In 2016, at least people have an understanding of anxiety and panic attacks. Back then, I suffered in silence. That was the way football was – and it was horrendous.'

Woodward did eventually move to Bramall Lane but he had been receiving treatment in the Priory clinic and his medication affected his weight and fitness. He made only three league appearances for his new club before moving to Scunthorpe on loan. He then had a short spell at Halifax and, finally, Northwich Victoria before giving up. In total, a player Warnock rated as one of the best defenders he had ever managed made only 154 league starts in 10 years.

In his worst moments, Woodward has been 'a mess, spiralling to the point where I wasn't going to be here any more. I've parked in my garage with a pipe. I've been to the woods with a rope. I've had tablets, ready to go. I took it to the point where I couldn't be here any more. I've been there, physically, and it frightened the life out of me. People talk about it being for attention or a cry for help but I can say, categorically, mine was because I didn't know how I could live. The only thing that ever stopped me was knowing the devastation it would cause others.'

Bennell, now 62, was jailed for two years in May 2015 for another historic case involving a 12-year-old boy in Macclesfield and admitted in a 2012 interview with the *Sunday Times* that Gary Speed was one of the youngsters who stayed at his house. Bennell told the newspaper he had not abused Speed, but added that even if he had done he would be unlikely to admit it anyway. When the reporter told him he would be left in peace, he replied: 'There's no peace now. How can you have peace when you've killed somebody?' He added: 'To me, killing someone is what you've done to them, because their life's never the same again.' Lawyers for Speed's wife, Louise, subsequently put out a statement saying they had been assured that the former Wales manager was not one of Bennell's victims.

Woodward strongly suspects Bennell, who adopted the name Richard Jones and was living in Milton Keynes before his last prison sentence, colluded for a long time with at least one other paedophile who has never been detected. This, fundamentally, is one of the reasons why he hopes other victims will feel able to come forward. 'I'm convinced there is an awful lot more to come out. I also know this will not be a total shock to some people within football that others were involved. This has taken an immense amount of strength and courage but I need closure. I can finally have a voice and I want to give others a belief. We were victims in a profession where we were all so desperate to succeed as footballers. Some of us were fortunate to experience that, yet others weren't. We all suffered the same pain.'

Woodward spent 12 years in the police after his football career had ended but encountered problems of his own and was dismissed last week after a disciplinary tribunal for having a relationship with the adult sister of a crime victim.

Life is a permanent battle but he is getting by, eternally grateful for the therapy he has received from the Sporting Chance clinic and clinical psychologist Dr Lee Martin. There are times when he does break down emotionally and, taking everything into consideration, it is remarkable he has kept his sanity. 'I didn't tell anybody until the police started their investigation. At first, I told them nothing happened but then I couldn't bottle it up any longer and that was the moment my family found out. That's been one of the hardest things, seeing the devastating effect it has had on my family. My sister has suffered massively. She left him immediately. My parents know everything and have to live with it every day. We have a good relationship considering everything but there's no doubt it has had a big effect on all of us and probably will do for the rest of our lives. Without the love and support of my partner, Zelda, I would not have survived the last 18 months.'

He tells his story with great courage and eloquence and it would be wrong to assume he is angry with the world at large. He does, however, feel let down by the sport he grew up loving, and the dressing-room culture of the day which, he says, meant keeping everything in-house. 'Throughout those years at Crewe, so many people used to talk about it. Other players would say directly to my face: "I bet he does this to you, we know he does that." There was all that dressing-room bravado. Then, outside the club, it was never discussed. That's how football worked back then: "We can talk about it within these walls, but we keep it watertight and it doesn't go any further." Nobody wanted to break that circle of trust.

'That club has never been held accountable. My belief, after all these years, is that it must have been well known within the club that he had young boys staying over. That's the reason why I feel let down by Crewe. I wasn't at school but I was at a professional football club who had a duty to protect children, and there were hundreds of children running around that place.'

Talking about what happened, he hopes, will give him some form of closure. But it will be always with him and he still suffers, every single day. 'Even now, when the results come through on a Saturday and it says "Crewe Alexandra" I get that awful feeling and my stomach turns. And that's me at 43.'

He did, however, play against them for Bury a couple of times, home and away. 'At Gigg Lane I had one of my best games for a long time. I was brilliant that day and it felt like it was me fighting back. Then at Gresty Road I scored – and I'd never scored. But the truth is that going back to Crewe haunted me. It took a lot of inner strength on the coach heading down the motorway and I haven't been there since. I avoid Crewe now. I will never set foot anywhere near that town again.'

20 NOVEMBER

Carrie Fisher on Harrison Ford: 'I love him. I'll always feel something for him'

SIMON HATTENSTONE

Perhaps the most surprising thing is that it has taken Carrie Fisher so long to fess up. The famously candid actor and memoirist has been asked numerous times whether there was a real-life romance on the set of *Star Wars*, to mirror the relationship between Princess Leia and Han Solo. No, of course not, she would invariably reply: she was a teenager, Harrison Ford was 14 years older, they couldn't have been more different, what a daft idea.

Now she has written *The Princess Diarist*, in which she calls on the journals she wrote at the time, to reveal that she had an intense affair with Ford. The diaries, and accompanying poems, make for painful reading. Here is a 19-year-old riddled with self-loathing and angst, already in therapy but yet to be diagnosed as bipolar, pretending to be a woman of the world. She falls obsessively in love with Ford, who, while happy to sleep with her, does not appear to feel the same way.

Fisher has always written about herself with self-lacerating honesty (notably in *Postcards from the Edge*, the fictionalised account of an overdose). Why has she waited so long to tell this story? A number of reasons, she says, talking down the line to me from Los Angeles, her voice thick with bronchitis (our interview in London was cancelled when she fell ill). The most important was the discovery of the journals, which she found in boxes under the floorboards when she was renovating her house. 'I hadn't seen them in 40 years. After all this time, I had genuinely forgotten they existed. And I thought they were this incredible archaeological find.'

Enough time has passed, she says, to enable her to tell the story. 'It wasn't just my secret to keep,' she says, meaning that Ford was married at the time of their affair, to Mary Marquardt. Shortly afterwards, he divorced, and married *ET* screenwriter Melissa Mathison, a close friend of Fisher's, who died last year. Was it out of respect for Mathison that she did not write about their relationship? 'No, not at all. Melissa always felt it was not that big of a deal. But then she wasn't the wife.'

Is she doing it for the money? Fisher laughs. 'Oh, it wasn't that much money. I had a pre-established deal, so it wasn't like they said, "We'll pay you a million dollars to tell some secret thing." I was just wondering if I'd have the nerve to do it.'

Rereading her diaries, Fisher says she was startled by her passion. It enabled her to write about herself in a way she never has before – not sugar-glazed with irony or wisecracks, but straight from the heart. Her daughter, Billie Lourd, read it with her for the audiobook, and 'she thought it was so emotional, she had never seen me like that. No one has. This is the most personal thing I have written.'

One of the questions she repeatedly asks herself in the diaries is whether Ford has a clue how she feels. What does she think now? 'I don't think, until now, he knew the intensity of my feelings.' As for herself, she says she has probably tried to bury those emotions over the years. 'Even in the diary I don't like to admit it, because it's a failure.' She pauses, and starts again. 'No, it's not a failure – it's unreciprocated love.' Another pause. 'Which I guess is a type of failure.'

I ask her what Ford, now married to the actor Calista Flockhart, thinks of the book. She says she doesn't know. 'I told him I was writing the book, and I would give it to him and if he didn't like anything in it I would take it out, and he seemed surprised at that. Then I called him and said I'm going to send it to you, and I did and I never heard from him.'

She knows he is unlikely to thank her for making the story public. Ford is as taciturn as she is garrulous, as private as she is confessional. 'I don't think he wants anything known about his life,' she admits, 'and he's lived it accordingly. I certainly don't want to say anything that would do more than embarrass him. Anything private embarrasses him.'

The affair with Ford took her by surprise. 'I was shocked by the fact that he fancied me. I was a very insecure girl and had only had one boyfriend.' She writes that he whisked her off when she was tipsy, and asks herself whether he took advantage of her. What does she think now? 'Oh no, never. It wasn't that kind of thing at all.' In fact, she says, there was no way he could have known how innocent she was, because she had deliberately painted a false picture of herself. 'He perceived me as this very confident, experienced girl. I don't think he had all the information! And when he got it, he behaved accordingly, and he didn't have to do that.'

In what way? 'He softened a bit, you know, to the degree that Harrison can soften. And we stayed together for the remainder of the film. It was never going to be more than that. I didn't think it was going to be even that.'

While Ford was the number one thing on her mind throughout filming, she reckons she was probably around 15th on his list of priorities. She often sounds desolate in the journals. 'I do not want to take part in my life,' she writes. 'It can just go on without me.' Was she suicidal? 'No, I was never suicidal. I was just extremely insecure, especially around men.'

Yes, she says, there is a huge amount of pain there, but some of it is teenage angst and some of it was a reflection of her mental health. 'I think some of that could have been being bipolar, though I hadn't been diagnosed then. I had started going to therapy when I was 15. I realised something was a little too much with me. The doctor said, "Why are you here?" and I said, "I want to stop crying so hard."'

Looking back, she says, her feeling that Ford did not really care for her couldn't have helped. 'Certainly the situation didn't make me feel that much better about myself.' Again, she pauses. 'But in a way it did.' How? 'Because he'd chosen me.'

Even now, she says, her feelings about that time are mixed. 'I wouldn't want to live through that again, ever. It's just so obsessive, and self-obsessed, and confused.' Was it one of the most intense experiences of her life? 'I think so, because everything was exciting and new. We all became famous at that time, but there were other things to focus on, and certainly [the affair] was a formidable distraction. And maybe that made the fame less confusing, because it didn't have all of my focus.'

Was he as good in bed as you'd expect Harrison Ford to be? Fisher gasps with faux shock. 'Oh come on, I can't answer that question! I was very infatuated with him. Look at him. Look at those pictures of him. Can you imagine what I thought, given what I thought of myself?' How does she feel, looking back at her teenage self now? 'I felt sorry for myself, and I don't like that at any age.' She says she's thankful that, at 60, she is not so lacking in self-belief.

I ask if her relationship with Ford shaped future relationships. 'Freakishly, yes.' How? 'Well, I went with Paul after that, and Paul was not dissimilar.' Fisher dated Paul Simon for six years, was married to him for 11 months, and then dated him again after they divorced. 'Paul was much more verbal. But there was something very diffident again. He was the same amount older. I was 21 and Paul was 36. They were both very cerebral and serious. And they were witty, which is different from being funny. Funny, there's a sort of pleading in it. Witty is a much more cerebral self-expression. They both had that. And they're both better after a couple of beers.' She says there was one crucial difference in her relationship with Simon. 'This time it was reciprocal, which was a huge relief.'

What astonishes me is that Fisher says she and Ford never discussed their relationship, neither at the time nor afterwards. 'He's not a big talker,' she says drily. 'You know, he wasn't Mr Chuckles.' But what happened when they met on set for the sequels – *The Empire Strikes Back* and *Return of the Jedi*. Nothing, she says; it was just their secret. 'I think it was reabsorbed. You can see in our body language that we are comfortable with each other.'

Last year they were reunited as characters for the first time in 30 years, for *Star Wars: The Force Awakens*. Surely by then they could talk about it? 'No,' she says. 'On this last film I noticed that two people were flirting and they had a big age difference like we had, and I pointed it out to him, and he said [she puts on his deep-voice deadpan], "Well, I hope it goes well for them." I think it's the only time we've ever referred to it.' Did he wink? 'No. He's not a wink person.'

What did emerge over the years, she thinks, was a lasting friendship. Recently, she told Mark Hamill, who played Luke Skywalker, about her affair with Ford. How did he react? 'He was shocked.' Does she still love Ford? 'Yes, I love him. I'll always feel something for him. I love Mark, too, but I love Mark more like a sibling. You can't pretend something for so long without some of it coming true.'

For a long time, Fisher had been ambivalent about the *Star Wars* franchise. Yes, it had made her, but it had also stultified her – for many people, she will always be Princess Leia. Now, she is simply thankful. 'It has been an enormous thing in my life. And it's been the motor that's run everything else.'

As for her current not-so-private life, she lives with her dog, Gary Fisher (who has his own Twitter account), is single, looking to move to Britain (particularly post-Trump) and is more than ready for another man. 'I want to find a British professor who will be able to put up with me, so you can put the word out. Good sense of humour, intelligent, not hideously unattractive, and sort of confident without being arrogant.'

I ask if she will be embarrassed next time she meets Ford. 'Yeah, I'll be embarrassed,' she says. How long for? 'Not that long. I think it's worth a flush or two!' She laughs.

I tell her that, as she has been talking, I've been picturing that scene in *The Empire Strikes Back*, where Princess Leia finally professes her feelings to Han Solo. 'I love you,' she says. 'I know,' he replies. It feels so true to life, I say. 'Yes,' she says, 'I think that's definitely informed by our relationship. It is much more me to say, "I love you" and much more him to say the other. He improvised his bit.'

Five weeks after this article was published, Carrie Fisher died.

Just about managing? In towns like Pontypool that's a dream

ADITYA CHAKRABORTTY

A health worker in Pontypool told me what happens when people lose their sense of purpose. 'You don't get up in the morning. You might see a spiral in depression,' she said last week. 'You lose contact with the outside world.' The dismal list went on: no self-worth, no self-confidence …

As she talked, I realised her description didn't apply only to people. Places and communities can be stripped of their purpose too. That is certainly what's happened to Pontypool.

If I could send Theresa May and her chancellor, Philip Hammond, anywhere before tomorrow's autumn statement, it wouldn't be to some love-in with big business at a swanky London hotel – but to this south Wales market town. It might make them think.

The story of Pontypool is a story of riches squandered, of dynamism blocked, of an entire community slung on the slagheap. Sat atop vast deposits of iron ore and coal, it was probably the first industrial town in Wales. For a time, under Victoria, it was richer than Cardiff. Even now, to look along its skyline is to see traces of wealth: the park with its Italian gardens and bandstand; the covered market with its olde price list for snipes or a brace of pheasants; the 25 listed buildings that make this one of the most sumptuous small town centres in Britain.

Then look down. On a typical weekday, the indoor market is a desert. Those bits of the high street that aren't to let are betting parlours, vaping dens and charity shops: the standard parade for hollowed-out towns across Britain. The reason isn't hard to fathom: the mines shut down decades back; the factories have pretty much disappeared. Those big employers still left aren't big employers any more. One of the staff at BAE tells me that when he joined in 1982, it had 2,500 workers on its shop floor; now, he reckons, it has 120.

Swaths of Pontypool and the surrounding region of Torfaen now rank among the poorest in all Britain. On part of one of its housing estates in Trevethin, 75 per cent of all children under four are raised in poverty. Over half – 53 per cent – of all households who live on that stretch are below the poverty line. With that come all the usual problems: families that can't pay the rent, that are more likely to fall prey to a whole range of sicknesses, from mental health to cancer. Those people can expect to die 20 years before their near-neighbours in some of the better-off areas in Pontypool. First the economy died out, now its people are too.

Pontypool is like the rest of south Wales, like many other parts of Britain I have reported from. It's what politicians and economists call 'post-industrial'. That term, though, implies something coming after; here, hardly anything has come after. A few years ago Pontypool town centre was declared on the verge of death by a local councillor, who bore a coffin lid in a mock funeral procession.

It's a similar story in Hull, Sunderland, in so many places across Britain. For three decades Tories and Labour thought they could buy the acquiescence of residents with benefits and public-sector jobs. Then came the 2008 crash and the cuts that have followed. Then came the Brexit referendum.

I visited Pontypool a few weeks before that vote – and it was on that trip that the suspicion dawned that the remain camp didn't have it in the bag at all. True to form, Torfaen voted nearly 60 per cent to 40 per cent to leave the EU.

If May is to have any hope of lasting in No 10, it will be places such as Pontypool that she needs to pacify. The early signs do not look good. Everything promised or leaked from the autumn statement so far this week – the cuts in business taxes, the extra billion pounds for new roads and infrastructure – south Wales has had some version of already, and nothing has worked.

After the heavy industry went, the future for south Wales was meant to lie in luring new business investment. Mark Hooper, a local social entrepreneur, terms it the 'Welsh dowry': the advance the Welsh elite gives to any multinational that promises to settle down with them. Count among that the millions the Cardiff government spent on bringing in an Amazon distribution centre, even building billionaire Jeff Bezos a new road. Add the millions lavished on Ford in Bridgend. Most of all, look at the LG factory into which Westminster and Cardiff pumped so much political and financial capital – and which was soon abandoned. As the first Brexit chancellor, Hammond's growth strategy mostly consists of doing the same across the rest of the UK. I see no reason why it should work any better.

In the heart of Trevethin, the poorest stretch in all of Pontypool, I asked two community councillors how many of their residents would count as 'just about managing' – May's latest coinage. One in three families, they reckoned, were not managing at all, simply landing themselves in more debt. As for the rest, they were barely holding it together in the face of the benefit cuts.

'I have good working people knocking on my door for help,' Jon Harlor told me. He remembered how 'one girl came to me in tears'. A young mum of three and a shop worker on zero hours, she never knew how much her income would be from week to week – and the tax credits were no help. 'They're reliant on the food banks to smooth out the peaks and the troughs.'

What would it take to fix a place such as Pontypool? First, reverse the benefit cuts – which are a wrecking ball for communities of the working poor. Second, drop the hi-vis and hard hats of infrastructure spend. Such offerings might draw multinationals into central London; they don't work here.

Finally, learn one of the hardest lessons of Brexit: the reason the political geography of Britain is so divided is because its economic geography is so unequal. Treasury levers and Bank of England billions are barely any use here. Instead, what's needed is an attentiveness to place.

In his 'Deep Place' studies of local Welsh economies, the academic Mark Lang starts from what places like Pontypool already have, and what can be built on. He pulls together members of the community and asks them what they need. His new report on Pontypool shares a lot with the work on the foundational economy done by the Centre for Research on Economic and Social Change, which I've written about here before. It starts from a recognition that chasing multinationals and chain retailers pays only limited dividends in a place that's had its purpose stripped out. It argues for focusing on what locals need: social care, good schools, broadband. This isn't Westminster politics with its big announcements, or even Cardiff politics and its ribbon-cutters' charter. It's more modest, perhaps even pessimistic. To me, it rings more true.

26 NOVEMBER

I fell in love with a woman, and everything changed

ALYS FOWLER

I have buried myself in my garden at times. Lost myself in the depths of rich loam, renewed myself in new growth, scattered parts of me like self-sown seeds. I am my garden.

So every time I come here to write about my garden, I am writing about myself. Between the beetroot seedlings and the apple prunings, there's a little bit of me here and there.

I'd like to hope this doesn't get in the way of any growth, but recently I've felt more and more at odds with this column and the place I call home, my garden. It turns out you can hide quite successfully under leaf mould, but the page isn't quite such an easy place. If I'm rambling a little, it's because I'm still trying to make sense of why I need to write this down, here of all places.

The good thing about the garden is that it doesn't give a fig for my existential crises – it just gets on with being. While I was pondering the meaning of things, it filled all the blank spaces. It speaks its truth very plainly: 'You're not tending to this place, so we grew you some wild strawberries.' That's pretty honest.

Here's another truth: last year I came out. I fell in love with a woman. I went from whispering, 'I am a lesbian', to saying it out loud. Everything shifted, everything changed, yet the world stayed the same. The garden grew more wild strawberries.

I guess this has little to do with gardening or my passion for it. So why do I need to tell you this? Well, one thing passion has taught me is that it matters: when you find that thing you can be passionate about, that you can enthuse about, your world grows a little wider. It teaches you respect, because it helps you connect to people, to other things. It matters to me that who I am in this column is as honest and passionate as who I am out there in the soil.

Coming out later in life left me racked by guilt and slumps of shame, and there's a kind of grief, too. My marriage had ended. But there's also an internal peace I could barely have dreamed about before. Those are quite rolling emotions to run with – so extreme at times.

It took me a long time to come right back to the garden, to tend to all those wild strawberries. There have been moments when I've looked out on the garden and its wild, seemingly chaotic state felt like a metaphor for the inside of my head. But in kinder moments, when I wandered down into this storm of seed-heads and tendrils, I found unexpected joys. A plant I was quite sure I'd killed a number of years ago was not only flourishing, but in flower. A vine that I was convinced would never do well was now upwardly marching and declaring its health. When I was ready to come back to all of this and I pulled up a blanket of strawberries, there it was, my good earth, rich, welcoming and ready to go again.

26 November

Havana in mourning: 'We Cubans are Fidelista even if we are not communist'

STEPHEN GIBBS, JONATHAN WATTS AND TED FRANCIS

'Revolution ... is sacrifice,' echoed the trembling voice of an elderly Fidel Castro around the streets of Old Havana at dawn on Saturday, as Cuban state radio began replaying his speeches, the day after his death.

Dani, 37, who takes tourists around the cobbled streets on his bicitaxi, had woken to be told the momentous news by a neighbour. 'I didn't believe it,' he said. Like many Cubans of his generation he had begun to assume that Castro would be around for ever. El Comandante's 80th birthday, a decade ago, had been celebrated with posters declaring '80 more years'.

Outside the art deco Bacardi building, one of many private businesses expropriated in the 1960s by a young, triumphant Castro, Mario Astoria, a security guard, was sitting on his own. 'I feel this in my heart,' he said. 'When Fidel came to power this country was a pebble in the ocean. Now everyone knows about us.'

The previous evening, at Havana's current hippest spot, the cavernous art gallery and nightclub Fábrica de Arte, there was a different atmosphere. At midnight, it began closing its bars, without explanation. The rumour spread that the reason was a forthcoming momentous announcement. When the news finally came, it drifted out slowly. Castro was always suspicious of the internet, and Cuban mobile phones are still not able to connect to it. Locals were depending on foreign tourists with connectivity to tell them their 'historic leader' had died.

Liset, 26, a dancer, gasped with shock when she heard. Like many Cuban artists she had met Fidel. 'I was once besotted with him,' she said. But she confessed to being more intrigued than sad to hear of his death. 'I began to feel that what he was saying, and what we were living, were two different things,' she said.

Out on Havana's dimly lit streets people began to make their way home. Many seemed reluctant to talk about the man whose mortality was once such a sensitive subject that foreign ministry officials cut short conversations with diplomats and journalists who dared mention it.

By morning, close to Castro's relatively modest bungalow home in the east of the country, there was no sign of the major state security operation planned had he died when still in power. One of Castro's mantras was that 'revolutionaries never retire'. Had a serious intestinal ailment not almost killed him in 2006, forcing him to step down, few imagine that the world's longest-serving non-royal head of state would have willingly handed control of the nation to anyone, even his younger brother.

But in his twilight years Castro appeared to enjoy stepping back from the onerous duties of the presidency, if not the lime-light. He abandoned his trademark khaki uniform, instead opting for a more comfortable tracksuit, in which he would occasionally be photographed meeting visiting dignitaries.

'He had his good days and his bad days,' said one Havana-based European diplomat. On those 'good days' he would make his views clear, writing an often-rambling newspaper column, which was dutifully read out in its entirety on the nightly news. He avoided praising – or criticising – his brother Raúl's unravelling of some of the more pedantic rules which he had imposed, such as a prohibition of Cubans staying in tourist hotels, or having mobile phones in their own names.

As relations between Cuba and the United States improved, Castro came as close as he had to directly criticising his brother, saying the Cuban president had the right to make his own decisions, but 'I don't trust the policy of the United States'.

Castro died at 10.29pm on Friday, but the Cuban public were not informed until a midnight broadcast by President Castro.

In a southern suburb of the city, the Rodríguez family watched in a stunned silence that continued long after the broadcast had ended. '*El Caballo* is dead,' said Leo, finally, referring to Castro by his nickname of 'the Horse', as his voice cracked with emotion.

The airport worker is a devoted Fidelista who still drapes a revolutionary flag from his apartment window on national day. He met his wife Clarita at the Union of Young Communists. They credit the government for subsidised housing, free university education and free healthcare, which is of particular importance to their daughter, who needs to see a doctor every two weeks for treatment of a chronic condition.

Given such benefits, they expect huge crowds to gather at the capital's Plaza de la Revolución to show their respect. 'The plaza will be overflowing,' Clarita predicted.

Their neighbour was also shocked. Like many of her generation, 36-year-old Elena hates the restrictions imposed on free speech in Cuba and has long wished that the 'dictatorship' would collapse. But she was in tears when she heard the news. 'Of course I'm crying,' she said. 'We Cubans are Fidelista even if we are not communist.'

Elsewhere in the city, residents expressed their sense of loss.

'I'm speechless. Many Cubans are dismayed,' said Mercedes Copa, 59. 'Fidel's death opens a period of uncertainty. Perhaps today is the start of a new stage in Cuban history,' said Irma Guzman, her neighbour.

Castro's death opens up many uncertainties in a country that has long become used to an exceptionally slow pace of change. The crisis in Venezuela, which for over a decade has sent cheap oil to Cuba, is being acutely felt. Power cuts and gasoline shortages are once again commonplace.

In his presidential campaign, Donald Trump has pledged to reverse President Obama's opening up to Cuba, which has included the restoration of diplomatic ties and easing of travel restrictions. Raúl Castro has himself said he will stand down from the presidency in 2018.

Cuba now begins nine days of national mourning. Castro's ashes will be taken to his family home in Birán, in the far west of the island, retracing the path of his 1959 revolution.

'Cuba won't be the same without him,' said Mario Astoria, as the sun rose over Old Havana.

16 DECEMBER

Don't call it post-truth. There's a simpler word: lies

JONATHAN FREEDLAND

Sixteen years ago, I sat in court 73 of the Royal Courts of Justice in London and felt the ground crumble beneath my feet. I was following the libel trial brought by David Irving, the Holocaust denier and 'pro-Nazi polemicist' – to quote the judge's eventual verdict – against Penguin Books, which had dared publish a text which told the truth about him.

I watched as Irving discarded the usual rules of evidence. The eyewitness testimony of survivors was dismissed as lies. Confessions by the guilty were waved away as fake. Inconvenient documents were written off as forgeries. All that was left was what he wanted to believe.

At the time, it struck me that Irving was threatening something greater even than the memory of the Holocaust: he was undermining the very idea of facts, history and truth. If every item of evidence could be rubbished as bogus, then how could anyone ever prove anything? How would we know that Henry VIII had six wives or that Napoleon fought at Waterloo?

Hence the queasy sensation the ground was falling away. As I wrote at the time: 'If we start to doubt corroborated facts, how can we prevent ourselves being swallowed up in doubt, unable to trust anything we see? It might all be a conspiracy, a legend, a hoax. This is the bizarre, never-never world inhabited by David Irving. Now the court has to decide: is this our world too?'

That feeling returned to me this week, brought back by a screening of the film *Denial*, released next month, which dramatises the Irving trial of 2000. But it was also prompted by the reaction to events in Aleppo and, more widely, by the way 2016 has punched truth in the face, leaving it bruised and bleeding.

As Aleppo endured its final agonies, the simple act of circulating any account – a video, a photograph, a news report – would trigger an unnerving response. Someone, somewhere would reply that the photograph was doctored, the source was a stooge, the rescued child was not really a child or not really rescued.

Of course, we're used to people taking different sides on conflicts far away, arguing bitterly over who is to blame. At its most extreme, it results in a newspaper like the *Morning Star* sinking so low that it hails the human devastation of Aleppo – where every hospital was bombed and where the slaughter of civilians became routine – not as a crime, but as a 'liberation'.

But this is about more than assigning blame for this death or that bombing. This is about refusing to accept that the death or bombing occurred at all. This is about defenders of Bashar al-Assad, and his Russian and Iranian enablers, coming on television to say that what is happening on the ground is not happening, that it is all an illusion. The late US senator Daniel Patrick Moynihan used to say: 'You're entitled to your own opinion, but you're not entitled to your own facts.' But that distinction seems to have broken down. Now people regard facts as very much like opinions: you can discard the ones you don't like.

This problem is not confined to Syria. This week the CIA joined 17 other US intelligence agencies in concluding that Russia was behind the hacking of Democrats' emails, adding its conclusion that Moscow had done so in order to tilt the US election towards Donald Trump. 'Ridiculous,' said Trump, who has not looked at the CIA's evidence and has refused to receive the daily intelligence briefing provided for all incoming presidents on the grounds that he is 'like, a smart person'.

After Iraq and the weapons of mass destruction that never were, plenty are understandably wary of accepting the word of the intelligence agencies. But Trump's scepticism – cynicism is a better word – operates on a different level. 'Nobody really knows,' he says about the hacking charges, the very words he uses about climate change, in the face of a vast body of evidence. Recall that he also says that he won the US popular vote 'if you deduct the millions of people who voted illegally', a flagrantly false claim for which there is no evidence whatsoever.

We've been calling this 'post-truth politics' but I now worry that the phrase is far too gentle, suggesting society has simply reached some new phase in its development. It lets off the guilty too lightly. What Trump is doing is not 'engaging in post-truth politics'. He's lying.

Worse still, Trump and those like him not only lie: they imply that the truth doesn't matter, showing a blithe indifference to whether what they say is grounded in reality or evidence.

Back in 2000, such a posture left you isolated in that never-never world inhabited by Irving. Today you'll have a US president, a British foreign secretary (never forget the £350m Brexit bus), as well as a ready army of fake news consumers to keep you company.

How has this happened so quickly? Technology has clearly played a part. Social media allows fact-deniers to spread their anti-history fast and wide. Distrust in elites is also central. People are no longer prepared to take their leaders' word on trust. Iraq poisoned that relationship, but its roots go deeper. In the US, Watergate broke public faith; some suspect the rot set in even earlier, with the Kennedy assassination.

But a crucial shift is surely the trend towards deeper and more bitter partisanship. Once people have aligned themselves with a tribe, studies show their first instinct will be to believe what favours their side and disbelieve what favours their opponent. One telling poll this week found Vladimir Putin's approval ratings have shot up among US Republicans. They once hated him, but now their guy Trump is Putin's buddy they're ready to see the Russian autocrat in a favourable light – and to ignore all evidence to the contrary.

This is making our public sphere a dizzying place. Without a common, agreed set of facts, we can hardly have any kind of public conversation at all. Writer David Roberts, one of the first to use the phrase 'post-truth', says that these days: 'There are no more referees. There are only players.'

We have no group of non-partisan arbiters, trusted to define at least the factual basis for our collective discussion. When actual judges enter the picture, as they have in the Brexit article 50 case, one side rushes to discredit them, branding them as biased, ideological partisans, no less tainted and untrustworthy than everyone else: enemies of the people.

What's so odd about this is that we are happy to accept that there are facts, and judges of fact, in every other aspect of our lives. Philosopher Quassim Cassam notes if a car mechanic says your brakes have broken, you don't denounce him as biased and drive on: you listen. If a doctor says you have a tumour, you don't mock him as a member of the medical elite. We even accept expert judgment on reality TV: no one minds Mary Berry deciding who should win *Bake Off*.

Only in the political realm have we somehow drifted into a world in which no one can be trusted, not on questions of judgment, nor even on questions of fact. But we cannot live in such a world. Evidence, facts and reason are the building blocks of civilisation. Without them we plunge into darkness.

26 December

Talented and unique: George Michael took a singular path to stardom

ALEXIS PETRIDIS

On Christmas Eve, the night before George Michael's death was announced, BBC4 broadcast a repeat of a 34-year-old edition of *Top of the Pops*. Wham! appeared, performing their second single, 'Young Guns (Go for It!)'.

It was a fantastic single, clearly made by someone with an innate understanding of how to turn what was happening at the cutting edge of black music into brassy, funny, hook-laden pop, and it confirmed Wham! as 1982's other big new pop phenomenon after Culture Club.

But many felt they were not a band who seemed destined to leave a lasting mark. Quite the contrary. The more their records sold, the more they were sternly derided as symbolic of a shift in British pop from the socially and politically engaged post-punk era to something flimsy and depthless.

On 'Round Here', a song about his youth in Hertfordshire from his 2004 album *Patience*, Michael sang about Wham! being inspired by the Specials and the Jam, among others.

They didn't feel the same way. Jerry Dammers of the Specials was so incensed by Wham!'s debut single 'Wham Rap' – with its apparently blithe attitude to rising unemployment – that he wrote a song mocking it, 'Bright Lights'. The Jam's Paul Weller was equally dismissive about 'Young Guns (Go for It!)': 'Go for fucking what?' he'd complained in *NME*.

As it turned out, those first impressions were wrong. Wham! were a noticeably smarter and more complex band than their brash front suggested. 'Wham Rap' was a song not so much about indifference to unemployment as resilience in the face of it.

A powerful streak of knowing irony and camp ran through their music that's perhaps easier to see in retrospect than it was at the time. Frequently depicted as the musical incarnation of the Thatcher era, they played benefit gigs for miners during the 1984–85 strike.

Marketed as rampantly heterosexual – on their first tour, Michael and his partner Andrew Ridgeley earned a degree of notoriety by stuffing their shorts with shuttlecocks, which they then threw to the screaming audience – their songs kept offering oblique suggestions that all was not quite as it seemed: 'I choose to cruise,' sang Michael on 'Wham Rap'; there's something intriguing about quite how furious the narrator of 'Young Guns (Go for It!)' is about his friend announcing he's going to get married. And its beautifully turned pop songwriting was no fluke. Michael, it quickly transpired, was capable of knocking out hits to order. Every single Wham! released over the next four years entered the top 10, save for a 'Megamix' of previous hits released without their consent: four of them went to number one.

Their success clearly wasn't enough for Michael. He was maturing quickly as a songwriter, as evidenced by the six and a half minutes of 'Everything She Wants', a lyric about being trapped in a relationship with an increasingly demanding woman to a sublime synth-funk backing, improbably stuck on the other side of the deathless 'Last Christmas'.

It was hard to avoid the suspicion that he felt constrained by Wham!, by their image, by the exclamation mark at the end of their name that seemed to suggest everything they did would be fun and frothy. At Live Aid, he appeared not with Wham! but duetting with Elton John on 'Don't Let the Sun Go Down on Me', Ridgeley relegated to the ranks of backing singers, alongside Kiki Dee.

Tellingly, Michael released the lovelorn 'Careless Whisper' under his name, as if he felt it didn't fit with the brand he had helped create. More telling still was the release of his second solo single, 'A Different Corner', shortly before Wham! announced their split.

Wham!'s later hits increasingly tended towards irrepressible 60s soul pastiches: 'Wake Me Up Before You Go-Go', 'Freedom', 'The Edge of Heaven'. 'A Different Corner' was something else entirely: a sombre, fragile, drumless drift of a song with no hook-laden chorus. The fact that it went to number one perhaps said more about the degree of success Wham! were enjoying at the time – their farewell concert was in front of 72,000 people at Wembley Stadium – than its commerciality.

Michael had clearly been laying the groundwork for a solo career that was very distinct from Wham!. The transition from teen pop star to adult artist is one of the trickiest moves to pull off successfully. He made it look bizarrely painless: Michael seemed to know exactly what he wanted and how to get it.

His next solo single was a duet with Aretha Franklin, 'I Knew You Were Waiting (for Me)', a transatlantic number one that went on to win a Grammy for best R&B performance. Moreover, the very fact that Michael was now working with the Queen of Soul automatically conferred a certain gravitas upon him – like the Live Aid duet with John, it suggested he had been fast-tracked from *Top of the Pops* into the orbit of musical legends – cementing the idea that he was now an entirely different artist to the shut-tlecock-stuffing singer of 'Young Guns' and 'Bad Boys'.

In case anyone had missed the point, his debut solo album, *Faith*, opened with the sound of Wham!'s 'Freedom' played on a church organ, as if at a funeral. It went on to sell 25 million copies – as many records as his former band had sold over their entire career. You could see why. *Faith* had it all.

There was attention-stoking controversy in the shape of 'I Want Your Sex' (anyone looking for evidence of how times have changed might alight on the fact that in 1987, not only was its video banned, some TV and radio presenters refused to even mention the song's title).

Its contents offered a succession of beautifully crafted hit singles – six in total – that ran the gamut from slick funk to pop to heartbroken ballads. It crossed musical boundaries to such a degree that it became the first album by a white artist to top the US R&B charts, something Michael was proud of.

He was now arguably the biggest pop star in the world, but Michael still seemed dissatisfied with the nature of his success. 'You look for your dreams in heaven, but what the hell are you supposed to do when they come true?' he sang, glumly, on 'Waiting', a track from *Faith*'s follow-up.

He called the album *Listen Without Prejudice Vol 1*, as if he felt something of Wham!'s frivolity still clung to his image, and he refused to make a video for its first single, 'Praying for Time'. The album noticeably failed to repeat *Faith*'s blockbuster success, although it still sold 8 million copies.

There were far fewer pop hooks on offer, more social commentary, a sense of melancholy introspection that infects the only two songs you could reasonably describe as up-tempo.

As with Wham!, you occasionally get the feeling that the still publicly closeted Michael was trying to alert fans to the truth about his sexuality: 'I think there's something you should know, I think it's time I stopped the show, there's something deep inside of me, there's someone I forgot to be,' offers 'Freedom! '90'.

If you're occasionally struck by the sense of an artist who had made his rise to fame seem effortless trying a little too hard to be taken seriously, it also contained some of his greatest songs, not least the impossibly lovely confection of jazzy drums and floating synthesiser on 'Cowboys and Angels'.

The projected follow-up, *Listen Without Prejudice Vol 2*, never appeared: he gave music intended for it away to an Aids charity album and also donated the proceeds of another, 'Too Funky', when it was released as a single in 1992.

An acclaimed appearance at the Freddie Mercury tribute concert and an EP of covers aside, Michael more or less vanished for the next four years: when he reappeared, it was with 'Jesus to a Child', a shattered-sounding lament for Anselmo Feleppa, who had died in 1993 from an Aids-related brain haemorrhage.

The subsequent album *Older* was, understandably, even more bleak and solemn than its predecessor. Even the solitary dance track, the brilliant 'Fastlove', had a noticeable darkness to its tone: 'In the absence of security, I made my way into the night.'

Michael later claimed the album was another attempt to quietly reveal the fact that he was gay to his fans without involving the press. When the newspapers finally did get their story two years later, with his arrest for engaging in a lewd act in a Beverly Hills toilet, it seemed to reignite the sense of sly humour that had been largely absent from his work since Wham!'s demise.

His musical response was a witty celebration of the pleasures of cottaging, 'Outside', complete with a video depicting him performing in a toilet cubicle decked out like a disco. The police officer who arrested him claimed the video caused him 'emotional distress'; his subsequent attempt to win damages was dismissed.

On his covers album *Songs from the Last Century*, he amended the lyrics of 'My Baby Just Cares for Me' to make a reference to the pulchritude of singer Ricky Martin: when he released a protest single attacking Tony Blair and George W Bush over the invasion of Iraq, it arrived with an animated video that variously depicted Michael in drag, dressed as Homer Simpson and seducing Cherie Blair.

Over the past decade, stories about Michael's drug use, sex life and ill health overshadowed the music he made. He remained defiant in interviews and onstage, but it still seemed a shame: what turned out to be his final album, *Patience*, was often opaque, overlong and frequently required effort on the part of the listener – it really did sound like an album made by a man who smoked a lot of marijuana – but its highlights suggested his songwriting abilities were unimpaired: 'My Mother Had a Brother', 'Round Here', the glittery spectacular of 'Flawless (Go to the City)'.

His first tour in 15 years, 2006's 25 Live, was an unmitigated triumph: boldly staged so that Michael essentially faced arena audiences alone, with his backing band relegated to the shadows. It grossed more than $200m.

The feeling that whatever else might have been going on in his life, he could be relied upon to create interesting music never faded: this month there was news that he was planning to make an album with Beyoncé producer Naughty Boy.

It sounded like the start of an intriguing new chapter, but Michael's musical legacy was already sealed years ago. His career showed that you could escape teen pop stardom with aplomb, or at least you could if you were Michael.

It says something about the singularity of his talent that scores of artists have tried to follow it, and almost none of them have succeeded in quite the way he did.

When Michael's life ended he was an entirely different artist to the one he began as. Once mocked as flimsy and depthless, he turned out to be anything but.

29 DECEMBER

Reporting while Muslim: how I covered the US presidential election

SABRINA SIDDIQUI

'We should exterminate them.'

The words rolled off the voter's tongue as though he was merely discussing a pest invasion in his home. He was talking about Muslims.

I froze as I became suddenly aware of my own Muslim identity, my long hair just barely covering my necklace that bears the name of Allah in Arabic script.

The conversation had begun just as any interaction with a voter does. The man had come to see Rand Paul speak at a luncheon in Rock Hill, South Carolina, and I approached him to gauge his thoughts on the Kentucky senator's candidacy.

It was when the topic turned to national security, which he listed as his top priority, that he expressed his desire to purge Muslims from the United States.

'When you say exterminate, do you mean we should kill Muslims living in America?' I followed up, masking my incredulity as I've been trained to do as a journalist.

'Yes,' he confirmed. 'If they don't leave, we start killing them.'

I had never feared for my personal safety while on the road covering previous US elections. But it occurred to me in that moment I was travelling alone, clocking up countless hours in my rental car across a state I did not know.

Although his words remain with me 19 months later, I didn't make too much of it then. Only now, in retrospect, does the encounter foreshadow the anger and fear that was a dominant theme of the 2016 campaign.

I was among the hundreds of reporters who spent nearly two years living out of a suitcase and hotel rooms to cover an election that soon became the biggest story in the world. But as a Muslim, I was just one of a handful.

I covered candidates as a member of the travelling press – first Marco Rubio, then Hillary Clinton. In between the shuffle of rallies, buses and planes, I pursued stories on the ground in battleground states seeking to capture the mood of the electorate.

Unlike my friend Asma Khalid, who eloquently chronicled her experience, there was nothing obviously Muslim about me.

I don't wear a hijab and, to most who have a certain image of what Muslims look like, the woman in the sleeveless, knee-length dresses wasn't it.

It was perhaps because they did not make the connection that voters often opened up to me with their candid thoughts about Muslims.

There were many more chilling conversations with those who, like the man in South Carolina, wished aloud for violence and concentration camps.

Others were somewhat humorous, like the sweet old lady who pulled me aside at a New Hampshire diner. She warned me that Isis was looking for brides and was genuinely concerned I might be kidnapped. Tell your editors to get you some security, she lectured.

But as the campaign dragged on, so did the toll of separating my personal identity from my professional obligations.

I recall the day when Ben Carson stated in an interview he did not believe a Muslim should be president of the United States. I went about my task of gathering reaction from the other 16 Republican presidential contenders almost robotically, until the tears dropped on my keyboard as I typed.

That same week, I kept myself composed when offering political analysis of the moment on MSNBC. But I nearly lost it again later when my cousin's daughter, raised as my niece, bounded over to me at a family party.

She was seven years old at the time and typically watched my television appearances to see what I was wearing or to admire the glossy makeup and hair.

But this time she had a question.

She asked: Is it true someone said we can't be president?

I felt as though someone had punched me in the gut.

To this American-born Girl Scout, then in just the second

grade, someone hadn't simply said a Muslim shouldn't be a president. Someone had said she should not be president.

I told her not to worry – she could be anything she wanted to be, even president.

Cynically, I didn't believe my own words and was tempted to tell her parents perhaps she shouldn't watch my segments during the election. But that seemed an overreaction. Besides, I thought, how much worse could it get?

On the evening of 7 December, I was in the midst of dinner when Donald Trump called for a total ban of all Muslims from entering the US.

Sparking controversy was nothing new for the Republican frontrunner, but I thought surely this time he had been taken out of context. It was then that I switched to CNN, where Trump stood at a rally in South Carolina, reading the statement himself.

I had hesitated to use my personal voice in the election, mindful of maintaining my professionalism. But it dawned on me that some newsrooms in America had one or two Muslims at best; most of them had none.

I've always advocated for more diversity in the media. What good came from pushing editors to hire more minorities, only to feel it would be somehow inappropriate for us to share certain perspectives unique to us?

And so I sent a tweet noting my family was American but had spent 10 years living abroad in Italy during my childhood. Would we not be allowed to return home under Trump's proposal today?

His campaign soon clarified the ban would not apply to US citizens. But it would affect all Muslim foreign nationals until, as Trump put it, the US government could figure out 'what the hell is going on'.

I tweeted once more about how much of my family would still be barred from coming to visit.

My goal was not to push an agenda, but to make clear who would be affected by such a proposal. Even to some of my colleagues in the media, Muslim-majority countries can conjure frightening images.

They ought to at least know that my version of people coming from Pakistan is my aunts, uncles and cousins joining our family for Thanksgiving or spending their summer holidays here. And so it is for the vast majority of Muslims who enter the US, as tourists, students or workers.

I carried on, as usual, reporting the news that stemmed from Trump's comments: the politics, the policy implications, the condemnation from members of his own party that had become routine.

It was always at the night's end, as I settled into another hotel bed, that it hit me. I was often so exhausted that I could no longer remember which part of the country I was even in, and yet there were so many nights I simply couldn't sleep.

The more Muslim profiling rose to the forefront of the debate, the more I wrestled with how to navigate my background

The week before the New Hampshire primary, Marco Rubio criticised Barack Obama's visit that day to a mosque during a rally. His comments drew instant headlines and posed an obvious follow-up question when he appeared before reporters the next day.

Since I was embedded with the campaign, I knew I would get a question and indeed I did. I prepared to ask Rubio why he took issue with Obama's visit and if he was suggesting he would not go to a mosque as president. But something came over me.

With the nominating contests in full swing, there was a much larger media presence and I hesitated upon realising I was the only Muslim there. Am I going to be the Muslim reporter asking the Muslim question? I thought.

I chose a different topic, certain that one of the many reporters there would ask the senator about the main reason he was in the headlines that day.

But as the press conference came to an end, the question went unasked.

I realised my error immediately, not as a Muslim but as a journalist.

When George Stephanopoulos asked Rubio to clarify his comments about Obama's mosque visit at a Republican debate days later, it was an instructive moment for me. It was a valid question, and I should not have doubted my authority to ask it.

My reticence was born in part from how my increasing visibility on the campaign trail was met by a faction of readers.

On any given day, some following my work, most of them Trump supporters, would fill my mentions with photos of suicide bombings and other violent images from terrorist attacks. I dealt with threats which I reported to Twitter, but they were often of the variety that were batted away as part and parcel of social media, where anonymity allows for no limits.

There were times when I felt as though I may not have it in me to continue.

I had been hired by the *Guardian* to cover the campaign and jumped at the chance to go out on the trail. On the surface I was having the time of my life, but internally I struggled a great deal.

That's not to say it was not an unforgettable experience. I learned a lot by travelling to parts of the country I would not have otherwise seen, built lasting friendships and grew as a reporter.

I realised, too, that my community was counting on me.

There was the Syrian couple who approached me at a Rubio rally in Virginia asking me to keep at it, and the Bangladeshi immigrants who told me at a Hillary Clinton rally in Iowa they were pleasantly surprised to see a Muslim face on TV talking not about national security but about general politics.

There were also routinely words of encouragement, from friends, professional acquaintances and strangers who came from both parties, spanned all backgrounds and reminded me why my parents chose America as their home nearly 40 years ago.

I'd be lying if I said that alone was enough to make up for feeling at times like an outsider in my own country. It didn't change that I underestimated just how many of my fellow Americans wouldn't say aloud what they really think of Muslims or immigrants.

My approach to eradicating Muslim stereotypes has always been to try to put forth the best version of myself. I learned from this election that the real work begins now.

Winter

I've left Twitter. It is unusable for anyone but trolls, robots and dictators

LINDY WEST

I deactivated my Twitter account today. It was more of a spontaneous impulse than a new year resolution, although it does feel like a juice cleanse, a moulting, a polar-bear plunge, a clean slate (except the opposite – like throwing your slate into a volcano and running). One moment I was brains-deep in the usual way, half-heartedly arguing with strangers about whether or not it's 'OK' to suggest to Steve Martin that calling Carrie Fisher a 'beautiful creature' who 'turned out' to be 'witty and bright as well' veered just a hair beyond Fisher's stated boundaries regarding objectification (if you have opinions on this, don't tweet me – oh, wait, you can't); and the next moment the US president-elect was using the selfsame platform to taunt North Korea about the size and tumescence of its nuclear programme. And I realised: eh, I'm done. I could be swimming right now. Or flossing. Or digging a big, pointless pit. Anything else.

Twitter, for the past five years, has been a machine where I put in unpaid work and tension headaches come out. I write jokes there for free. I post political commentary for free. I answer questions for free. I teach feminism 101 for free. Off Twitter, these are all things by which I make my living – in fact, they comprise the totality of my income. But on Twitter, I do them pro bono and, in return, I am micromanaged in real time by strangers; neo-Nazis mine my personal life for vulnerabilities to exploit; and men enjoy unfettered, direct access to my brain so they can inform me, for the thousandth time, that they would gladly rape me if I weren't so fat.

I talk back and I am 'feeding the trolls'. I say nothing and the harassment escalates. I report threats and I am a 'censor'. I use mass-blocking tools to curb abuse and I am abused further for blocking 'unfairly'. I have to conclude, after half a decade of troubleshooting, that it may simply be impossible to make this platform usable for anyone but trolls, robots and dictators.

Surprisingly, none of that is the reason I left. I still loved Twitter – the speed of information, the breadth of analysis, the jokes, the gifs, the fortifying albeit intermittent solidarity, the chance to vet your instincts against those of people much smarter and better informed than you. Every day, people on Twitter – particularly people of colour, trans activists, disabled activists and sex workers – taught me how to be a better person and a better neighbour, a gift they persisted in dispensing even (always) at great personal cost. I still believe, at least in the rear-view mirror, in Twitter's importance as a democratising force – facilitating direct, transparent access between the disempowered and the powerful, the marginalised and the ignorant. But I'm leaving anyway, for a while.

I hate to disappoint anyone, but the breaking point for me wasn't the trolls themselves (if I have learned anything from the dark side of Twitter, it is how to feel nothing when a frog calls you a cunt) – it was the global repercussions of Twitter's refusal to stop them. The white supremacist, anti-feminist, isolationist, transphobic 'alt-right' movement has been beta-testing its propaganda and intimidation machine on marginalised Twitter communities for years now – how much hate speech will bystanders ignore? When will Twitter intervene and start protecting its users? – and discovered, to its leering delight, that the limit did not exist. No one cared. Twitter abuse was a grand-scale normalisation project, disseminating libel and disinformation, muddying long-held cultural givens such as 'racism is bad' and 'sexual assault is bad' and 'lying is bad' and 'authoritarianism is bad', and ultimately greasing the wheels for Donald Trump's ascendance to the US presidency. Twitter executives did nothing.

On 29 December, Twitter CEO Jack Dorsey tweeted: 'What's the most important thing you want to see Twitter improve or create in 2017?' One user responded: 'Comprehensive plan for getting rid of the Nazis.'

'We've been working on our policies and controls,' Dorsey replied. 'What's the next most critical thing?' Oh, what's our second-highest priority after Nazis? I'd say number two is also Nazis. And number three. In fact, you can just go ahead and slide 'Nazis' into the top 100 spots. Get back to me when your website isn't a roiling rat-king of Nazis. Nazis are bad, you see?

Trump uses his Twitter account to set hate mobs on private citizens, attempt to silence journalists who write unfavourably about him, lie to the American people and bulldoze complex diplomatic relationships with other world powers. I quit Twitter because it feels unconscionable to be a part of it – to generate revenue for it, participate in its profoundly broken culture and lend my name to its legitimacy. Twitter is home to a wealth of fantastic anti-Trump organising, as well, but I'm personally weary of feeling hostage to a platform that has treated me and the people I care about so poorly. We can do good work elsewhere.

I'm pretty sure 'ushered in kleptocracy' would be a dealbreaker for any other company that wanted my business. If my gynaecologist regularly hosted neo-Nazi rallies in the exam room, I would find someone else to swab my cervix. If I found out my favourite coffee shop was even remotely complicit in the third world war,

I would – bare minimum – switch coffee shops; I might give up coffee altogether.

Apparently that sentiment is in the air because, as I was writing this column, I came across a post by my friend Lauren Hoffman, a writer for *Vulture* and *Cosmopolitan*: 'I've made many real/good friends on Twitter but I guess if I met all my friends working at, like, the mall and the mall became a tacit endorsement of fascism I would keep the friends but stop going to the mall.'

Keep the friends. Ditch the mall.

17 JANUARY

May can think big all she likes. Britain's about to find out just how small it is

RAFAEL BEHR

Maybe the European Union is God's way of teaching the British about Belgium. Specifically, it is a mechanism that forces UK politicians to confront the idea that Belgium matters. And not just Belgium but countries like it – the small countries.

This concept doesn't come naturally to a nation that is neurotically worried about its greatness. Naming famous Belgians is a parlour game for British foreign secretaries. Cultivating small-state alliances feels like something less ambitious countries do. The UK struggles to see itself in perspective because it is richer and more powerful than most countries, yet so much less influential than it used to be.

We are not alone in suffering from post-imperial angst, but we have tied ourselves in uniquely existential knots where relations with our European neighbours are concerned. Theresa May understands the deep cultural and psychological attraction of Brexit as a great unpicking – a disentanglement from continental ties, the benefits of which feel obscure to much of the public.

Therein lies the emotional cleverness of the prime minister's formulation of a 'clean Brexit', as laid out in her speech on Tuesday. Pro-Europeans probe the agonising detail of the negotiations to come without recruiting any more of the public to share their pain. If anything, the balance of opinion is swinging the other way. The prime minister's message was tailored to the large segment of voters, including many ex-remainers, who see the big in/out question as settled and say they want the job done without any more palaver.

The effectiveness of May's account of future relations with the EU – no 'partial membership', no messy overlaps with the past – is its simplicity. Her Europhile critics want to talk only about complexity, which is the least catchy tune in politics. May paints Britain with the crispness of its outline restored, its place in the world made clearer by the erasure of all those fiddly lines that connect London to Brussels and then to Paris, Berlin, Ljubljana, Tallinn and the rest. She offers liberation from the need to care about Belgians.

That obligation endures whether the prime minister wants it or not. Small states will have a say in the divorce contract terms that Britain signs with the EU. Their voice will be heard in the negotiations and in chambers where the deal must be ratified. It was opposition in Belgium's Wallonian regional parliament that nearly scuppered a Canada–EU free-trade agreement last year.

No less important than pragmatic attention to small-state sensibilities is the strategic and moral duty that Britain owes to lesser powers. The EU has historically been good at inflating the influence of minor capitals, to the frustration of major ones. It has also allowed the most powerful economies – Germany, France and the UK – to throw their weight around, to the annoyance of lesser players. This voluntary national surrender of autonomy in some dimensions for greater influence in others is the essence of the European project, and it mystifies the kind of politician who wants international relations to be a league table of countries, with an obvious champion at the top.

When, earlier this week, Donald Trump described the EU dismissively as 'a vehicle for Germany' likely to lose more members after Brexit, he was aggravating diplomatic vandalism with historical ignorance. The apparatus of European integration first came into existence, and has been sustained in large part, by German atonement for its 20th-century crimes, expressed as willingness to subordinate a narrowly defined national interest for wider continental cooperation.

But Trump struggles with the concept of mutual arrangements that guarantee stability without yielding a fist-pumping victory or cash payout to one party. He craves the firm smack of a deal. He appears to find the idea of big countries lending power to smaller ones for the sake of anything so sissy as 'shared values' contemptible. He sees Nato as a European tax on the US military.

It is one of the ways in which his instincts and those of Vladimir Putin are aligned. The Russian president also has no interest in a system of international relations based on rules and protocol. For Putin, the EU has always been an obstacle to the pursuit of a divide-and-rule strategy within the former Soviet sphere of influence in the old Eastern bloc. He and Trump would both prefer a Europe of disparate and disorganised nation states, all potential clients of Washington and Moscow, without an organising principle of their own.

This is not May's vision. In her speech she emphasised a hope that the EU succeed post-Brexit, and underlined her belief that the union should not unravel. That such a wish even has to be expressed testifies to a world in alarming flux.

The US is about to acquire a president who is relaxed about the dissolution of essential pillars of European security, when not actively undermining them. And this is the president whose offer of a trade deal is meant to give Britain confidence that Brexit will work. Given Trump's known views on trade and the aggressive protectionists whose company he keeps, it is safe to presume that the non-negotiable terms of that deal will be total vassalage to US corporate interests. It will require a surrender of economic sovereignty every bit as great as that involved in EU membership, with none of the accompanying diplomatic clout.

May's speech on Tuesday was meant to be a beacon illuminating Britain's future outside the EU. But, coming days before Trump's inauguration, it should be read also as an unwitting requiem for the global order that is passing away. It imagined a place where the contours of power are neatly defined and stable, where Britain has freedom to choose its friends and decide its status in the world. Viewed from Trump Tower, Britain sits in the bottom half of the first division of world players: a leading G7 economy, a nuclear-armed security council member, but not a superpower. Our interests matter, but probably not that much more than Belgian interests currently matter in Whitehall.

It's a question of perspective. For decades Britain has struggled to get a comfortable sense of its scale relative to the rest of the world. We are about to find out how big – or small – we really are.

20 JANUARY

A morning with 'adorable deplorables': why Trump supporters are optimistic

LOIS BECKETT

On the bus, in the morning darkness, Steph and Brandi put on their makeup, using a phone as a mirror.

Stephanie Friess and Brandi Tillman have been friends since high school, and now they are on their way from Wilmington, Delaware, to Washington to celebrate the man who has given them a brand-new country.

On election night, Steph stayed up past 3am to see Trump's victory being announced. The next morning, remembering the night before while driving her car, the 24-year-old felt jubilant to be living in Trump's America.

The two women made matching Trump caps – blue and black – decorated with sequins and the slogan 'Adorable Deplorable' in honour of the inauguration. Hillary Clinton had tried to attack Trump for lifting up the most 'deplorable' among his followers: 'the racist, sexist, homophobic, xenophobic, Islamophobic – you name it'. Trump's followers had proudly reclaimed the term, and now Brandi and Steph had bedazzled it.

On Saturday, hundreds of thousands of women will be marching in Washington in protest of Trump's presidency in a demonstration called the Women's March.

While large majorities of black and Latina women voted against Trump and for Hillary Clinton, white women didn't.

Brandi and Steph are part of the majority: early exit polls showed that 53 per cent of white women voted for Trump, including 45 per cent of women with college degrees.

The two women, both college students, were not entirely convinced by Donald Trump at first. But, Steph said, 'he definitely grows on you'. Both friends say they appreciate Trump's bluntness, his toughness, his lack of greed, and what seems like a genuine love for America.

'He wants everyone to be successful,' Stephanie said. 'He isn't putting people down.'

Brandi liked Mitt Romney, but 'he wasn't strong enough', the 25-year-old said. 'He wasn't empowering us enough. He plays that innocent politician role that all politicians play. Trump doesn't do that.'

On the bus to Washington, many of the women's fellow white Trump supporters expressed frustration at constantly being labelled racist. It was a term, some argued, that liberals just threw around whenever they were losing an argument.

A local bakery in Pennsylvania had just produced tiny hat-shaped 'Make America Great Again' cakes in honour of the inauguration, and a short post about the themed cakes on Facebook had sparked a long debate, with some commenters labelling the bakery racist, or saying they would not longer patronise it. 'Why not a "grab 'em by the p*ssy" cake?' one commenter asked. 'Or a "deport all immigrants" cake?'

The bus supporters were indignant. They had won. It was supposed to be a day to celebrate. And yet the news was full of protests and threatened disruption, and even a bakery making an inauguration dessert had somehow become divisive.

'A cake can't be racist,' Dave DeFries, a longtime Trump supporter from Delaware County, Pennsylvania, said in exasperation.

In the seat behind Brandi and Steph, Laura Ann, 34, who asked that her last name not be used, had bought two of them. She sliced them and handed them out. The cake was moist, the frosting tasting faintly of marshmallow.

Laura Ann had voted for Obama twice. She worked in health-care, and had wanted the president to fix the health insurance system. He had failed. She was still kicking herself for voting for him. As a gun owner with several AR-15 rifles – she found them light and easy to handle as a female shooter – she had also been frustrated by the constant attacks on 'the so-called "assault rifle"'.

'I'd really like to see [Trump] help the inner cities more,' she said. She thought Ben Carson, who grew up in Detroit and went on to become a surgeon, would be a great force in helping urban America.

Eileen, at 46, had cast her first ballot ever for Trump. 'I want the jobs to come back to America,' she said. Her brother, a systems analyst, had lost his job to workers in India and had been forced to personally train the Indian worker who was taking his place, under threat of losing his pension.

Eileen also felt Obama had failed to bring insurance compa-nies in line to bring healthcare costs down. Worried that her high-school friends who voted for Clinton would attack her, she asked not to publish her last name.

Many of the supporters said they had never been politically involved before Trump ran for president. Several had voted for Obama at least once. Some of the new activists said they were amazed by the energy of Trump's movement. 'It doesn't seem like a political environment,' Dave Ennis said. 'It seems like we're going to a football game.'

Some said that their friends or family were worried that something might happen on inauguration day, that the protests might make DC dangerous. One man mentioned that he had seen a video produced by the conservative provocateur James O'Keefe about activists discussing a plan to throw acid on Trump supporters.

At the back of the bus, another Dave (who did not give his last name) sat opposite his wife and 16-year-old son, Brian, who he called a liberal 'snowflake'. The two of them argued constantly, the father said, especially about Black Lives Matter.

Brian said he believed that the Black Lives Matter protesters and the Boston Tea Party rebels were identical – except for their race. Protesters had to be loud to make themselves noticed. His father was more sceptical that black Americans were being unfairly victimised. His own interactions with the police when he was younger had taught him that when people chose a certain lifestyle, the police would target them – and there was nothing wrong with that.

Brandi and Steph said they felt that racism towards black Americans had been given a disproportionate platform compared with other kinds of racism. They disapproved of Obama supporting the Black Lives Matter movement, which they saw as racist.

'Why is it Black Lives Matter, not all lives?' Stephanie asked.

'I just don't think most cops are out to get black people,' Brandi replied.

'The media blows a lot of this out of proportion,' Stephanie said.

'I didn't think it's bad that we had a first black president. That's not bad. That's great,' Brandi opined. But Obama 'should not have been elected to a second term. I think his colour had a lot to do with that.'

In school, Brandi said, some black girls had bullied her, and when she complained, 'my teacher told me to grow a thicker skin'.

Asked about the systemic inequality black Americans face – in the criminal justice system, or in education – Brandi said that, because she's been living in Delaware, a relatively liberal state, 'maybe I haven't seen that as much'.

'I, like, see the opposite. Black people get free college,' she said. 'My mom's a single mom. I'm not white privileged, and I'm sick of being told I am.'

Both said they felt they had grown up and gone to school while constantly being told things 'trying to make us feel bad for being white'. Slavery was a topic of discussion again and again, the schools focused on black authors, 'it's always black history month'.

'It's like, I get it, I get it, slavery was bad. I didn't do it,' Brandi said.

Brandi said she felt bad for her other minority friends – Hispanic, Asian, Indian – who also faced racism, but seemed to get less attention. Her Indian American friends faced job discrimination, she believed, by people who might not think they fit the look they wanted, or who bought into the stereotype that they might be terrorists.

Both friends also had some concerns about Trump. Stephanie didn't believe for a long time that Trump could really pull off a presidential demeanour. That's why she thought Clinton would win. Brandi said she did not believe new environmental protections should be rolled back, and her stepmother had serious concerns about Trump's pick for education secretary, Betsy DeVos, a billionaire philanthropist and school choice advocate whose understanding of basic educational concepts and laws came under question during her confirmation hearing. 'I know teachers aren't very happy about that,' she said.

'I'm a little bit worried about the tweeting,' Brandi added. She was concerned, she said, that 'he might say something ...'

'That he can't take back,' Steph broke in.

But for the most part, the two friends were optimistic that Trump would tackle the economy, create jobs, address cyber-attacks, and make America stronger. Brandi, who was waitressing as she went through college, said: 'I'd like to see more money. I'd like to see more tips.'

Neither of the friends had been concerned about his comments about grabbing women by the pussy. 'That was 10 years ago, and people change,' Brandi said.

Brandi said if a famous billionaire had tried to grope her, she would have sued immediately, not stayed silent for years until the man ran for president. 'Damn straight, if someone gropes me, I would want to sue,' she said. Steph disagreed. She probably would have stayed quiet, she said.

A Belgian journalist who was also on the bus then took his turn and interviewed the two women about their support for Trump, and asked them to comment on the fears many Americans have about the coming months.

Brandi said her faith as a Christian kept her from being too anxious, and that Americans should calm down. Trump, after all, was just the president.

'He's not God. He's not Hitler. It's not the end of the world,' she said.

20 JANUARY

Trump's first speech in office was an unapologetic appeal to nationalism

GARY YOUNGE

Even the heavens wept. As Donald Trump stepped forward to become America's 45th president the cold shower that broke over Washington offered no end of metaphors. His address, however, was literal to a fault. There was no higher calling, no sense of a greater purpose, no florid imagery or impassioned idealism. This was as crude and unapologetic an appeal to nationalism as one might expect from a man incapable of rising to an occasion without first refracting it through his ego.

It is said that presidents campaign in poetry and govern in prose. Trump campaigned in graffiti – the profane scrawls of a mindless vandal – and, if his inaugural address was anything to go by, may yet govern in tweets – the impulsive, abbreviated interventions of a narcissist.

Were this a reality TV show, we would have switched off by now. All the better qualified, more sympathetic and empathic characters have been eliminated. The last man standing is a scheming, pathological misanthrope whose disrespect for the rules alone should have disqualified him. The producer would have been fired; the advertisers would have bolted. Nobody in their right mind would want anything to do with it.

But there is a difference between reality TV and something surreal that you can watch on TV. From the robed supreme court chief justice holding aloft Lincoln's Bible for Trump to swear on to the gathering of former presidents, the entire purpose of an inauguration is to celebrate a mature democracy. As the White House is bequeathed to the popular choice, it's intended to symbolise continuity and stability – a common destiny in a shared polity.

Friday achieved the opposite. To watch Trump take the oath was to bear witness to democracy's fragility. It marked not simply the transfer of power from one leader to another but the erosion of the very values that give that power legitimacy.

That frailty stems not from any question about whether Trump won the election but how he won it and what that victory portends. There is more to democracy than elections and more to elections than simply voting. Democratic traditions are underpinned by norms that he not only disregarded (on that score he would not be the first) but brazenly and gleefully violated – advocating violence at his rallies, haranguing the media, fuelling racial animus, religious exclusion and misogyny.

As such, his inauguration represents an indictment of an entire political culture. It leaves condemned a Democratic party that could not defeat him, a Republican party that would not disown him, a mainstream media that failed to scrutinise him and a social media that spread his lies far faster than any scrutiny could travel. All were found wanting. Now all will be tested.

This is no local problem. Those who take to the streets across the globe to demonstrate against Trump's presidency over the next few days would do well to stay there and resist his counterparts in their own backyards. Where this particular threat to democracy is concerned, America is by no means exceptional.

In Washington, the moment was all the more disorienting because of what it replaced. Barack Obama's approval ratings are higher now than they have been for some time, reminding us of the stratospheric expectations of that freezing January day when he first took office eight years ago. It's as though his presence could never compete with his promise or his passing.

To watch him accompany Trump through the process was to see the civility of pageantry triumph over the candour of politics. Several of those with front-row seats, from both parties, had concluded Trump was unfit for the office he now holds. 'When making life or death or war or peace decisions,' Michelle Obama said six weeks before election day, 'a president just can't pop off or lash out irrationally ... If a candidate traffics in fear and lies on the campaign trail ... well that is the kind of president they will be.'

That is the president who was sworn in on Friday. No amount of pomp and finery can mask that. That is why what was billed as a ceremony felt more akin to a charade.

It is also why many in the US, and beyond, are not simply concerned about what comes next; they are genuinely terrified. An impulsive braggart and bigot is now in control of the world's most powerful military and economy. Fear and malevolence won. The hands that once grabbed pussy now have access to the nuclear launch codes.

21 JANUARY

The Women's March reminded us: We are not alone

JESSICA VALENTI

It's hard to explain what it feels like to walk alongside a sea of joyful, but fed-up women. My friend Ann Friedman, taking a plane almost entirely filled with women on their way to Washington DC yesterday, described it as 'like drugs'.

And it's true. As I rounded a corner this morning at the Women's March – which at last count had over 500,000 protesters in DC alone – I felt a rush of euphoria when I saw the crowd. Later, as I passed by a group of older women carrying 'Why I March' signs adorned with pictures of their daughters and granddaughters, it was difficult not to weep.

After watching a serial misogynist take the highest office in the nation, after the devastating loss in November, it's overwhelming to remember that we are not alone. That there are more of us who care about equality – 3 million more to be exact – than there are those obsessed with walls and fear.

And so it made sense that the women who arrived in DC today arrived with energy and joy. They flashed peace signs, smiled and shouted greetings at each other as they walked towards the main staging area.

There were women with their babies, women with their grandmothers, women with signs, women in pink 'pussy' hats, and some in Wonder Woman costumes. (Even the actress who plays Super Girl got in on the action, toting a sign that read: 'Don't try to grab my pussy, it's made of steel.')

And although there are plenty of reasons to be angry, this was not a march of anger. None of them were. When you look at the pictures of the protests that took place in hundreds of cities across the world today, putting millions of women on the street, you see something amazing: you see joy. There is singing, dancing, drums, costumes. All of us strangers, but somehow, in that moment, not unfamiliar to each other either.

Even better, the happiness of the day didn't detract from the seriousness that women felt about the political moment. I spoke to a young woman from Toledo, Ohio, in a 'Make America Nasty Again' hat who had spent the whole night on a bus with a friend to get here because she's worried about women's rights. The women I sat next to on my train from New York took a red-eye from California because they were horrified with Trump's immigration stance and misogyny.

And while political experts analysed from afar – David Axelrod, for example, tweeted out that the march's energy would 'mean little' unless 'channelled into sustained political action' – actual protesters and speakers reminded us that they know more than pundits give them credit for.

There were signs making links between feminism and environmentalism, one protester in Boston pointed out that 'Being scared since 2016 is a privilege' and in DC activist and author Janet Mock shined a light on violence against trans people, saying: 'My sisters and siblings are being beaten and brutalised, neglected and invisibilised, extinguished and exiled.'

While today might have been the first moment of activism for some of the people who showed up in their city, or travelled across the country to be in DC, there were just as many who knew that activism didn't begin or end today and that the movement is about more than just showing up.

For the moment, though, it felt beside the point to strategise on what comes next. Today was important – necessary, even – to simply have a day for a mass catharsis, a showing of hope and a reminder that we are in the majority.

And when you walk among crowds of joyful women – women not willing to go back, women ready to fight – it's hard not to feel like we're the winners after all.

29 January

The making of an education catastrophe – schools in Knowsley were dubbed 'wacky warehouses' (extract)

IAN COBAIN

To the east of Liverpool is a local authority area known as the metropolitan borough of Knowsley. It was created in 1974 and whoever drew its boundaries had a magnificent sense of humour.

To start with, its shape: in the north, Knowsley begins at the point where the open farmland of south Lancashire gives way to Kirkby, a postwar expanse of social housing and light industry. In the south, it ends at Halewood, where an enormous Jaguar Land Rover factory whirrs and grinds around the clock, rolling out a finished vehicle every 80 seconds. The distance between the two is more than 11 miles. At its narrowest point, however, Knowsley is less than two miles wide. It is a long, thin streak of a place.

Its illogicality is not confined to its shape. Within those borders are half a dozen places that have no firm connection with each other, historically, geographically or socially.

Almost half the borough is countryside: partly farmland and partly the vast estate of Edward Stanley, the 19th Earl of Derby. The remainder bundles together the old Lancashire towns of Prescot and Whiston, and several unattached areas of housing in Huyton, Kirkby and Halewood that were developed in the 1930s, and again in the 50s and 60s, as so-called 'overspill' from the poorer neighbourhoods of Liverpool.

Today, Knowsley is at the top and the bottom of every British economic and social league table whose top or bottom you would be anxious to avoid.

Around 20 per cent of working-age people are receiving some form of out-of-work benefit. Some areas of the borough suffer from the worst income deprivation in the country; more than a third of local children live in these conditions.

In some households, unemployment has become trans-generational: children are growing up in families where the parents, the grandparents and even, sometimes, the great-grandparents have not worked.

Ethnically, meanwhile, Knowsley is the least diverse corner of Britain. According to the census, around 97 per cent of its population are white. In other words, it is the most white working-class place in the country. At last year's referendum, its people revealed themselves to be very keen to leave the EU, while most of those living elsewhere in the Liverpool area voted firmly to remain. It is also the area where the greatest proportion of people – some 81 per cent – describe themselves as Christian.

Writing in 1965, shortly after the Labour MP for Huyton, Harold Wilson, had been elected prime minister, the political journalist Anthony Howard described the area as home to thousands of Irish families from the slums of inner-city Liverpool. 'The birth rate is said to be the highest outside Red China and the crime rate is one of the highest in Britain,' Howard wrote. 'It has fine skyscraper flats and bright new schools; but the telephone boxes are constantly smashed, litter lies thick on the verges and there are frequent fights in the streets.'

Today, there is less litter and few telephone boxes. Many adjectives are applied to the tower blocks, but 'fine' is rarely heard. And the bright new 60s schools? Well, Knowsley's problems are at their most acute – and most visible – when it comes to education. Its GCSE results are the worst in the country. The government believes that every education authority should, at an absolute minimum, be able to secure five GCSEs at grades A* to C for 40 per cent of its pupils – a target Knowsley has failed to hit for several years.

More than 15 per cent of the borough's working-age population have no educational qualifications, compared with a national average of 8 per cent. And there is worse: in September, Knowsley became the first local authority in the country to cease to offer its young people A-level education. None whatsoever.

Arriving in Huyton, at the centre of the borough, many visitors are struck by just how vast some of the old council estates are; mile after mile of solidly built prewar terraces, now all managed by housing associations.

Turn right and you pass by the Bluebell estate, where Steven Gerrard, the former England football captain, grew up. This area produces a prodigious number of top professional footballers, and despite the globalisation of the game it is not unusual, when Everton play Liverpool, to see three or four men from Huyton and Kirkby on the pitch. It also produces an unusually high number of playwrights and screenwriters specialising in comedy and social realism: Alan Bleasdale, Phil Redmond, Willy Russell.

At the end of Bluebell Lane, you find yourself facing the seven-storey office block that is home to Knowsley metropolitan borough council. Like the borough it serves, the council is a place of extremes. Until last May there were 63 seats on Knowsley council. The Labour party held all of them. In last May's election the number of seats was reduced to 45 and the Liberal Democrats won three. But there hasn't been a Tory on Knowsley council since 1995.

And there is no close media scrutiny either: the *Liverpool Echo* has a reporter spending half their time reporting on the borough but, since the closure many years ago of the local paper, the *Prescot and Huyton Reporter*, no media organisation focuses entirely on local affairs.

All this may go some way to explain one of the more bizarre episodes in Knowsley's recent history: one that served to demoralise teachers, bewilder their pupils and drive educational attainment down still further.

In 2005, the Labour government launched Building Schools for the Future, a programme to invest in secondary-school buildings, aiming to ensure that every child would be educated within a 21st-century environment by 2020.

During the Blair–Brown years, according to some former Knowsley officials, the council would on occasion enthusiastically act as an experimenter for Labour policies. Building Schools for the Future was no exception. Knowsley took the programme to its utmost degree: all 11 secondary schools in the borough were flattened and seven new ones constructed at a cost of £157m. What is more, following an audit of local children's 'learning styles', the council's senior education officers had decided that most were 'kinaesthetic learners': rather than sitting behind desks, they needed to use their bodies and senses, and trial and error.

The new schools were built accordingly. When they opened in 2009, they were not called schools, however, but 'centres for learning'. The kids, when they walked inside, quickly dubbed them 'wacky warehouses'. The teachers – or rather 'progress leaders' – were furious that their warnings had been ignored. Instead of classrooms and corridors there were vast open spaces known as 'base areas', with curtains on runners to create different zones. A child's misbehaviour would be witnessed not by the rest of the class, but by half the school. Keeping track of pupils' movement became a major problem, with teachers resorting to the use of walkie-talkies.

And the acoustics were dreadful. The design and technology classes were next to the science laboratories – with no wall in between – with the result that a child who was hammering a nail into a piece of wood could reach out and touch a child who was trying to learn about the structure of an atom.

One of the new schools, Christ the King in Huyton, was hailed as an exciting centre of learning for the future. It was consigned to history after just four years: parents simply did not wish to send their children there, and fewer than half of its 900 places were filled.

At the other new schools, most headteachers insisted they be given classrooms and corridors. The rebuilding work took place gradually, over several summers. And all the time, the borough's exam results remained stuck to the foot of the national league tables.

As executive director of children's services for the past three years Paul Boyce, a former social worker and social services manager, has the responsibility of sorting out this mess. He could not be more scathing about the way in which Knowsley embraced the concept of kinaesthetic learning. 'Education gurus have been in charge of education here, and I think they used that opportunity to experiment rather than to deliver,' he says. Some aspects of the centres for learning fiasco he derides as 'spaceships and the internet'.

Boyce is quite clear about the principal reason why GCSE results are so poor in Knowsley, and why A-level education is no longer being offered: it is because 43 per cent of Knowsley's children leave to be educated in Liverpool or the neighbouring boroughs to the east, St Helens and Halton, when they are 11 years old.

There are three underlying reasons for this. The first lies in the damned geography of the place; it is such a long, thin borough that very often a child's nearest school – and certainly the nearest good school – will be outside Knowsley. The second is that many parents – particularly, but not exclusively Catholic parents – want to send their children to single-sex schools, and Knowsley has none. And the third is that Knowsley's schools are now seen as second-rate. If you are an aspiring parent in Knowsley, the first thing you do is push your child out of the borough. Those pupils who remain are from families that are the least mobile, and often among the poorest.

There was a further sieving at the age of 16, with many of those children who wished to take A-levels travelling to a sixth-form college outside the borough, particularly the highly regarded Carmel College in St Helens. In 2015, 52 per cent of Knowsley's 16-year-olds opted to study A-levels, which amounted to 981 young people. But only 29 of them were studying in the borough.

Each year, the disappearance of all these children sucks out tens of millions of pounds of government funding that would otherwise be available for Knowsley's education budget. It was only a matter of time before sixth-form education became financially unviable.

Four of Knowsley's six remaining secondary schools have become academies. The remaining two are administered jointly by Knowsley and by the Roman Catholic archdiocese of Liverpool.

By last year only one of these six schools, Halewood Academy, was offering A-level education. But it estimated that it needed at least 155 sixth-formers to break even, and had only 83. In March it announced that its sixth form would need to close in order to balance its books. Parents were powerless to do little more than set up a protest page on Facebook.

At this point, I should probably declare an interest. I grew up in Huyton, attended my local primary school and, aged 11, won a place at the boys' grammar school that then existed in the borough. Prescot grammar school had been founded in 1544 and its black-gowned masters maintained its time-honoured ways: a traditional curriculum, lots of sport, and a predilection for corporal punishment.

We knew we were receiving a good education, however, and this became even clearer once we started studying for our A-levels, when classes became places for inquiry and discourse. The rules became few and far between as we were permitted to explore new boundaries. In one of the sixth-form classrooms we had a record player and were permitted to smoke. We couldn't light up during the lessons, but we could during the breaks, after which the masters would teach us in a fug of smoke, without batting an eyelid. It seems unthinkable today – but this was the 70s, and the teaching was very effective. I learned a great deal about politics, rather less about economics, and acquired a lifelong love of poetry.

Had A-levels not been available at Prescot, I'm not sure whether I would have taken them elsewhere. Others who went on from Prescot to enjoy illustrious and useful careers are similarly doubtful. Professor Sir Michael Brady, for example, who has held two chairs at Oxford University – in information engineering and oncology – says: 'I'm not sure that I would. The idea of getting on a bus and going all the way into the centre of Liverpool every morning would have been quite a disincentive.'

Andrew Burrows QC, professor of law at Oxford, says he probably would have found a way of taking A-levels elsewhere. 'But some of the boys I studied A-levels alongside would not, as travel, and the cost of travel, would have been an issue.' Burrows' old school friends include teachers, a solicitor, a doctor and a professor of medicine.

Friends and neighbours who did not pass the 11-plus and attended one of the local secondary moderns have a different story to tell. Most left education at 16, sometimes with few qualifications, and only a handful attended a further education college.

Prescot grammar eventually merged with the girls' grammar school, became a comprehensive, moved location, merged again, and in time – because councillors could not agree on a shorter name – became the Knowsley Park Centre for Learning, Serving Prescot, Whiston and the Wider Community.

By the late 70s, some of the comprehensive schools in Knowsley were enjoying a brief period of great success; Ruffwood in Kirkby, for example, under the leadership of headteacher Alan Barnes, attracted visits by educationalists from across the globe, became a place where teachers queued up to work and sent entire cohorts of working-class pupils off to university.

At the heart of Paul Boyce's plan is the newly created Education Commission for Knowsley. The ultimate aim will be 'to make education irresistible', Boyce says. A new generation of headteachers are running the six secondary schools, and their determination to achieve change is palpable.

Boyce hopes that in the not-too-distant future, Knowsley will be able to secure government funding for a new sixth-form college, one that would be run jointly with a high-achieving education institution from outside the borough.

Knowsley Park Centre for Learning, Serving Prescot, Whiston and the Wider Community became an academy in September. Headteacher Judy Walker immediately ditched the name. Today it is simply Prescot school, and the pupils arrive in new uniforms with a badge that incorporates a date, in very large numbers: 1544. The interior has been remodelled. 'The council asked me what I needed, and I replied: "Walls, and windows that open,"' says Walker. 'It was bonkers.' She says she is aiming to provide an academic curriculum. 'I want that grammar school ethos and high academic achievement, but without selection.'

But like other secondary schools in Knowsley, Prescot is obliged to give literacy classes for the large numbers of children who arrive, aged 11, with a reading age of nine or 10. And while Walker would like to open a sixth form and offer A-level education, she is frank that there is a need to improve GCSE results first.

At Lord Derby Academy in Huyton, headteacher Victoria Gowan and her staff keep detailed statistics on each child's performance at each stage of their school career and in each subject. Some 60 per cent of pupils at Lord Derby are classed as disadvantaged – meaning they are eligible for free school meals or have been looked after in local authority care – compared with a national average of 29 per cent. The school is determined that this fact will not damage their prospects.

Gowan places strong emphasis on discipline. Pupils are expected to surrender their mobile phones at the start of each day, walk on the left in corridors and stand when giving lengthy answers to questions.

After visiting Lord Derby, the commission's chair, Christine Gilbert, noted that 'the children are now arriving with pens and bags, which wasn't always happening before'. Exclusions, which had been running at 13 per cent a year, were down to 3 per cent in 2016, as children began to be taught in a well-staffed inclusion unit.

Lord Derby pupils are expected to look immaculate, on the premises and off, as Gowan attempts to give the community a new confidence in their school. She has also changed the curriculum; gone are the two- and three-hour lessons, during which pupils were taught several subjects by groups of teachers. 'Both the pupils and the staff were relieved when we reintroduced 50-minute lessons,' she says.

Raising educational attainment in Knowsley is a matter not only of local concern, but of regional and national importance. With the attainment of white, working-class children remaining stubbornly low compared with other groups, Gilbert takes the view that if the commission can crack it in Knowsley, their methods can be used to raise standards everywhere.

Meanwhile, Sir Michael Wilshaw, the outgoing head of Ofsted, has warned that any attempts to achieve a geographic rebalancing of the British economy will be fatally undermined if children in the north of England are not better educated. In a speech in which he singled out Knowsley but also condemned Labour-controlled Rochdale, Salford and Oldham, Wilshaw warned that any attempt to create a northern powerhouse would 'splutter and die' if young people lacked the skills to sustain it.

In its attempt to establish what more it could be doing, Knowsley asked a London-based public policy thinktank, ResPublica, to examine its schools' problems. ResPublica's report, presented at a conference in the borough last June, made no mention of grammar schools.

In October, with Theresa May in Downing Street and grammar schools firmly back on the political agenda, ResPublica published a new version of its report, and says it had Knowsley's permission to do this. There was a new preface that raised the possibility that schools in the borough could become selective, and a new recommendation: that the government should ensure that any future grammar schools target the most disadvantaged areas. The return of grammars, said the thinktank's director Phillip Blond in the accompanying press release, is 'potentially a transformative idea for areas where there are little or no middle classes'.

In Knowsley, councillors, education officials and headteachers were furious. ResPublica declined to answer a number of questions about the way its report was altered. Instead it issued a statement in which it attacked the council and threatened to sue the *Guardian* if it published anything that damaged its reputation.

Senior civil servants at the DfE are said to share Knowsley's view that there is no case for a new grammar school in the borough. But in Downing Street, officials seized upon ResPublica's newfound conversion to the grammar school cause. At prime minister's questions in late November, May hailed 'the report commissioned by a Labour council in Knowsley' and quoted from Blond's press release.

After years of academic decline, the draining away of many of the more able pupils and the self-inflicted damage of wild experimentation, Knowsley appears finally to be starting to get to grips with its education catastrophe, and may be moving in the right direction.

Is this the moment when it is to be turned into a laboratory once more; subject to trial – and no doubt errors – directed not from within, but from Whitehall, and No 10?

11 February

'How are you enjoying the break?' I ask my wife. She shudders

TIM DOWLING

My wife and I are sitting opposite one another on a train heading north. Planned engineering works have added an hour to the journey, but we have a table, and the landscape rolling by is pleasingly misty. My wife is asleep with headphones on and my coat draped over her, mouth slightly ajar.

I distinctly remember her once responding to an idle proposal of mine with the words, 'Never, ever try to take me on a minibreak', but the weekend away was her idea, even though it's not quite a weekend.

'Sunday to Monday,' she said. 'The hotel is half the price.' I don't mention that I associate this kind of cost-cutting exercise with old age, like eating in restaurants at 6pm, or wearing down vests in the house. Suddenly the carriage seems chilly. I eye my coat with envy.

When I next look up, my wife is awake, and wholly focused on whatever is happening in her headphones. I turn again to the world outside the window: a felted stillness occasionally interrupted by the degraded silhouettes of spindly trees. I look at my wife, and she looks at me.

'What?' she says, lifting the headphones off one ear. I repeat myself.

'"Foggy"?' she says. 'You interrupted my thing to say "foggy"?'

'What are you listening to?' I say.

'It's a podcast about a woman whose husband is having an affair,' she says. 'She's not happy.'

For the rest of the journey I switch between the window and my wife. Sometimes her eyes are wide with shock; sometimes she looks stern. Through the window I see a man with a camera standing on a lonely platform. When I turn back, my wife is wagging an admonishing finger in my direction.

'I'm not the man in your podcast,' I say.

'What?' she says, pulling back her headphones.

'Trainspotter,' I say, pointing.

'What are you, five?' she says.

Despite our late arrival, we're still too early to check into our hotel. We go to the pub beneath it and order two beers.

'How did your podcast end?' I say. 'Are they reconciled?'

'Yes, but ...' my wife says.

'But what?' I say.

'The wife can't stop being snide,' she says.

'A snide wife,' I say. 'How does he cope?'

'Shut up,' she says.

'How are you enjoying your mini-break so far?' I say. My wife shudders a little at the word.

'It *is* a sort of mini-break,' she says. 'But we're also visiting our middle son at university.'

'A combined visit and mini-break,' I say. 'This is the mini-break part.'

'I've texted him,' she says. 'He's on his way.'

'Do you want to hold hands?' I say.

'No, thank you,' she says. We look towards the door for a long moment.

'Name a kind of bird that has a penis,' my wife says. 'I'll start: goose.'

'OK,' I say. 'Wait, what?'

'If you don't know, just say, "I don't know,"' she says. 'Duck.'

'I believe some flightless birds have penises,' I say. 'Like ostriches.'

'Emu,' she says.

'Are you sure about that?' I say. 'I'm not sure about that.'

'We'll look it up, shall we?' she says, pulling out her phone.

'Do owls have penises?' I say.

'Emus and other large flightless birds, yes,' she says. 'Swans have penises.'

'I was about to guess swan.'

'It says I last visited this webpage on 10 January.'

'This does seem familiar,' I say. 'Sitting in a bar, just the two of us, looking at the bird penis page.'

'Christ,' she says. The door opens, but it's just another couple of about our age, standing on the threshold in silence.

'Check owls,' I say.

11 FEBRUARY

'It's always high drama.
It's somebody's life at stake.'
Inside British rape trials (extract)

MELISSA DENES

Newcastle crown court is an imposing red sandstone building that dominates the quay by the river Tyne, fronted by pillars and a wall of tinted windows. From the glass elevators, there are views across the water to the Baltic art gallery and the Sage concert hall, silhouetted like a Russian doll on its side.

Up on the second floor, in courtroom number five, the jury files in – nine women, three men – and the defendant takes the stand. He is 19 and nervous, fidgeting with a new shirt and tie. The public gallery is full, five rows of chairs filled with family and friends: a boy in a leather jacket and buzz cut who sits stiff and still, another in a shirt so tight his tattoos show.

It is the morning of day two; the defendant is accused of raping his former girlfriend. His barrister, who chews the arm of his glasses between questions, picks up where he left off yesterday: when did the relationship turn violent? When she started drinking, the defendant says; she elbowed him between the eyes and broke his nose. Another time, she pushed a hot pizza in his face. He speaks rapidly, flushing when the judge asks him to speak up.

Did they argue about sex? Yes, he says, there was a position that hurt so he stopped. But then one day she said: you raped me. What was your response? 'I nearly had a heart attack. That was it, the start of world war three.'

'Why would she accuse you?'

'To make me feel guilty.'

'And did you?'

'Yes.' The defendant begins to cry.

His barrister reads out a series of text messages:

What I done to you you didn't deserve I love the bones of you. I never regretted anything so much.

What was he referring to?

'Pushing her off the bed: it was the first time I laid hands on her.'

The room fills with the rustle of paper as the jury goes through hundreds of texts, highlighted one colour for him, another for her.

Him: Sorry for being a proper horrible cunt.

'And,' says his lawyer, 'that one ends with a kiss.'

Her: You're only with me because you're scared I'll tell.

Him: Do it, I deserve it.

Her: I'm not keeping your dirty little secret.

Sitting alongside the defendant's family, Keith Woodhouse is making notes. A 63-year-old former magistrates clerk, his hand-writing is illegible, a scrawl that travels up and down the pages. But it makes sense to him: when he types them up in the evening, his observations are clear and unemotional and succinct.

Today Woodhouse will have noted: that the judge reminded the jury there is no such thing as a stereotypical rape; that he granted a Section 41 application, allowing the defence to cross-examine the complainant about her sexual history; that the complainant gave evidence by video link yesterday. She was asked if she had broken her boyfriend's nose. No, she smiled, but she wished she had.

Woodhouse is part of a groundbreaking new scheme, one of 12 volunteers – nine women and three men – working as observers on rape trials in Newcastle. Since January 2015, they have sat on 30 trials and made a string of recommendations: that barristers meet clients before a trial (this is rare); that complainants are better informed about the ways they can give evidence (behind screens, by video link); that prosecutors attend specialist training. Their reports are shared, and there is much the observers have praised (judges who universally gave 'myth-busting' directives), and some things they have not (a complainant asked by the defence if she was a 'bunny-boiler').

The panel is the only one in the country, and was launched by Northumbria's crime commissioner Vera Baird, who sits along-side Woodhouse today. At 66, she has the loping, long-legged walk of a teenage boy, six feet tall in a burgundy trouser suit and brogues, cropped red hair sticking up on her head. A former Labour MP and solicitor general, Baird has represented victims of domestic violence, as well as miners during the 80s strikes.

After lunch, it is the female prosecutor's turn. She is younger than the defence, sceptical and coolly polite with her witness. Was he controlling, she begins.

'At the start.'

'In what way?'

'Actually, I wasn't.' She picks away at his phone messages: 'It doesn't make sense, does it, "your dirty little secret"?' The defendant says this was a reference to anal sex. But why would she want to tell her family about that? The lawyer loses her patience: 'Oh come on, that's utter rubbish.' The defendant raises his voice: 'I'm just a jack the lad!' The judge sums up, reminding the jury that, to convict, they need to be absolutely sure consent was not given.

The lift down to the street is full, barristers in yellowing wigs with armfuls of paperwork crammed in next to witnesses, their mothers and sisters. There was no one in court today for the complainant; her friend gave evidence yesterday, Woodhouse says, but she struggled in front of the defendant's family. The accused is in the lift, too, leaning against the glass wall, pale and drained between two friends. On the steps outside they sit to share a cigarette.

In the five years since Jimmy Savile's death, Britain has seen an unprecedented surge in the reporting of rape. Figures released in October 2016 showed a rise of more than double since 2011, or an increase of 123 per cent; 90 per cent were reported by women. This has unfolded at the national, institutional level – through Operation Yewtree, the Jay inquiry, the Football Association inquiry. But it has also happened on a local, individual level – away from the cameras, involving nobody famous. Can the police and courts keep up?

Many of the alleged crimes are decades old. One counsellor I spoke to, Sue Pearce at Rape Crisis in Newcastle, described what is happening in the UK as a 'mass triggering'. She had recently treated a woman who at different times had undergone electric shock therapy and been sectioned; finally, in her 70s, she told her daughter she had been abused as a child. Pearce's shelves are stacked with tubs of toys, plastic dinosaurs, crayons – not because clients bring their children, but because people come to talk about something that happened when they were pre-verbal, when they were last playing with bricks.

The conviction rate for rape has gone up in the past year, from 56.9 per cent of cases brought to trial, to 57.9 per cent. But this masks a bleaker statistic: of every alleged rape reported to the police, only 7.5 per cent will result in a conviction. The majority of cases do not go to trial, and it remains very hard to prosecute: forensic evidence is rare, because few people report immediately; it is often the word of one witness against another; juries are directed to convict only when they are absolutely certain – something that can seem an impossible ask.

In this country alone, there will be hundreds of thousands of women who have not reported rapes, for a hundred thousand reasons – because he was family, because they did not want a trial, because they did not expect to be believed.

And I understand them, because it happened to me – and to many women I know. It was a long time ago, and I did not go to the police because he was the police. He lives in a country where it is too late to bring a prosecution, but it doesn't stop me feeling horrible guilt. If women like me say nothing, rape continues to look like a freak occurrence – something to be instinctively disbelieved. I won't be telling my story here – it has taken 20 years to write four sentences – but I do know what it is to be shocked into silence, and to keep it that way.

There is no family in court the following day, just me and observer Val Cottier. It is day one of a different trial. The complainant will give evidence from behind a screen, and there is a delay while the clerk closes a one-inch gap with a peg. The defendant sits in the dock, wearing a navy fleece and trousers; it is 10am and he is drunk, muttering and shaking his head.

The jury comes in – five men, seven women – and the male prosecutor outlines the case. The man in the dock is the complainant's uncle, he explains; she alleges he raped her six years ago.

The complainant begins to give evidence, her voice clear and confident. What was she wearing when she went to bed? Pyjama bottoms and a vest. Underwear? No. Cottier makes a note. She writes fast; when the lawyers pause, she goes back with a yellow highlighter to mark the important bits.

The prosecutor continues. How long did the assault last? 'It felt like ages.'

'What did you do then?'

'I checked my daughter was still asleep and I held her hand.' She begins to cry, and a clerk walks around the screen with tissues.

She continues: 'I shouted at him to leave.'

'Liar,' the defendant mutters.

'But in the morning he was there, and he told me to get him a cup of tea.'

'I drink black coffee!' the defendant shouts.

The complainant is not rattled. She had planned to give evidence by video link, but at the last minute changed her mind, wanting to look the jury in the eye. Why did she go to the police all these years later, asks her barrister? 'A storyline on *EastEnders*,' she says.

The defence lawyer begins. Is she sure she physically resisted, he asks. Or might she wish she had? 'I didn't want him to,' she says, firmly. Has she heard about people receiving compensation for this crime? 'I just want justice,' she says, raising her voice. The judge calls a break for lunch.

Val Cottier retired from her job in child protection two years ago, she tells me, but was bored within weeks, kicking around the house, her children both grown up. This is her ninth trial as an observer. Like Keith Woodhouse, she aims to be impartial. 'I make no judgments. I am not the jury.' But this is not the same as being emotionally detached, and she has found herself thrown by convictions ('to see a mother's distress: that was her child, no matter what'). They all walk a fine line between empathy and objectivity, but her previous job trained her in just that. 'Sometimes you want to cry for a person, but you can't because then you're no help. It's always high drama here,' she adds, 'people sobbing or having a good snog. It's somebody's life at stake.'

After the break, the accused takes the stand. 'Is it possible you had sex?' his lawyer asks. 'I don't know.'

'Yes or no?'

'Yes.'

'Did you rape her?'

'I wouldn't do that.'

'How much did you drink?'

'Nine pints and 20 bottles.'

'And you don't have a drink problem?'

'Guinness is good for you,' he says wildly.

The odds seem heavily stacked against the accused: the lawyers in their wigs who unpick his every sentence; the jury who ignore him, looking to the lawyers to make sense of things. His testimony is an alcoholic's blend of localised recall and the fog of amnesia. 'Do you know what you did three months ago?' he challenges the prosecutor. 'But I'm not the one charged with rape,' the lawyer counters, and runs with it: 'How can you not recall sex with your niece? You raped her, didn't you?'

'She's a rat!' he shouts. 'And you're cross-examining us!'

'Yes, I am,' says the prosecutor, and even the defence can't help a smile.

The prosecutor sums up, and it is a good speech. It is a staple of TV drama, he says, the innocent man wrongly convicted. What is less often portrayed, and something I'd like to see, is how it feels to see your attacker acquitted. He tells the jury to focus on the accused's inconsistencies.

The defendant stands: 'That statement is total bollocks.'

His lawyer begins. 'In the interests of realism,' he says, 'the defendant was all over the place. But this case is more complicated than that. It is possible that none of you have been drunk. But I suspect that there are those of you who are drawing on personal experience – of that uncomfortable morning after the night you can't quite remember. I would argue that this was a clumsy sexual encounter.' If the prosecutor's speech was good, the defence's is cleverer: an argument that asks the jury if they would convict themselves after a messy night out.

The accused does not look at them as they file out, his eyes down and miles away. Suddenly there is muffled screaming in the courtroom next door: the verdict is in on yesterday's trial. Not guilty. The defendant's family fill the corridors, whooping.

An hour later, the jury returns their verdict on today's trial: another not guilty.

What should the conviction rate for rape be? Not 100 per cent: there will always be defendants who are innocent. But it's an interesting question, says the director of public prosecutions, Alison Saunders. It is lower than most crimes, and probably always will be, because rape is more complex: it usually takes place in private, between people who know each other. This is both the most common scenario, and the one a jury finds hardest to convict – because the myth of the stranger and the blameless victim, Ken Clarke's infamous 'serious rape', still has enormous currency. Scotland's former director of public prosecutions, Elish Angiolini, who in 2015 published a critical review of rape trials in London, tells me that 'most people still think of a Doris Day character dragged down a dark alley'.

Both Angiolini and Saunders argue that a conviction isn't everything. They know this is a difficult message, and Saunders says she would always encourage someone to go to court. 'But if we focus too much on prosecution, we don't help people who don't want that. For some it is about feeling safe, knowing it won't happen again.' Angiolini argues that the very low report-to-conviction rate of 7.5 per cent is misleading, because it is not the case that 100 per cent of people want a trial. 'They may wish to be removed from a position of danger, to be believed.'

Saunders thinks the Jimmy Savile effect is overstated. 'The increase in reports is also down to the incredible amount of work that's been done to encourage people to come forward – success stories like the conviction of the Oxford grooming gang.' Like Angiolini, she argues that the conviction rate is a crude measure of success. 'Just because there was an acquittal doesn't mean a case shouldn't have been brought, or that a woman wasn't believed. The guilty verdict is a very high test.'

The process is improving, she says. 'We have doubled our specialist units. We work much more closely with the police, embedding prosecutors into police stations, and police at the prosecution level.'

Angiolini is cautiously, similarly optimistic, despite what she describes as a 'tsunami of cases'. 'There is a change in how people are understanding this crime. And those people are potential jurors, who will bring different verdicts. Back in the 1980s, nobody had the word grooming in their vocabulary unless it was to do with horses. Since then there has been a sea change in the way people understand child abuse. I think we are on the cusp of that with rape.'

Sue Pearce is a young-looking 55, blonde and energetic. Originally from Devon, she has lived in the north-east half her life, and spent years hustling for the small amounts of money that keep the Rape Crisis centre she runs in Newcastle going.

She is also a founder member of Baird's observers panel. 'My life is 98 per cent sexual violence,' she smiles ruefully. 'I'm no good at sticking up for myself – but if it's someone else, I'm off.' When Baird first floated the idea of the panel, Pearce was sceptical. 'I thought, "Woah, will they really let you?" But she did it.

'We paired up on the first trial. Vera's got a legal head on: why hasn't the prosecution done this? I'm more victim-focused. I'd notice that the barristers talk, and that in the public gallery you can hear. If they were talking about my daughter – well, it doesn't feel right. Or you'd see a woman giving evidence by video link from a room so tiny the male court usher would be practically in her lap.'

Pearce tells me about a woman she counselled who took her former boyfriend to court. 'I was called as a witness, and it made me see I had stuff to offer. Only one person had stayed with her from start to finish, and that was me. She never met the barrister, apart from a hello before the trial started. There were masses of texts, and they'd transcribed them the wrong way round, marking hers as his – so she almost had to bring the case herself on the stand.'

The verdict was not guilty. 'And the family erupted like something on *Jeremy Kyle*.' The two women have stayed in touch, and 'there isn't a day goes by that she doesn't think about that trial. But she doesn't regret it. Her life has panned out differently.

'She was a doctor. She was slightly older, and they played on that: "You're older, you're very educated" – while he was a cheeky chappy. And because her job was used as a detail that made her less likable, less believable, that job she loved was never the same. She's given training for judges, and you could hear a pin drop. So she is different. But a good different.'

I didn't go to the police 20 years ago because I didn't expect to be believed. I was glad to be alive, and wanted to move on. I'm not proud of that: it is the people speaking up now, who are bringing difficult cases even when they are dismissed as fantasists and money-grabbers, who will force real change.

Would I win a case today? I'd probably face similar odds – a little better than 50/50, his word against mine. But beyond that I think I would be believed, and that is something surprisingly, powerfully new. Believed not by everyone, but by counsellors and lawmakers like Pearce and Baird and Saunders, who, step by step, are making a difference. Is it enough?

Some details have been changed.

15 FEBRUARY

In an age of robots, schools are teaching our children how to be redundant

GEORGE MONBIOT

In the future, if you want a job, you must be as unlike a machine as possible: creative, critical and socially skilled. So why are children being taught to behave like machines?

Children learn best when teaching aligns with their natural exuberance, energy and curiosity. So why are they dragooned into rows and made to sit still while they are stuffed with facts?

We succeed in adulthood through collaboration. So why is collaboration in tests and exams called cheating?

Governments claim to want to reduce the number of children being excluded from school. So why are their curriculums and tests so narrow that they alienate any child whose mind does not work in a particular way?

The best teachers use their character, creativity and inspiration to trigger children's instinct to learn. So why are character, creativity and inspiration suppressed by a stifling regime of micromanagement?

There is, as Graham Brown-Martin explains in his book *Learning {Re}imagined*, a common reason for these perversities. Our schools were designed to produce the workforce required by 19th-century factories. The desired product was workers who would sit silently at their benches all day, behaving identically, to produce identical products, submitting to punishment if they failed to achieve the requisite standards. Collaboration and critical thinking were just what the factory owners wished to discourage.

As far as relevance and utility are concerned, we might as well train children to operate a spinning jenny. Our schools teach skills that are not only redundant but counter-productive. Our children suffer this life-defying, dehumanising system for nothing.

The less relevant the system becomes, the harder the rules must be enforced, and the greater the stress they inflict. One school's current advertisement in the *Times Educational Supplement* asks: 'Do you like order and discipline? Do you believe in children being obedient every time? ... If you do, then the role of detention director could be for you.' Yes, many schools have discipline problems.

But is it surprising when children, bursting with energy and excitement, are confined to the spot like battery chickens?

Teachers are now leaving the profession in droves, their training wasted and their careers destroyed by overwork and a spirit-crushing regime of standardisation, testing and top-down control. The less autonomy they are granted, the more they are blamed for the failures of the system. A major recruitment crisis beckons, especially in crucial subjects such as physics and design and technology. This is what governments call efficiency.

Any attempt to change the system, to equip children for the likely demands of the 21st century, rather than those of the 19th, is demonised by governments and newspapers as 'social engineering'. Well, of course it is. All teaching is social engineering. At present we are stuck with the social engineering of an industrial workforce in a post-industrial era. Under Donald Trump's education secretary, Betsy DeVos, and a nostalgic government in Britain, it's likely only to become worse.

When they are allowed to apply their natural creativity and curiosity, children love learning. They learn to walk, to talk, to eat and to play spontaneously, by watching and experimenting. Then they get to school, and we suppress this instinct by sitting them down, force-feeding them with inert facts and testing the life out of them.

There is no single system for teaching children well, but the best ones have this in common: they open up rich worlds that children can explore in their own ways, developing their interests with help rather than indoctrination. For example, the Essa academy in Bolton gives every pupil an iPad, on which they create projects, share material with their teachers and each other, and can contact their teachers with questions about their homework. By reducing their routine tasks, this system enables teachers to give the children individual help.

Other schools have gone in the opposite direction, taking children outdoors and using the natural world to engage their interests and develop their mental and physical capacities (the Forest School movement promotes this method). But it's not a matter of high-tech or low-tech; the point is that the world a child enters is rich and diverse enough to ignite their curiosity, and allow them to discover a way of learning that best reflects their character and skills.

There are plenty of teaching programmes designed to work with children, not against them. For example, the Mantle of the Expert encourages them to form teams of inquiry, solving an imaginary task – such as running a container port, excavating a tomb or rescuing people from a disaster – that cuts across traditional subject boundaries. A similar approach, called Quest to Learn, is based on the way children teach themselves to play games. To solve the complex tasks they're given, they need to acquire plenty of information and skills. They do it with the excitement and tenacity of gamers.

The Reggio Emilia approach, developed in Italy, allows children to develop their own curriculum, based on what interests them most, opening up the subjects they encounter along the way with the help of their teachers. Ashoka Changemaker schools treat empathy as 'a foundational skill on a par with reading and maths', and use it to develop the kind of open, fluid collaboration that, they believe, will be the 21st century's key skill.

The first multi-racial school in South Africa, Woodmead, developed a fully democratic method of teaching, whose rules and discipline were overseen by a student council. Its integrated studies programme, like the new system in Finland, junked traditional subjects in favour of the students' explorations of themes, such as gold, or relationships, or the ocean. Among its alumni are some of South Africa's foremost thinkers, politicians and businesspeople.

In countries such as Britain and the United States, such programmes succeed despite the system, not because of it. Had these governments set out to ensure that children find learning difficult and painful, they could not have done a better job. Yes, let's have some social engineering. Let's engineer our children out of the factory and into the real world.

23 FEBRUARY

The destruction of Britain's high streets is no accident

SIMON JENKINS

Children should not play with bombs. Business rates are the cluster munitions of fiscal policy, and the chancellor, Philip Hammond, and his 'communities' secretary, Sajid Javid, have been playing with them all week. They have duly exploded in high streets all over southern England. There is blood everywhere.

When I discovered that the resident of one of the most expensive flats in London was paying £1,400 a year in property tax, while Javid wants a watch shop in the same building to pay £244,000, I realised that whatever else Britain is good at, it is terrible at taxation.

The point is not that the building concerned, One Hyde Park, so stinks of money that no one is likely to notice what anyone pays. It is that such discrepancies are so grotesquely unfair as to ridicule an activity that still relies on honesty to work – that of paying taxes. If government were a profession, the ministers and civil servants involved in business rates would be debarred from further practice.

Ministers have long recognised the adage that we pay income tax in sorrow and council tax in anger. They have duly grubbed votes by not increasing either. Council taxes since 1993 have declined steadily against property prices and become ever more regressive. There has been no domestic property revaluation for a quarter of a century. Ministers can thus boast how 'we' have held local taxes down, while blaming councils for the resulting 30 per cent cut to social care since 2010. Such is the cynicism of modern politics.

For its part, the Treasury has had to seek 'stealth' revenues, such as VAT, stamp duty and business rates. The cost of the last to big companies has roughly doubled in the past decade, yielding £29bn last year, as much as council tax and on a quarter of the number of properties.

The south-east needs to be careful how it moans. Businesses in the north and west will benefit from the revaluation, while London is badly hit because it has grown richer and its properties are more valuable. Newly fashionable Islington and Hackney have seen their business rates soar by 45 per cent. Javid, clearly a born-again leftwinger, said last week that he was hurting only the wealthy. He in effect told novelist Jeanette Winterson that if she wanted to shut her sourdough and quinoa outfit in Spitalfields, she could always move to Hull, and leave London to the hedgies. That is his London, not mine.

I have no problem with the south-east paying more tax. It is plainly wrong that London should get half of England's spending on transport, and disproportionate amounts on housing, education and the arts. Under both Tony Blair and David Cameron, every lever of domestic policy was directed towards boosting London.

What was daft was to heap the entire burden of seven years of non-revaluation on to what would inevitably be small and poor as well as big and rich shops, pubs and workplaces. In inner

London, the valuation cap on H-band houses means that home-owners would pay no extra council tax, however far above £1m their houses might rise in value. In Belgravia, a tiny flat pays the same council tax as a palatial mansion.

Shops and pubs are therefore seeing their taxes soar, in part because neighbouring houses have been rising in value yet incurring no extra tax. It is not the rich who are paying these new business rates, it is those who service them.

The business rate penalises the one feature of local geography that emphatically aids community cohesion, the high street. It taxes inner-city shops, and thus benefits out-of-town supermarkets and online warehouses. It taxes places where people can walk, and thus encourages shopping by car. It taxes town centre jobs in favour of commuter sprawl and rural colonisation. A business tax is a mansion tax on the Old Curiosity Shop – whose rates in Lincoln's Inn are rising from £7,225 to £12,005. It makes the poll tax look intellectually sophisticated.

If Treasury officials ever dirtied their shoes in pubs or high streets, they would have seen this fiasco coming a mile off. Since Thatcher crushed the discretion out of local democracy in the mid-1980s, the Treasury's grip on the public sector has tightened and yet grown more insensitive. The failure to stop the poll tax was its Waterloo. Since then, its avid centralism has supported ministers in their assaults on council tax and postponed revaluation. Britain's total dominance of central over local sources of revenue is shared nowhere else in Europe.

My local publican, an independent, has to find another £11,000 in rates next year, in effect an £11,000 impost on his income. He might have to close, as have roughly a third of the shops in my high street in the past two years. Shops are struggling under a blitzkrieg of local hypermarkets and squadrons of Ocado and Tesco home delivery vans.

This is not 'market forces' at work. It is policy at work. It is policy that, in my district, allows the development of acres of empty luxury flats, starving shops of custom. It is policy that promotes out-of-town retail. It is policy that allows changes of use from commercial to residential, sending land values soaring. The free market is not sent by God. It is what happens when ministers and councillors go home to bed.

Theresa May yesterday promised 'some appropriate relief' from business rates, but that is mere palliative. Hammond has talked of taking 'another look' at the rates. There is no need. They are clearly honouring government policy, which is to turn town centres into housing estates and ensure every shopping bag arrives at every home with an internal combustion engine attached. Big development and big retail are this government's friends.

The basis of local taxation in Britain is unfit for purpose. It needs reform, preferably along lines proposed by the London mayor's recent finance commission. This suggested that all property taxes be fixed by local councils, subject only to redistribution from rich to poor areas. Central government, said the commission, should get the hell out of a policy where it was helplessly at sea. But I can tell that May, Hammond and Javid are already screaming in the opposite direction.

26 FEBRUARY

Grey squirrels

PASS NOTES

Name: Grey squirrels.
Age: First introduced to the UK in the 1870s.

Arch-enemy: HRH Prince Charles.

Are you sure? I thought Charles was arch-enemies with Donald Trump. Well, yes, but he hates squirrels, too. He must just really have a thing about American interlopers with titchy hands.

Why does he hate squirrels so much? Because there are just so many of them.

There are? Oh God, yes. There are approximately 3.5 million of them in the UK at the moment. They're an infestation.

And what's wrong with that? They aren't British, are they? Red squirrels are British. Red squirrels have a stiff upper lip. Red squirrels cry at the national anthem. Red squirrels have a fundamental understanding of decent British values. Not like these invading greys.

Bloody hell, all right Farage. More importantly, grey squirrels carry the squirrelpox virus, which is causing the number of reds to dwindle. And this is where Prince Charles comes in.

Is he going to eat all the grey squirrels? Even better. He's going to sterilise them!

Really? Is he going to start climbing up trees and perform squirrel vasectomies? It's much smarter than that. He has backed plans to conceal oral contraceptives inside Nutella hidden around the country's forests.

Really, though, what's he going to do? No, that's actually the plan. You hide the contraception in Nutella, put it inside a trap that only squirrels can fit through, then watch in delight as they stop being able to have kids.

This all sounds a bit Children of Men *to me.* Well, yes, but the argument is basically that we have to either gradually decrease the number of grey squirrels by humanely limiting their ability to reproduce, or we go around the country smacking them with the back of a shovel.

Well, fine. This is the least awful option. Yes, it is. If everything goes according to plan, then the contraceptives will be introduced five years from now. Four years after that, we will have reduced the grey squirrel population by two-thirds, and the red squirrel will be able to mount a gloriously patriotic comeback. God save the Queen!

Did you vote for Brexit, by any chance? You lost! Get over it!

Do say: 'Well, that's me gone off Nutella for a bit.'

Don't say: 'STERILISE ALL IMMIGRANTS, SAYS PRINCE.'

3 MARCH

At last a new Oscars cliché: I'd like to blame all the little people

HADLEY FREEMAN

And the award for best hasty salvaging of reputations goes to ... Hollywood and the Oscars! Ooh, but have we opened the right envelope? Hahaha! Well, of course we have, given that Brian Cullinan and Martha Ruiz, the PricewaterhouseCoopers (PwC) accountants responsible for last Sunday's snafu, have been not so much thrown under a bus as chucked off a plane, ripped apart by a freight train and crushed under a Hummer, and therefore can't screw this one up. So congratulations to celebrities and the Academy Awards for this prize!

Last Sunday, as I'm sure we all remember, was WrongEn-velopeGate/this generation's Kennedy assassination/the most important cultural event that ever happened – in other words, the wrong winner was read out at the Oscars. Emma Stone, who had won the best actress Oscar moments before, declared this mix-up 'one of the most horrible moments of my life', leading one to wonder what were the others – room service toast that was slightly too burnt? A faintly disappointing VIP lounge?

While the losers (*La La Land*) and winners (*Moonlight*) have apparently moved on from this upset, it seems increasingly clear the Academy Awards will never recover from this three minutes of pain. A week on, stories about HOW, CRUEL GOD, HOW? the mix-up happened are still being churned out in the press, and I surely speak for the world when I say the prospect of the endless rib-ticklers we'll get at next year's Oscars about wrong envelopes makes me want to move to Siberia and stick icicles into my brain.

We could query the behaviour of quite a few people that night: Warren Beatty, who was apparently incapable of simply saying that he'd been given the wrong envelope when he knew he had; *La La Land*'s producer, Fred Berger, who gave a thank-you speech even though he knew he'd lost; Beatty (again) for seizing the mic after the error was revealed and insistently telling the world that none of this was his fault, thereby cutting into the *Moonlight* team's time even further.

But this is Hollywood, dammit! And if there is one thing this town knows how to do it is protect its own. And so screen grabs from backstage on the night were released and pored over by the media like the 21st century Zapruder film. Investigations were demanded with greater urgency than, say, investigations into President Trump's Russian connections, and before the sun had set on Monday, Cullinan and, soon after, Ruiz had been duly named as the execs to blame.

Well, the buck had to stop somewhere. Whether that buck-stopping really needed two individuals' names and photos to be released to the world's media, given that they are private citizens who flubbed up at an awards ceremony and not, say, treason-committing politicians, is a debatable issue.

Well, I say it's debatable, but it isn't at all, apparently. Because this week has been open season on the two of them, with humiliating details about their professional and personal failings being eagerly leaked to the world's obliging media. Photos of Cullinan tweeting backstage were sneered at by people on Twitter, apparently unaware of the concept of irony. Cullinan, *Variety* solemnly reported on Thursday, 'enjoyed the spotlight'. The trade paper went on to justify this claim by suggesting he had 'been angling for a spot on stage' during the ceremony. In fact, it is mentioned in the fifth paragraph that he quite possibly wanted no such thing – according to PwC, he was trying to ensure that his firm wouldn't be mocked on stage again as it had been the year before, when Chris Rock pretended three Asian children were PwC accountants, a low point in the Oscar annals which, after protests, eventually wrung a classic non-apology apology from the Academy.

Ruiz and Cullinan 'just didn't have the disposition' for the Oscars, Gary Natoli, the event's stage manager, claimed in an extensive interview in which he repeatedly stressed the event's total innocence and Ruiz and Cullinan's total culpability. 'It was very upsetting to us. It still is. You work really hard on a show, and then something like that happens. You feel bad about it, even though it's not your responsibility,' Natoli said.

And for sure, the pain is real. Though not perhaps as real as the pain of Ruiz and Cullinan, who now have to have security in their homes because their addresses were widely disseminated and they and their families have received death threats, because that is how the world works now when individuals are singled out in the media and most people have access to the internet.

This, incidentally, is mentioned just as an aside at the bottom of articles sneering at Cullinan and Ruiz, because what really matters is that for two minutes people thought the wrong movie won, not that some poor muppets are currently living in fear. After all, God forbid Warren Beatty should feel awkward for even a second.

Leaving aside the very strong urge to shout, 'FOR GOD'S SAKE, GET A GRIP – IT WAS A MIX-UP AT AN AWARDS CEREMONY', there is no doubt that Cullinan and Ruiz had one job, and they fumbled it. But if anyone thinks this means they now deserve to be humiliated and traduced on a global scale, well, they care about the sanctity of the Oscars a lot more than I do, and I've been four times.

The Academy found the mix-up humiliating; the truth is, it's been the reaction of all the key players afterwards – the Academy, the celebrities, the media – that has been embarrassing. To err is human, to kick people in the face to salvage the egos of the beautiful folk – well, that's Hollywood.

21 MARCH

Martin McGuinness: Sinn Féin leaders help carry coffin home in Derry

HENRY McDONALD

As sleet began to fall on the funeral procession, an Irish tricolour at half-mast fluttered in the bitingly cold wind. Another was draped over Martin McGuinness's coffin.

The mourners were passing down William Street, not far from where McGuinness grew up in the republican Bogside district. Once, these streets were some of the most dangerous in Ireland, echoing to the sound of gunfire and explosions. Today, there was only the sound of applause, as hundreds of people watched Gerry Adams help carry his old friend's coffin home.

Helping Adams shoulder the coffin of his longtime ally, with whom he steered the Irish republican movement from 'armed struggle' to democratic politics, was Michelle O'Neill, the leader of Sinn Féin and potentially the next deputy first minister of Northern Ireland.

Between them was Raymond McCartney, a Sinn Féin assemblyman and former hunger striker and member of the Provisional IRA. They walked past the iconic preserved gable wall known as 'Free Derry Corner' – once a self-declared autonomous nationalist area and still featuring murals commemorating the events of the Troubles.

Derry is still bitterly divided. But in the Bogside where McGuinness was a teenager, he witnessed riots after civil rights marches, and then the slaughter of 14 civilians by British paratroopers in 1972. It was once the scene of many gun and bomb attacks he would have directed as Derry's IRA commander. Today, the mood was different.

Some locals were preparing a traditional Irish wake in honour of the dead republican leader. At the Gasyard Centre, not far from the McGuinness family home in Westland Avenue, mountains of sandwiches were being prepared for the hundreds expected to pay their respects to his house.

Through tears, the centre manager, Linda McKinney, said the 66-year-old Sinn Féin peace process chief negotiator was 'a gentleman' who 'did so much for this area'.

John Kelly, whose brother Michael was shot dead in the Bloody Sunday massacre, echoed that sentiment in the newly opened Museum of Free Derry nearby. 'I have known him for a long time,' he said. 'Yes, he was a member of the IRA, but he turned that around and became a man of peace.

'You can't take that from him. He was a great friend of the Bloody Sunday family over the years and was there for us from day one. It is a great loss to Derry and Ireland.'

Yet despite McGuinness's journey from IRA leader and vocal defender of its violent campaign to a politician who made peace with many of his former enemies in unionism, Derry remains split along sectarian lines.

Beyond the city's 17th-century walls is the last Ulster Protestant/loyalist enclave on the western bank of the Foyle river that bisects Derry. A mural on the Fountain estate reminds those living there that they are still surrounded. Echoing back to the 1688–89 blockade of then Protestant Derry by the forces of the Catholic King James II, it reads: 'West Bank Loyalists Still Under Siege'.

That siege mentality was reflected in the fear of one woman in the Fountain who would speak about her feelings towards McGuinness only if she could remain anonymous. She recalled an IRA massacre in the same year as Bloody Sunday, when on 31 July 1972 three car bombs exploded in the centre of Claudy, a village outside the city in the County Derry countryside. The woman remembered one of the nine victims of the explosions, a child called Kathryn Eakin.

'Many people from this community have lost loved ones to the IRA,' she said. 'Two friends of mine lost their little girl in the Claudy bomb. Her name was Kathryn. She was just eight years old.

'Both her parents died a few years ago and went to their graves without getting closure. The loss of their child destroyed them. A lot more people will never get closure now Martin McGuinness is dead, taking his secrets with him. They will find no comfort in his death.'

Others took a different view. A former Royal Ulster Constabulary officer, who served in Derry on and off between 1978 and 2003, acknowledged that McGuinness had moved from being the man who directed an organisation that tried to kill him several times to 'grow into the role of statesman'.

Peter Sheridan, a Catholic police officer, rose through the RUC's ranks and ended up as an assistant chief constable. He had to move his family from two different homes during his time in Derry after intelligence reports indicated the IRA was poised to assassinate him.

He was injured in an IRA gun and bomb attack that left two RUC colleagues and a prison officer dead at Magee College in 1987, when McGuinness sat on the Provisionals' ruling army council.

But 25 years later, Sheridan, retired from policing and working as chief executive for the Co-operation Ireland cross-border peace group, found himself in the same line-up as McGuinness while they waited to greet the Queen at a charity event in Belfast.

'I had already accepted that Martin McGuinness had moved on,' he said. 'When I witnessed his historic handshake with the Queen I realised it was as much about reaching out the hand to the unionist community as doing so with her.'

22 March

Solidarity against terror

It was only ever a matter of time. This strike at parliament took aim directly at the heart of British democracy. It was perhaps meant to reach the prime minister – for today, the day of prime minister's questions, was the one day when her movements would be well known – but more probably it was, like the attack in Berlin just before Christmas, simply an attempt to hit at a European centre of power. The earlier car attack on the dozens of tourists and office workers and three police officers on their way back from a commendation ceremony, caught walking across Westminster Bridge around 2.45pm, was plainly intended to magnify the terror.

'This is the moment that everyone planned for and hoped would never happen,' the Metropolitan police acting deputy commissioner, Mark Rowley, said at his first news conference afterwards. It was also the hardest kind of attack to stop, an apparently lone terrorist using low-tech weaponry seeking to do maximum harm, almost certain of death himself. He got through, but a dozen or more attacks have been foiled in Britain since 2013, 10 of them in the past two years. More than 500 live counter-terror investigations are under way at any given moment, Mr Rowley said recently. The police and the security forces have to be right all the time. The terrorists only need to be lucky once. It is important to hold on to that truth, and to remember that, terrible as the loss of life has been and grim as the aftermath will be, no one would want to live in the kind of world where such an attack had been made entirely impossible.

The security forces acted swiftly and courageously to protect parliament and the public. For the families of the dead, and for the injured, this is a horrendous, life-changing event. The shock and distress of eyewitnesses, trapped on buses or simply walking along the pavement, was evident in their voices and their faces as they spoke to reporters. Some of them behaved with impressive presence of mind, including the foreign office minister Tobias Ellwood, who tried to revive the fatally injured policeman.

The security forces and police have planned for what they call a 'marauding attack' for years. The awful choreography of the response to terror was fast and well rehearsed. The police officer who later died of his injuries stopped the attacker at the gates off Parliament Square. Before the man had gone a pace or two further, he himself was shot by an armed officer. These two courageous interventions almost certainly saved scores of lives in a busy area thronged with politicians, visitors and some of the hundreds of staff who work in the palace.

There will be many questions to ask in the coming days about what was known of the attacker and his associates, but for now, there can only be a wholehearted appreciation of the professionalism with which the police did their job.

What now? We often mock our political class, but it is worth remembering that being an MP has never been risk-free. In 1979, the IRA murdered the senior Tory MP Airey Neave with a car bomb only yards from where today's attack took place. An MP died in the Brighton bomb in 1984, and another was murdered at his home in 1990. Last June, Jo Cox died at the hands of a rightwing extremist, Thomas Mair, as she made her way to her constituency surgery. Security at parliament is tighter than it has ever been. Its one obvious weakness was the main vehicle entrance into New Palace Yard, off the road linking Whitehall with other government offices. This is the very heart of government. It's where tourists stand taking selfies through the open gates of the place that is still regarded around the world as the birthplace of modern democracy.

Today's attack has long been anticipated. It is not an act of war. It must not be allowed to divide us one from the other. Terror's purpose is to spread hate and division. The first protection against it must be solidarity.

23 MARCH

Look out, America! Here comes Katie Hopkins with her London-loathing hate speech

MARINA HYDE

Is there any animal, vegetable or mineral less London than Katie Hopkins? There are bits of the Outer Hebrides that have more of the capital to them than Katie, with her dull, self-satirising snobberies and clear sense that the city – perhaps all cities – are a joke in which no one cares to include her.

Needless to say, madam has rushed straight from the traps to put her stamp on the Westminster terror attack, with a gazillion-word *Daily Mail* thunk-piece on London. Or as Katie has it: 'An entire city of monkeys: see no evil, hear no evil, speak no evil. Blind. Deaf. And dumb.' Mmm. It's like that bit in *Mean Girls* where the girl makes a histrionic speech in front of the whole school and the guy at the back says: 'She doesn't even go here!?'

'Liberals in London,' Katie also declared, 'actually think multi-culturalism means we all die together.' Um, you don't even go here!? YOU LIVE IN DEVON, MATE. I'm not going to say where, because it's not fair to cause a house price crash (and her exact location may be covered by some sort of Shitness Protection Programme).

Still, even as the police urge caution on the Westminster attack, Katie's intemperate intervention serves as a reminder that where some people see tragedy, others see tragitunity. 'No anger for me this time,' wrote Katie. 'No rage like I've felt before. No desperate urge to get out there and scream at the idiots who refused to see this coming.'

There was, however, a desperate urge to get booked on Fox News. And since this is a showbusiness column, may I congratulate Katie and her publicist in pulling the gig off this time. Katie seems marginally more frantic to break America than even Robbie Williams once was. The problem is that Over There hardly lacks for its own supply of reactionary wingnuts. And with a protectionist president openly demanding a return to American-made goods and services, a foreign purveyor of discord will only be first choice in rare situations. Katie knows there are only going to be a few times a news producer is going to call her instead of Ann Coulter. The Westminster attack is one of them.

Consequently, we are in what Katie and her agent may well regard as a golden window. These are the hours and days you need to make count. She wants that phone ringing off the hook. She wants to graduate from Tucker Carlson to helping Sean Hannity talk about anything but Trump and the FBI. Deep down, she wants a *Vanity Fair* cover saying 'The Alt-right Brits Are Coming', in which she and Nigel Farage are in bed like Patsy and Liam were.

To read Katie Hopkins is to know that she would have disagreed with the Enlightenment if she thought there was a *Loose Women* appearance in it. She writes like a not-very-bright sixth-former

Los Angeles, 26 February: Chaos at the Oscars as the award for Best Picture is mistakenly announced for *La La Land*, before correctly being given to *Moonlight*. AARON POOLE/AMPAS/EPA

Windsor Castle, 25 April: The Queen inspects a classic 'invalid carriage', as she hosts a ceremony to celebrate the 40th anniversary of the charity Motability. RICHARD POHLE/AFP/GETTY IMAGES

Washington, 20 January: President-elect Donald Trump waits to emerge onto the portico for his presidential inauguration at the US Capitol.
PATRICK SEMANSKY/AP PHOTO

Barcelona, 21 January: Demonstrators in Spain join millions around the world in a Women's March for equality and inclusivity, prompted by Trump's ascent to power. DAVID RAMOS/GETTY IMAGES

Santa Clara, California, 2 October 2016: Eli Harold, Colin Kaepernick and Eric Reid of the San Francisco 49ers kneel for the national anthem, protesting police brutality and racial inequality. In September this year, Trump called for kneeling NFL players to be fired. THEARON W. HENDERSON/GETTY IMAGES

Charlottesville, Virginia, 12 August: People fly into the air as a car ploughs into a crowd of demonstrators protesting at a white nationalist rally, at which one anti-fascist campaigner was killed. RYAN M. KELLY/AP

London, 22 March: A policeman points a gun at a man on the floor after an attacker ran over passers-by and fatally stabbed a policeman in Westminster. The terrorist was shot dead. STEFAN ROUSSEAU/PA WIRE

Outer Hebrides, 5 June: The body of 14-year-old Eilidh MacLeod, who was killed in the terrorist attack at the Ariana Grande concert in Manchester, is laid to rest on the Hebridean island of Barra. ANDREW MILLIGAN/PA WIRE

London, 14 June: A local resident's view of Grenfell Tower after fire broke out in the 27-storey block of flats in Kensington, leaving at least 80 people dead. NATALIE OXFORD/AFP/GETTY IMAGES

London, 16 June: A man holds up a poster of two missing children from the Grenfell fire. DANIEL LEAL-OLIVAS/AFP/GETTY IMAGES

Paris, 14 May: France's newly elected president, Emmanuel Macron, kisses his wife, Brigitte, during the handover ceremony. PHILIPPE WOJAZER/REUTERS

Maidenhead, 9 June: Theresa May listens as the declaration at her consistuency is made after her disastrous decision to call a snap election.
ALASTAIR GRANT/AP PHOTO

Glastonbury, 24 June: Just a fortnight after Labour made surprise gains in the election, Jeremy Corbyn salutes the crowd on the Pyramid Stage at Glastonbury Festival, as they chant his name. DAVID LEVENE/GUARDIAN

Brussels, 17 July: Brexit secretary David Davis (left) smiles for the cameras with the EU chief negotiator Michel Barnier ahead of the second round of Brexit negotiations. STEPHANIE LECOCQ/EPA

Bonneville, Washington, 4 September: The Eagle Creek wildfire rages as residents play at a local golf course. The fire, allegedly started by teenagers, burned for nearly a month and covered 76 square miles. KRISTI McCLUER/REUTERS

Puerto Rico, 27 September: Irma Maldanado stands, with her parrot and dog, in what is left of her home after it was devastated by Hurricane Maria. JOE RAEDLE/GETTY IMAGES

trying to ape the prose style of Tony Parsons – no argument, just a portentous moodboard. Her Westminster article reads like a series of Google calendar reminders to herself. 'Shots fired. An Asian man rushed to hospital. And I grew colder. And more tiny.'

Here she is on the rest of the country's relationship with London: 'We are taken under the cold water by this heavy right foot in the south, a city of lead ...' Oof. Prose of lead. The concrete shoe of no verbs. Too many. Staccato sentences. Passing for gravitas. In fact, having performed a highly scientific linguistic analysis, I can confirm Katie uses fewer active verbs than even Tony Blair or John Keats. Presumably it's because she really doesn't have anywhere to go, philosophically. Still, were Katie on hand now, I expect she would retort that what we say is more important than how we say it. In fact, I know she would, because it wasn't long ago that she said the diametric opposite. 'The thing that would hurt me,' she told an interviewer, 'is if people suggested that I was bad at writing.'

For now, it falls to her to explain London to the Americans. 'Londoners can't even be honest about these attacks,' she told Fox News. 'Because it would mean everything they believed in was false.'

Ah, the false idols of the decadent metropolis! Had Katie spent more than 10 minutes in the World History aisle of Wikipedia, she would know there have always been people who hated cities for what they stood for. The metropolis has at many times served as shorthand for a kind of moral decay and wicked permissiveness that requires (usually forcible) regression.

'This place where monsters lurk and steal lives away in an instant,' thunders Katie of the capital's wickedness. 'For nothing.' Dear, dear – it does all seem rather terminal. I wonder what Katie would do with the failed, corruptive experiment that is London? The Khmer Rouge decided that the only solution was to empty the cities, and send their suspiciously educated denizens to the countryside. Come Katie's revolution, perhaps Londoners will be forcibly migrated too.

Yes, in a sledgehammer irony that will nonetheless have escaped her, Abu Hopkins detests the liberalism of the city. A serial preacher of hate, she speaks of humans as cockroaches, and of non-military matters in terms of struggle and war. 'We stand divided,' she tweeted at Sadiq Khan, 'cowed by your religion.' She now seeks to demonise London among her faithful, calling for an end to its degenerate values in the most apocalyptic terms she can muster.

Fortunately – and I hardly need to state this – she will get about as far with such smallness as she will with breaking America. Devon's loss remains the capital's gain. For all the tragedies and assaults enfolded into its history, London is a city that will never be so defeated as to have the time to explain itself to Katie Hopkins.

26 MARCH

Populism is the result of global economic failure

LARRY ELLIOTT

The rise of populism has rattled the global political establishment. Brexit came as a shock, as did the victory of Donald Trump. Much head-scratching has resulted as leaders seek to work out why large chunks of their electorates are so cross.

The answer seems pretty simple. Populism is the result of economic failure. The 10 years since the financial crisis have shown that the system of economic governance which has held sway for the past four decades is broken. Some call this approach neoliberalism. Perhaps a better description would be unpopulism.

Unpopulism meant tilting the balance of power in the workplace in favour of management and treating people like wage slaves. Unpopulism was rigged to ensure that the fruits of growth went to the few not to the many. Unpopulism decreed that those responsible for the global financial crisis got away with it while those who were innocent bore the brunt of austerity.

Anybody seeking to understand why Trump won the US presidential election should take a look at what has been happening to the division of the economic spoils. The share of national income that went to the bottom 90 per cent of the population held steady at around 66 per cent from 1950 to 1980. It then began a steep decline, falling to just over 50 per cent when the financial crisis broke in 2007.

Similarly, it is no longer the case that everybody benefits when the US economy is doing well. During the business cycle upswing between 1961 and 1969, the bottom 90 per cent of Americans took 67 per cent of the income gains. During the Reagan expansion two decades later they took 20 per cent. During the Greenspan housing bubble of 2001 to 2007, they got just two cents in every extra dollar of national income generated while the richest 10 per cent took the rest.

The US economist Thomas Palley says that up until the late 1970s, countries operated a virtuous circle growth model in which wages were the engine of demand growth.

'Productivity growth drove wage growth which fuelled demand growth. That promoted full employment, which provided the incentive to invest, which drove further productivity growth,' he says.

Unpopulism was touted as the antidote to the supposedly failed policies of the postwar era. It promised higher growth rates, higher investment rates, higher productivity rates and a trickle-down of income from rich to poor. It has delivered none of these things.

James Montier and Philip Pilkington, of the global investment firm GMO, say that the system which arose in the 1970s was characterised by four significant economic policies: the abandonment of full employment and its replacement with inflation targeting; an increase in the globalisation of the flows of people, capital and trade; a focus on shareholder maximisation rather than reinvestment and growth; and the pursuit of flexible labour markets and the disruption of trade unions and workers' organisations.

To take just the last of these four pillars, the idea was that trade unions and minimum wages were impediments to an efficient labour market. Collective bargaining and statutory pay floors would result in workers being paid more than the market rate, with the result that unemployment would inevitably rise.

Unpopulism decreed that the real value of the US minimum wage should be eroded. But unemployment is higher than it was when the minimum wage was worth more. Nor is there any correlation between trade union membership and unemployment. If anything, international comparisons suggest that those countries with higher trade union density have lower jobless rates. The countries that have higher minimum wages do not have higher unemployment rates.

'Labour market flexibility may sound appealing, but it is based on a theory that runs completely counter to all the evidence we have,' Montier and Pilkington note. 'The alternative theory suggests that labour market flexibility is by no means desirable as it results in an economy with a bias to stagnate that can only maintain high rates of employment and economic growth through debt-fuelled bubbles that inevitably blow up, leading to the economy tipping back into stagnation.'

This quest for ever-greater labour market flexibility has had some unexpected consequences. The bill in the UK for tax credits spiralled quickly once firms realised they could pay poverty wages and let the state pick up the bill. Access to a global pool of low-cost labour meant there was less of an incentive to invest in productivity-enhancing equipment.

The abysmally low levels of productivity growth since the crisis have encouraged the belief that this is a recent phenomenon, but as Andy Haldane, the Bank of England's chief economist, noted last week, the trend started in most advanced countries in the 1970s.

'Certainly, the productivity puzzle is not something which has emerged since the global financial crisis, though it seems to have amplified pre-existing trends,' Haldane said.

Bolshie trade unions certainly can't be blamed for Britain's lost productivity decade. The orthodox view in the 1970s was that attempts to make the UK more efficient were being thwarted by shop stewards who modelled themselves on Fred Kite, the character played by Peter Sellers in *I'm All Right Jack*. Haldane puts the blame elsewhere: on poor management, which has left the UK with a big gap between frontier firms and a long tail of laggards. 'Firms which export have systematically higher levels of productivity than domestically oriented firms, on average by around a third. The same is true, even more dramatically, for foreign-owned firms. Their average productivity is twice that of domestically oriented firms.'

Populism is seen as irrational and reprehensible. It is neither. It seems entirely rational for the bottom 90 per cent of the US population to question why they are getting only 2 per cent of income gains. It hardly seems strange that workers in Britain should complain at the weakest decade for real wage growth since the Napoleonic wars.

It has also become clear that ultra-low interest rates and quantitative easing are merely sticking-plaster solutions. Populism stems from a sense that the economic system is not working, which it clearly isn't. In any other walk of life, a failed experiment results in change. Drugs that are supposed to provide miracle cures but are proved not to work are quickly abandoned. Businesses that insist on continuing to produce goods that consumers don't like go bust. That's how progress happens.

The good news is that the casting around for new ideas has begun. Trump has advocated protectionism. Theresa May is consulting on an industrial strategy. Montier and Pilkington suggest a commitment to full employment, job guarantees, reindustrialisation and a stronger role for trade unions. The bad news is that time is running short. More and more people are noticing that the emperor has no clothes.

Even if the polls are right this time and Marine Le Pen fails to win the French presidency, a full-scale political revolt is only another deep recession away. And that's easy enough to envisage.

29 MARCH

Article 50: Ending a marriage of inconvenience

EDITORIAL

Britain's departure from the European Union, one of the largest economic powers in the world, is a historic and needless act of political folly, the consequences of which will shape this country and our neighbours' for years to come. But now it is happening.

It is thus the country's fourth big geopolitical shift since 1945. First we withdrew from empire, beginning with India in 1947. The second was joining what was then the European Economic Community in 1973. The third was the ending of the cold war between 1989 and 1991. They changed the world in ways no one could predict and we are still living today with the results. An abrupt severance from Europe without any transitional link to our nearest neighbours, with whom there are bonds of common endeavour, could still result in chaos. This would place at risk not only our prosperity and security but also deal a blow to the multilateral architecture that could presage a more volatile global era.

The sort of disorder that might be inflicted upon us in the coming years was there for all to see in the hours after Theresa May had sent Brussels our goodbye letter. It had all started so well. In parliament Mrs May wisely chose to make her pitch – both in tone and substance – in emollient terms. She had weighed her words carefully and was at her prime ministerial best at the despatch box where, after delivering her speech, she stood for hours taking questions. If Mrs May wanted to make a point about Brexit being accountable to parliament, she did so today. However, in Europe her letter was met with claims of 'blackmail' and outrage, some of it generated for audiences back home who cannot understand why Britain is leaving. Mrs May's unsubtle suggestion was that there could be a trade-off between Britain's security responsibilities and its desire for economic gain. This is anathema for those who translated it as a modern-day form of gunboat diplomacy: open your markets or we will leave you at the mercy of terrorists and Russia. Some of this is undoubtedly overblown. Mrs May knows it is in the interests of the EU and the UK that they should continue to act as close military allies, especially in uncertain times. She made the point several times in her Lancaster House speech. It remains her strongest – and weakest

– argument. After all who – if not Europe – will Britain ally with? Better if Mrs May had appreciated quietly that the UK contributes to European security, generating goodwill to secure a favourable trade deal.

This is a revealing error. Until now Mrs May has only had to deal with an audience composed of rabid Brexiters in the press and in her own party. They lapped up any Brussels bashing. However, now her critics are the people Mrs May has to do business with abroad. They cannot be bought off with *Daily Mail* headlines. They are also plainly unhappy with being presented with a trade-off between security and trade when wars are being fought in Europe's backyard. It shows that Mrs May understands her domestic audience but not her European interlocutors. Remember there are two years of this to come, so Mrs May needs to learn fast. What Eurosceptics have failed to understand is that the European Union is considered an existential inspiration, a destination for those who wanted democracy. To those living in the dictatorships of central and southern Europe which the magnetic power of the EU helped to overthrow, Europe meant freedom. For postwar Germans, a nation's power could not be exercised without the European Union. That perhaps explains the firm rebuttal from Angela Merkel, who also goes to the polls this year. Mrs May needs to lose her tin ear for European politics. It is obvious that the EU needs to deter others from following the UK's path. While anti-EU Geert Wilders failed to gain power in the Netherlands, Marine Le Pen remains in contention to become the next French president. Italy is even more troubling; two of the three leading parties in opinion polls are anti-EU.

It was not all bad news for Europe. Mrs May should be congratulated for saying Britain sought to 'guarantee the rights of EU citizens' and for putting workers' rights at the heart of Brexit. It would be an irony if those who voted for Brexit bore the brunt of its failures. There was, however, no mention of protections for the environment, the consumer or over data protection. These promises were made in the government's white paper and ministers should be held accountable for delivering such pledges. They already appear to be eating their words over claims that in post-Brexit Britain immigration would be reduced. While this newspaper wanted to remain in the EU, no one can be blind to the reality that some voters felt marooned by global forces beyond their control, which had, they thought, hollowed out their lives. However, this must not mean Brexit Britain should be a narrow-minded place, revelling in anti-immigrant isolationism. At stake is not Brexit, but what kind of Brexit. It was good to hear Mrs May say the world needs the liberal, democratic values of Europe – and Britain shares those values. Mrs May, a remainer, now leads a Brexit government. In January she warned 'supranational institutions as strong as those created by the European Union sit very uneasily in relation to our political history and way of life'. Mrs May was in effect saying a breach was always likely on the grounds of deep incompatibility.

What never went away was the bitter rancour of a peculiar British trait: a feeling that we had traded an empire we ran for one, bizarrely it was claimed, that ran us. Euroscepticism has existed ever since the European project has existed. But it was embedded in this nation's heart by Thatcherite cheerleaders who first wanted a separation, and then began to call for a permanent break-up. The strongest proof of Europe's feelings for Britain was all the trouble Brussels had put up with for the relationship's sake. In the end we have walked out, consciously uncoupling with a divorce letter that bitterly demands a special relationship after years in a marriage of inconvenience.

Spring

Darcus Howe: He translated the anger of street protests into political action

KEHINDE ANDREWS

When I heard the news of Darcus Howe's passing, it reminded me that one of the worst-told stories in Britain is the history of black struggle on these shores. It is almost impossible to trace the impact of his work, because we so poorly understand the context in which he laboured. I managed to go through 20 years of formal education without ever being told a single fact about black resistance movements in this nation. The closest we ever got was learning about Martin Luther King and Rosa Parks time and again during black history month.

Howe, who was born in Trinidad and Tobago in 1943, was an instrumental force for change in the black British struggle for equal rights and justice over five decades.

He migrated to the UK in 1961, a pivotal time for black activism in Britain. It had become clear that the movement of people from the former British colonies would not be temporary, with people going back to 'whence they came', as Conservative politician Enoch Powell had hoped. As subjects of the British crown who had fought and died for king and country in the world wars, Caribbean migrants had expected their children to get the best of the British schools system. Those dreams could not have been dashed more abruptly; by the mid-1960s, Caribbean communities were setting up supplementary schools in order to teach children the basics of maths and English, which the system was failing to provide.

It was not only in the schools that discrimination was rife. For young black people, the police were – and continue to be – the boots on the ground, the public face of state racism. Police harassment was rife, and the notorious sus laws – where you could be arrested merely on an officer's suspicion – were routinely abused and often ended in violence towards young black men. This treatment sparked mass reaction from black communities, who organised and protested and took to the streets. Howe is such an important figure because he managed to bridge the divide between the grassroots social movements, in which he participated, and the state-led campaigns to address inequality, which he influenced.

His key skill, as one of the main figures in the anti-racist, anti-police-brutality movement, was to translate the energy and anger of street protests into government action. He had a major impact on Lord Scarman, who was commissioned to investigate the causes of the 1981 riots. The rebellions in Brixton and elsewhere against the sus laws had shaken the nation; the Scarman Report was the first in Britain to take the police force to task for racial bias. As limited as Scarman was in his condemnation of police (he spoke of 'a few bad apples' rather than systemic racism), it was a landmark moment in opening up the forces to criticism. It laid the foundations for the Macpherson Report in 1999, which investigated the police's response to the racist murder of teenager Stephen Lawrence in 1993 and propelled an understanding of institutional racism into public discourse.

Howe was the nephew of Caribbean intellectual giant CLR James, who among many other works wrote *The Black Jacobins*, the definitive history of the 1804 Haitian revolution, when enslaved Africans rose up to overthrow their colonial French masters and formed the world's first black republic. Howe continued this intellectual tradition, giving a wider, more political voice to the street protests.

The radical journal *Race Today*, on which he worked as editor, was hugely influential in black political movements in the 1970s. Dr Denise Noble, a US-based professor of African American and African Studies, says it was especially powerful to have a 'serious black British journal that was both politically and theoretically nuanced'.

Reclaiming this history is important for me not only politically, but also personally. My father, Maurice Andrews, migrated from Jamaica at a similar time to Howe and was engaged in grassroots activism for decades. He was part of the African Caribbean Self-Help Organisation, which is still running after 50 years in Birmingham; he also founded the Harambee organisation, with which he is still involved. My mother, Carole Andrews, was also prominently involved in anti-racist campaigning, working for years at the organisation formerly known as the Commission for Racial Equality (CRE).

For both of my parents, Howe was a figure who could not be ignored and who made a major commitment to the struggle of the times. He was a central figure in many of the key activist movements over the past 40 years. He was a member of the British Black Panthers, along with key figures such as Althea Jones-Lecointe, Eddie Chambers and Olive Morris. *Guerrilla*, which airs this week on Sky Atlantic, dramatises that period; Howe was a consultant on the show. The series centres on the so-called 'black power' desk at the London Metropolitan police, which was set up to counter the perceived threat posed by black activism over 40 years ago.

In March 1981, the Black People's Day of Action drew 20,000 people on to the streets of London to protest the police investigation of the New Cross massacre. In January 1981, 13 teenagers had died in a fire at a house party in south-east London, in suspicious circumstances. Howe was a key figure in organising the demonstration, where one of the leading chants was '13 dead, nothing said'. But we would be wrong to memorialise events such as these as history. Over 30 years later, the Interim National African People's Parliament still organise annual marches because we still have no answers. Justice is too often suspended for black people; the long list of families waiting for justice for their kin who have died after police contact is chilling.

The Mangrove Nine trial in 1971 was a pivotal event in the black British struggle, and another in which Howe played a key role. Howe was arrested and charged after protesting against repeated police raids on the Caribbean restaurant Mangrove in Notting Hill in 1970. He and Jones-Lecointe insisted on representing themselves against the false charges brought against them and seven other defendants. After 55 days at the Old Bailey, the Mangrove Nine were acquitted and – for the first time – judges declared that there was 'evidence of racial hatred' in the Met.

Howe also served as chairman for the Notting Hill carnival in 1977 and resisted attempts to move the celebration from the streets of west London where it originated. The political nature of carnival is often overlooked, but it emerged from efforts to provide legal assistance to the black youth who were caught up in the racist riots in the area in 1958. The very concept of carnival is a political act that comes from the history of African enslavement. Enslaved people were given one day off a year and used this to celebrate and reconnect to their African past, which the slaveholders tried in vain to destroy. Attempts to stop carnival, which have been successful in Birmingham, and which are still hinted at in Notting Hill, can only be seen as an attempt to suppress political expression.

As we remember and celebrate his life and influence and mourn his death, the best way to remember Howe is as someone

who gave voice to a politics and community that was often overlooked. He made a lot of noise and he drew a lot of attention to
the struggle for equal rights and justice – and since these battles
are far from over, it's exactly what we should continue to do.

4 APRIL

My generation fought to be free. What happened to us?

POLLY TOYNBEE

Brexit has revealed a great many things about ourselves we might
prefer not to know, but in particular it has opened up a deep
cultural tug-of-war between the generations. My generation and
those older emerge in a bad light, a shocking disappointment for
those of us who once thought we were the avant garde; the tear-
ers-down of barriers; freedom fighters for the permissive society
in the vanguard of progress.

What's happened to us? The big baby boomer generation bears
down on a shrinking proportion of the young. In attitudes, we are
not ageing well.

A YouGov poll last week revealed how yearning for that imaginary 1950s golden age was a strong force that helped blow Britain
out of the EU. Remember, 64 per cent of over-65s voted for Brexit,
while 71 per cent of under-25s voted remain.

Yet the anti-immigrant sentiment, much stronger among
the old than the young, was only the topsoil on deeper strata
of backward-looking aches among the old. Brexiters are 53 per
cent for bringing back the rope (supported by just 20 per cent

of remainers). Bring back beating in schools, say 42 per cent of Brexiters (against just 14 per cent of remainers). Three times more Brexiters than remainers would bring back incandescent lightbulbs, blue passports, imperial weights and measures and pre-decimal currency – which would fox anyone under 55.

At the last election, 20 per cent more over-65s voted Tory than for Labour. Compare that to the under-30s who voted 4 per cent more for Labour. YouGov finds nearly three-quarters of the over-65s would ban burqas (36 per cent of the under-30s). A kindly 62 per cent of the young think we have a moral obligation to refugees, a view shared by only 39 per cent of the old. Same-sex marriage gets 83 per cent support from the young, but just 46 per cent of the over-65s.

Younger people could be wishing we of the Who generation really had all died before we got old. What's become of us? We who won all those freedoms on sex, contraception, abortion, gay rights, divorce, who saw the start of women's lib, an end to censorship, capital and corporal punishment, who threw off hats, gloves and conventions to wear and think what we liked? But no doubt many of my generation never bought into what seemed like the spirit of the age: abolishing capital punishment was never popular.

Pollsters can't tell how much this huge difference in generational attitudes is a cohort effect – the unchanging culture of a certain era – or how many people turn rightwards as they grow older. Will today's liberal-minded young follow a dismal trajectory towards conservatism as they age? Some people do turn meaner and more fearful as their own horizons close in.

My generation should count their blessings as the never-had-it-so-good beneficiaries of the NHS, better schools and overseas travel, with new opportunities in that great upward sweep from blue- to white-collar work. Now most of us sit on the proceeds of decades of booming house prices, enriched by an unmerited, untaxed property windfall. True, the over-60s are twice as likely to give to charity as the under-30s, though generosity may be easier with more cash than struggling 'generation rent'.

Growing old, too many in my generation seem unwilling to share all that experience of progress they have enjoyed. No, I know that's not you *Guardian* readers, many of whom grow more radical as they age; but all those backward-lookers should know better than to bring down the Brexit shutters on the young.

There is a mean-mindedness about the nearly half of over-65s who YouGov find think benefits (for others) are too generous – though they themselves have been shamelessly wooed with triple-lock pensions, winter fuel allowances, free TV licences and travel passes, regardless of their means.

Of course the poorer old need and deserve all these supports, but the biggest cohort ever to retire on decent pensions still keep their universal perks. The sheer numerical dominance of the over-65s over the shrinking proportion of the young invites political bribery. Labour is warned that if ever it is to win in England it needs to appeal to older voters – but quite how is unclear if so many of the old persist in voting with their pension books. What politician dare tell them to pay more attention to their grandchildren's generation?

The extreme £12bn benefit cuts starting this week take most money from young families and give 80 per cent of tax cuts to the richest, leaving the poorest third considerably worse off. The Institute for Fiscal Studies predicts there will be 5.1 million children in poverty by 2020, up 50 per cent – directly due to tax credit and working allowance cuts starting now. Those with children are hit hardest: children's services, health visitors and schools cut back, yet universal pension perks are protected.

Of course the old never willed any harm to the young, and the real blame lies with the government's draconian cuts, deliberately shared so unfairly. But the voting habits of the old are the underlying cause of a shift of wealth and income towards them and away from the impoverished young.

The one oddity is the care system, dysfunctional in every way and starved of funds, as described in a trenchant Commons report last week. If the grey vote is so politically powerful, why doesn't the social care crisis force the government to act? Partly because relatively few over-65s at any one time need care: many older voters don't confront the crisis until their very last years, when the average time in residential care is two and a half years.

Every report says the answer is to tap the accumulating property wealth of the old themselves: in 2010 Labour proposed that those with capital should pay a flat sum on retirement, but the Tories attacked it as a 'death tax'; and with great folly, chancellor Philip Hammond shut down any similar option by promising 'no death tax' in his March budget.

The *Daily Mail* thundered again last week about the unfairness of 'middle classes' in care homes cross-subsidising 'those who fail to save for their retirement', a rottweiler in defence of any raising of funds from the older generation who are the ones who own most wealth and will need the care.

What do we do about my generation? They have the voting power but too many seem to lack awareness of their good luck. If Brexit further harms the life chances of the young, the old who voted for it will owe them serious recompense.

18 APRIL

Dead-eyed Theresa May puts Tories' interests first

JOHN CRACE

Right to the end, Theresa May was unable to keep to her own time-table. For the past six months, the prime minister had repeatedly insisted she wouldn't be calling an early general election because it wasn't in the best interests of the country. Sometime over Easter, Theresa was blessed with a divine revelation – there are advantages to being a vicar's child – and came to the conclusion her own party's interests were rather more important than the country's. So shortly before 10am her office announced that she would be making a statement in Downing Street at 11.15.

Worried she hadn't caught enough people on the hop, Theresa darted out the front door of No 10 nine minutes early and made a dash for the wooden lectern that had been hurriedly placed outside. She paused to clock her surroundings. Satisfied that comparatively few journalists had made it in time, she got straight to the point. After overdosing on elections in recent years, the country was now going through cold turkey. People were literally crawling up walls out of desperation to vote, and to satisfy their cravings she was going to give everyone another fix on 8 June.

Not that she wanted to be seen as a prime minister who didn't keep her word. The problem was the opposition. They were doing the wrong thing by opposing her. Never mind that they weren't being very effective, the problem was that they existed at all. They were a nuisance. Come to think of it, President Erdoğan had a point in clamping down on any dissent. 'At this moment of national significance, there should be unity here in Westminster, but instead there is division,' May said. She had changed her mind over Brexit when she had spotted the opportunity to become prime minister and she couldn't for the life of her understand why other people couldn't be so flexible with their principles.

'The country is coming together,' she continued, waving away the inconvenient truth that no one could remember a time when it had been more split. 'But Westminster is not.' Labour MPs had said they might vote against a deal with the EU if they thought it wasn't good enough. How very dare they!

The Lib Dems – all nine of them – had threatened to grind government business to a standstill. The SNP had promised to be the SNP. Life had become just impossible for her. Her opponents had tried to take advantage of her small majority, so now she was going to punish them by wiping them out completely.

At this point Theresa almost imagined herself to be a latter-day Winston Churchill. Only her enemies weren't the Hun lining up to push the British Tommies into the Channel at Dunkirk, they were the enemy within. Those MPs who had dared to raise concerns on behalf of the 48 per cent of the country who had voted to remain in the EU would be ruthlessly crushed.

'Our opponents believe our resolve will weaken and that they can force us to change course,' she said, unaware of how sinister she sounded. And looked. Her eyes were almost as dead as her delivery: only by disconnecting from herself could she accommodate the cynicism of her position. 'They are wrong. They underestimate our determination to get the job done and I am not prepared to let them endanger the security of millions of working people across the country.' Quite right. If anyone were going to endanger the security of millions of working people, it would be her and her alone.

I. I. I. The longer Theresa went on, the more the statement became all about her. Her leadership. Her party. Her ego. Towards the end she made passing reference to the fact she had only last month declared she wouldn't be calling a snap general election. That had turned out to be just a resolution she had made for Lent. She had tried and tried to resist the temptation of capitalising on the desperate state of the Labour party, taking the opportunity to force through a hard Brexit that almost no one in the country had voted for and guaranteeing a Conservative government for the conceivable future.

But when push had come to shove, the spirit had been willing but the flesh was weak. In what was left of her heart, she knew that no one in the country really wanted another election and that this was being played out for her own vanity and insecurity, but she just couldn't help herself. 'Politics isn't a game,' she concluded severely. But it was and it is. Her actions spoke far louder than her words.

5 MAY

'We don't want you here': Muslims fearful as France prepares to vote

ANGELIQUE CHRISAFIS

In her apartment in a northern suburb of Paris, Hanane Charrihi looked at a photograph of her mother Fatima. 'Her death shows that we need tolerance more than ever,' she said. 'Tolerance does exist in France, but sometimes it seems those who are against tolerance shout the loudest and get the most airtime.'

Fatima Charrihi, 59, a Muslim grandmother, was the first of 86 people to be killed in a terrorist attack in Nice last summer when a lorry driver ploughed into crowds watching Bastille Day fireworks. She had left her apartment and gone down to the seafront to have an ice-cream with her grandchildren. Wearing a hijab, she was the first person the driver hit in the gruesome attack claimed by Islamic State. A third of those killed in the Nice attack were Muslims. But Fatima Charrihi's family, some wearing headscarves, were insulted by passersby who called them 'terrorists' even as they crouched next to their mother's body under a sheet at the site of the attack. 'We don't want people like you here any more,' a man outside a cafe told her family soon after the attack.

Hanane Charrihi, 27, a pharmacist, was so irked to find that, even after her mother's death, the so-called 'problem' of Islam in France was such a focus of political debate that she wrote a book, *Ma mère patrie*, a plea for living together harmoniously in diversity. The far-right Front National gained a slew of new members in Nice after the attack and now Marine Le Pen's presence in the final presidential runoff this weekend – after taking a record 7.6 million votes in the first round – has pushed the issue of Islam and national identity to the top of the agenda.

'I'm French, I love my country, and it seemed like people were saying to me: "No, you can't possibly love France,"' Hanane Charrihi said. 'All this focus on debating national identity by politicians seems like wasting time that could be focused instead on unemployment, work or housing.'

The runoff between the far-right, anti-immigration Le Pen and the independent centrist Emmanuel Macron has seen heated exchanges over Islam and national identity. In 2015, Le Pen was tried and cleared of inciting religious hatred after comparing

Muslims praying in the streets to the Nazi occupation. Macron has insisted that Le Pen still represents 'the party of hatred'. He told a Paris rally this week: 'I won't accept people being insulted just because they believe in Islam.' After more than 230 people were killed in terrorist attacks in France in just over two years, Le Pen has called Islamic fundamentalism a 'mortal danger' for France and accused Macron of having an 'indulgent attitude' towards it. He accused her of dividing France and stoking 'civil war'.

Le Pen's policy proposals include banning religious symbols, such as the Muslim headscarf, from all public places. She would outlaw ritual animal slaughter, namely Islamic halal slaughter, although Jewish kosher practices would also be affected.

When Le Pen's father and her party's co-founder, Jean-Marie Le Pen, reached the final round of the presidential election in 2002, the political class spontaneously united with anti-racism campaigners to block his vote, marching on the streets. This time anti-Le Pen demonstrations have been fewer, smaller and more fragmented. Comparatively few people have lined up behind anti-racism banners, and the Front National is now accepted as a part of the political landscape. The issue of diversity and France's divisions – between city and countryside, rich and poor, so-called 'native' French and immigrants – have haunted the campaign.

In Aubervilliers market – part of Seine-Saint-Denis, the leftwing and ethnically diverse area north-east of Paris, where young people on estates complain of discrimination that has underlined youth unemployment – Ezzedine Fahem, 62, worried there was a growing divide. 'In some places Le Pen's vote is increasing, yet here the very idea of Le Pen sparks fear,' said the former restaurant worker. 'To me, it feels like she targets Muslims, religion, foreigners. All this talk of integration. Look around here – everyone from abroad was pushed here into a ghetto. Now even if you're French and born here, you will always be brought back to your roots. You're French but you're always an Arab, you're still black, you're still Jewish.'

At the market, Alexandre Aidara is handing out election leaflets for Macron. He is one of the few parliamentary candidates already selected to run for parliament in June for Macron's 'neither left nor right' movement, *En Marche!* (On the Move). Aidara, 49, an engineer who was born in Senegal and studied in France, including at the elite civil service school, École Nationale d'Administration, has worked at a senior level in top government ministries. He said Macron's choice of more parliamentary candidates from ethnic minorities was a bid to renew the political class. Although Seine-Saint-Denis is one of the most ethnically diverse areas in France, only one of its 13 MPs is not white. Of France's 577 members of parliament, four come from ethnic minorities.

Le Pen's stance on the high-rise *banlieues* surrounding French cities is that security must come first. Macron's take is that discrimination is a growing problem and business opportunities hold the key. He has said that he wants 'social mobility' and would give a €15,000 bonus over three years to companies who hired people from 200 designated poor neighbourhoods.

'On diversity issues, Emmanuel Macron wants to show there are role models,' Aidara said. 'The role models here are rappers and footballers. That's good – art and culture is great. But you can also succeed through school, like me, through being an engineer. Discrimination represents a big economic loss to the economy and the state.'

Macron has argued that his line on fighting terrorism is to look at the 'roots' of why French-born children are growing up to take arms against their own country – a view that has sparked scorn not just from Le Pen but from Socialists. 'When people are born in France and attack France, it means integration has failed – you have to look at that, have to work on jobs, education, integration and schools. That's why we want to cut class sizes in priority zones,' Aidara said.

Macron also tried to take on the unresolved chapter in French history that is the colonial period and war in Algeria. On a visit to Algiers in February, he called France's colonial past a 'crime against humanity'. He later tempered his comments, but insisted: 'We must face this common, complex past if we want to move on and get along.' Le Pen this week accused him of slandering France's 'glorious history'.

Sara, 22, took a leaflet for Macron. A first-time voter and technology student who wears a Muslim headscarf, she voted in the first round for the hard-left Jean-Luc Mélenchon, 'because he was about everyone in France living together and getting on'. She felt anti-Islam feeling was becoming 'almost commonplace' in France. 'I'm not sure Emmanuel Macron has really understood that,' she added, but she would vote for him to keep Le Pen out. She liked the fact that Macron did not want to ban the Muslim headscarf from universities – an idea proposed by some on the mainstream right and even backed by the former Socialist prime minister Manuel Valls.

For years the French principle of secularism, or *laïcité*, has been caught up in a row over whether it has been twisted for political gain. The French republic is built on a strict separation of church and state, intended to foster equality for all private beliefs. But controversies – such as mayors banning the burkini full-body Muslim swimsuit from French beaches last summer – have seen commentators, and even the courts, warn of the 'violation of fundamental freedoms' in singling out Muslims. Macron has said his approach to French secularism would be 'tolerant', sparking accusations from Le Pen that he is 'lax'.

'Racism, racism, racism – that's what I'm afraid of in France,' said a 49-year-old French town hall worker who was born in Tunisia. 'I didn't vote in the first round but on Sunday I'm going to drag everyone I know out of their beds and drag them to vote Macron. I wouldn't normally vote for Macron, but what choice do we have? This election isn't over yet. The result is open. I worry Le Pen could win, and if she does, I think I might just leave France until her time in power is over.'

7 MAY

The French presidency goes to Macron. But it's only a reprieve

TIMOTHY GARTON ASH

Like someone who has narrowly escaped a heart attack, Europe can raise a glass and give thanks for the victory of Emmanuel Macron. But the glass is less than half full, and if Europe doesn't change its ways it will only have postponed the fateful day.

The next president of France will be a brilliant product of that country's elite, with a clear understanding of France's deep structural problems, some good ideas about how to tackle them, a strong policy team, and a deep commitment to the European Union. When a centrist pro-European government has been formed in Berlin after the German election this autumn, there is a chance for these two nations to lead a consolidatory reform of the EU.

Savour those drops of champagne while you can, because you've already drained the glass. Now for the sobering triple espresso of reality. First shot: more than a third of those who turned out in the second round voted for Marine Le Pen (at the time of writing we don't have the final figures). What times are these when we celebrate such a result?

Thanks to France's superior electoral system and strong republican tradition, the political outcome is better than the victories of Donald Trump and Brexit, but the underlying electoral reality is in some ways worse. Trump came from the world of buccaneer capitalism, not from a long-established party of the far right; and most of the 52 per cent who voted for Brexit were not voting for Nigel Farage. After Le Pen's disgusting, mendacious, jeering performance in last Wednesday's television debate, no one could have any doubt who they were voting for. She makes Farage look almost reasonable.

From the country which gave us the 1789 example of violent revolution, we now have the personification of today's worldwide anti-liberal counter-revolution. Le Pen is the very model of a modern national populist. She herself boasted in the TV debate that she is best placed to deal with this brave new world, 'to talk about Russia with Putin, to talk about the United States with Trump, to talk about Great Britain with Theresa May'. (How sickening to see a British prime minister listed in that company.) There is every reason to believe that this wave of populist reaction against globalisation, liberalisation and Europeanisation still has a lot of pent-up anger behind it.

Second espresso shot: Macron knows what needs to be done in France but is unlikely to succeed in doing it. To those who supported Le Pen you have to add the many who abstained, including leftwing voters who described this second round as a choice between cholera and the plague. The president-elect has no established party behind him, so it is totally unclear what majority will emerge from next month's French parliamentary elections.

He is already being described as 'Renzi 2.0', a reference to the Italian would-be-reformist former premier Matteo Renzi. His super-ambitious target is to reduce public spending from 56 per cent of GDP to just – wait for it – 52 per cent. The obstacles to change in France are enormous, from powerful unions and a bloated public sector to farmers who make a habit of blocking roads with tractors. If Macron fails to reform France, in 2022 we may yet have a president Le Pen.

Third espresso shot: it's great that Macron also wants to reform the EU, but that's not in his gift. With Brexit talks already turning nasty, Britain has moved from being a major ally in European reform to a massive distraction from it. Italy, with higher public debt than France, a fragile banking sector and fractured politics, may produce the next eurozone crisis. The underlying causes of the refugee crisis have not been addressed. Hungary and Poland are governed by anti-liberal populists.

Macron's proposals for eurozone reform – a common fiscal policy, a joint finance minister, some shared debt, and completion of the banking union – will not go down well with German voters. Above all, he has promised a 'Europe that protects'. Yes. But how?

So this is only a reprieve. Everything remains to be done. And Europe is still drinking in the last chance saloon.

15 MAY

'Each year the benefit system is more heartless'

NAZIA PARVEEN

In 2010, when David Cameron launched his 'big society' project in Liverpool, he talked a lot about empowering communities. The idea, he said, was 'a deep, serious reform agenda to take power away from politicians and give it to people'. But then austerity took the big society's place as the government's defining idea, and the phrase disappeared from the party's literature. It was dismissed as an 'enormous failure'.

Seven years on from that launch, on a sunny afternoon 100 miles south of Liverpool, Cameron's big idea is reluctantly being reheated in a Labour heartland. Today's 'empowered community', as Cameron would have it, are the leaders and volunteers of the many churches and mosques in Erdington, a Birmingham suburb. They might wish they didn't have to, but they are helping to meet the needs of some of the most impoverished people in society.

The Rev Gerard Goshawk invites me into the Six Ways Baptist church. It is peaceful, and there are no interruptions, but this is unusual, he says. Most days the church doubles up as an English-language college with free classes for immigrants, is home to one of the busiest food banks in the city and holds numerous other classes in an effort to get the community to engage with each other. It is a similar story across the suburb.

Goshawk says he works with local imams and church leaders to 'prop up a failing system'. The 53-year-old, who has lived in Erdington for the past decade and has a mainly African-Caribbean congregation, will not reveal his political affiliations, but talks of how the voluntary sector in recent years has been forced to step in because of harsh austerity cuts in his community.

'We are Christians and we can't just stand by and do nothing,' Goshawk says. 'Each year the benefit system is more heartless in the way that it deals with individuals with an economy that has shifted and left people feeling quite disempowered and left behind. In that sense we are filling a gap and providing for people's basic needs.

'Before I became a minister I was a nurse and then in the voluntary sector. It's the essential problem of any voluntary sector organisation that you end up propping up a system that is wrong, and trying to make it easier.'

In an election season, one question looms above all others: who is responsible for the problem? Goshawk is unsure. The answer is complicated, and the answer constituents settle on may prove vital to the area's political future.

On one hand, Erdington comes under the umbrella of Birmingham city council, which is Labour. On the other, in one of the constituency's wards which is also called Erdington, its three local councillors, Bob Beauchamp, Gareth Moore and Robert Alden, are all Conservatives. Alden is standing against Labour's Jack Dromey, the husband of former interim party leader Harriet Harman. And, of course, the government is Conservative.

So what do Erdingtonians do? Vote Conservative despite the current government announcing £43m cuts to Birmingham council's funding in 2015? Or stay loyal to the Labour candidate who some feel is 'struggling to affect change in the area'?

Whatever the answer, the softly spoken Goshawk is certain he has work to do. After the Brexit vote (Erdington voted 63 per cent in favour of leave) he was the minister who heard one leave voter give a withering verdict of the area on TV. He was outraged and decided to show that the community was not as divided as it was being portrayed. The result was #EverythingErdington, a community celebration that culminated in more than 100 people from many of the town's nationalities holding hands along the high street in a show of solidarity.

Just a few minutes' walk and we are in Oikos, another church – although that's just a small part of its colourful story. This one doubles up as the area's only up-and-coming restaurant. It is evening on the high street – deserted apart from the odd afternoon drinker making their way into one of the pubs. The exodus of big-brand stores and independent shops is a constant gripe for locals. But there is a buzz here at Oikos. Something different is at play.

Oikos, which means 'home' in Greek, was opened three years ago by evangelical pastor Jez Dearing. We meet just before an open-mic night to raise funds for mental health charity Birmingham Mind.

Dearing, 43, sits down with a flat white and handmade shortbread, opposite walls adorned in broken-down wooden pallets and shelves displaying works by local artists. This is a very different Erdington, says Dearing, one that appeals to the forgotten demographic in the area, the young working families and twentysomethings who want 'nice places to eat, sit and meet each other'.

But this is not just another trendy place to eat. Like Goshawk, Dearing – a father of two whose wife is a local mental health nurse – saw a need in the area for those who were the most impoverished, and a need that was not being fulfilled by the public sector.

Originally from the Forest of Dean, Dearing initially moved to Erdington because of its cheaper house prices, but 18 years later he is still here. In 2011, he entered negotiations with a private landlord to acquire the building, an eyesore that had been closed for 12 years. He spent every evening and weekend renovating the building with a band of volunteers, running electricity cables and plumbing in kitchens.

'It was most definitely a labour of love,' he says. 'But I had to do something. Every day I would walk past this building – it was so run-down. I wanted to do something good for Erdington. I love Erdington and wanted to bring new life to the high street. We had the opportunity to be a forerunner.'

Dearing isn't sure who is most to blame for the problems in the area: he describes himself as disenfranchised, and says he is 'on the fence' about the election. But it would be a mistake to see this as a lack of interest. His cafe provides more than just a brief beacon in an army of closed shops: he is also being called on to offer English language classes, apprenticeships, curry nights, knitting groups and board-game clubs. He wants to build a communal kitchen and run cookery courses to skill up the jobless.

'I guess if we didn't do it then it just wouldn't happen,' he says.

Musicians from across the city and from a spectrum of backgrounds bustle into the cafe as locals and others who have come from further afield settle in for a night of poetry and music. During a break between a rap solo and a rapturous ukulele performance, teacher Dan Mandley, 35, reflects on the political moment.

Mandley, whose wife runs the English classes at the cafe, reddens slightly and shifts uncomfortably in his seat when asked who he will vote for. There is a long pause. Eventually he says that he will vote Tory, for only the second time since he was 18.

'I voted to remain because the Polish immigration to this area has been one of the best things that could have happened to it,' he says. But unlike most people in the area, his outlook is more national than local. 'Now we are where we are, and as painful as it is I will probably vote Tory. I am traditionally a Labour voter but I feel Theresa May is more of a steady hand for Brexit negotiations.'

In 2015 Dromey won Erdington with a 5,129 majority. Optimists see this as a healthy margin – but there are those who believe Dromey is in 'the fight of his life'.

The constituency lies north of Edgbaston and Northfield, which have also become battlegrounds for the two main parties. Further clarifying the battle ahead, Ukip have announced that they will not be putting up a candidate in Erdington: even though they secured a healthy 6,040 votes at the last general election, they have asked voters in the area to vote tactically and support the Conservatives to keep out a Labour government on 8 June.

Even if the options have reduced, the choice remains difficult. In a district torn over its political affiliations, and where the voluntary sector is having to take up the slack caused by austerity, immigration and low wages, no one quite knows what will happen: blame the national government, or make the local MP pay the price?

Goshawk vocalises the difficult choice ahead: 'What we are here is part of the essential role of any religious organisation, but the danger is that we end up doing the dirty work for the government.

'I don't see it as a triumph, it's a tragedy and a shame that we are having to do that. There is a general societal need to provide for each other. To me, it is a sign of failure that we are having to do this. Where the blame for that gets lodged is complicated in somewhere like Erdington where we have a Conservative government, a Labour council, and Labour MP.'

23 May

Irreverent and knowing as James Bond: Roger Moore obituary

RYAN GILBEY

Sir Roger Moore, who has died aged 89, considered himself to be only the fourth best actor to have played Ian Fleming's secret-service agent James Bond on screen: in his estimation, he came in behind Daniel Craig (whom he called 'the Bond'), Sean Connery and George Lazenby. Though Moore was rarely regarded as the best or most definitive Bond, his inimitable humour and panache made him many viewers' favourite. His tally of seven films – beginning with *Live and Let Die* (1973) and ending with *A View to a Kill* (1985) – equalled that of Connery, though Moore occupied the role for a longer consecutive period. He was eloquent on the distinction between their portrayals. 'Sean played Bond as a killer and I played Bond as a lover,' he said. Only on Fridays did he resemble a cold-blooded mercenary: 'That's the day I received my paychecks.'

His casting was sometimes erroneously considered to be the catalyst for a newfound levity in the series; in fact, the two films prior to his arrival (*On Her Majesty's Secret Service*, 1969, and *Diamonds Are Forever*, 1971) had already tipped the tone towards silliness. What Moore did very cannily was to underline the absurdity of Bond himself. 'My whole reaction was always – he is not a real spy,' he said. 'You can't be a real spy and have everybody in the world know who you are and what your drink is. That's just hysterically funny.'

Irreverence and knowingness were integral to his interpretation. But he also seemed far more plausibly endangered as

Bond than Connery had ever been. Part of the viewer's affection and even concern for him could be attributed to his advanced age: Moore was already 45 when he was cast as Bond, whereas Connery made his debut at 32 and Craig was 37. This contributed to the sense that Moore's wellbeing was actively at risk on screen. Subjected to punishing levels of G-force on a flight simulator in *Moonraker* (1979) or dismantling a bomb while dressed as a clown in *Octopussy* (1983), he looked uniquely vulnerable. Clambering up the Eiffel Tower and the Golden Gate Bridge in *A View to a Kill* seemed inadvisable behaviour for a man of 56.

His range was modest, as he was the first to admit. He credited his success to '99 per cent luck', and singled out the 1970 supernatural thriller *The Man Who Haunted Himself*, in which he played a businessman who appears to be living two lives, as 'the only film I was allowed to act in'. Such self-deprecation only encouraged critics to contribute their own jibes: Anthony Lane of the *New Yorker* said that Moore 'needed a stunt double for his acting scenes' in the Bond films.

Moore became an object of mild mockery after the 1980s satirical TV show *Spitting Image* featured a puppet of him that expressed its emotions solely through its eyebrows. The joke proved robust, but not everyone realised that Moore had cracked it first. 'The eyebrows thing was my own fault,' he said. 'I was talking about how talentless I was and said I have three expressions: eyebrow up, eyebrow down and both of them at the same time. And they used it – very well, I must say.'

He was born in London, to Lily (née Pope), a housewife, and George Moore, a police constable whose responsibilities included drawing accident scenes to be used in evidence in court. Roger himself had artistic ambitions early in life. He left school at 15 to accept a job as a trainee animator at Publicity Picture

Productions, but was sacked a few months later when he neglected to collect a can of film.

Tagging along with friends in 1945 to auditions for film extras, Moore was picked to appear in a non-speaking role as a legionnaire in *Caesar and Cleopatra*, starring Vivien Leigh and Claude Rains. The film's first assistant director, Brian Desmond Hurst, took Moore under his wing and encouraged him to audition for RADA. When Moore was accepted, Hurst paid his fees. He left at 18 to become a supporting player in the repertory company of the Arts theatre, Cambridge, before he was called up for military service. Posted to Germany, he succeeded in getting a transfer to the Combined Services Entertainment unit. In 1946, he had married Doorn Van Steyn, a fellow RADA student.

After three years in the army, Moore returned to acting, landing small roles in theatre and film, as well as appearing as a model for knitting patterns and in photo stories. He moved to New York City in 1953 with his second wife, the singer Dorothy Squires (Moore and Van Steyn had divorced earlier that year), and began getting acting work on US television. He signed a contract with MGM and was cast in a series of unmemorable films, including *The Last Time I Saw Paris* (1954) and *Interrupted Melody* (1955). Returning to Britain, he took the lead in a 1958 television adventure series adapted from Walter Scott's novel *Ivanhoe*.

Other regular TV roles of increasing size followed, including two western series, *The Alaskans* and *Maverick*, before Moore finally became a bona fide star, playing the crime-fighter and playboy Simon Templar in the popular television crime series *The Saint*. Produced by Lew Grade, it ran from 1962 until 1969. Moore, who also directed nine episodes, brought a suavity to the part which makes it a clear precursor of his work as James Bond; even his habit in early episodes of looking directly at the camera prefigures the later Bonds, where he all but winks at the audience.

Two years after *The Saint* ended, Moore was cast once more as a playboy adventurer in another Grade TV series, *The Persuaders!*, in which he was teamed with Tony Curtis. The odd-couple pairing (Moore, as Lord Brett Sinclair, was dapper; Curtis, playing Danny Wilde, was a ruffian) and the action staged in glamorous locations made the series a hit. Moore also directed two episodes. During this period, he was appointed the head of Brut Films, an offshoot of the cologne manufacturer. He tried unsuccessfully to entice Cary Grant to make his acting comeback in a Brut production, but succeeded in recruiting him as one of the company's advisers. Moore was also instrumental in the making of *A Touch of Class*, the 1973 romantic comedy for which Glenda Jackson won her second Oscar.

His brief tenure as a mogul was abbreviated when he signed a three-film contract to play James Bond, a part which demanded no adjustment to the persona he had already established. *Live and Let Die*, an attempt to modernise the series with gritty blaxploitation trappings, still had its share of daftness; in one scene, Bond escapes across water using a row of alligators as stepping stones. Moore's performance here and in his second outing, *The Man with the Golden Gun* (1974), was cool and confident.

But it is his third Bond film, *The Spy Who Loved Me* (1977), which is rightly considered his pinnacle. The writing, direction and production design were impressive, the action more than usually taut, and the balance of comedy and suspense acutely judged – as in the iconic opening sequence in which Bond escapes falling to his death by opening a parachute emblazoned with the union jack. (The film was released in the Queen's silver jubilee year.) Moore appeared relaxed but never complacent. He even came up with some of the movie's nicest touches, such as the moment when Bond, emerging from an underwater drive, deposits a small fish out of his car window.

In between the Bond films, Moore moonlighted in other roles, including *Gold* (1974), a mining adventure shot in Johannesburg, the romantic comedy *That Lucky Touch* (1975) and the war movie *Shout at the Devil* (1975), co-starring Lee Marvin. But nothing came close to eclipsing his day job.

Outside the Bond series, he rarely deviated from action, appearing in quick succession in *Escape to Athena* (1979), *North Sea Hijack* and *The Sea Wolves* (both 1980). *The Wild Geese* (1978), a clunky, crypto-racist thriller about ageing mercenaries, was unusual in showcasing a more brutal side to Moore. Though he was seen pushing villains to their deaths in *The Spy Who Loved Me* and *For Your Eyes Only* (1981), nothing compared to the opening scene of *The Wild Geese*, in which he kills a drug dealer by forcing him to ingest large quantities of cocaine at gunpoint.

Moonraker (1979), among the silliest of the Bond series, was rushed into production to capitalise on the *Star Wars*-inspired craze for all things space-related. Moore had a gas playing a mummy's boy who believes himself to be Roger Moore in the US ensemble comedy *The Cannonball Run* (1981), before returning to Bond in the comparatively sober *For Your Eyes Only* and the positively quaint *Octopussy*. Moore bowed out, not before time, with *A View to a Kill*, where he looked understandably wary to be sharing the screen, not to mention a bed, with the ferocious Grace Jones.

Though the producer Albert R. 'Cubby' Broccoli suggested in his autobiography that Moore had refused to accept that his time in the role was over, the actor later denied this. Once free of bondage, Moore lost his appetite for acting and took on only a handful of roles, few of them distinguished. He had been due to return to the stage in Andrew Lloyd Webber's *Aspects of Love* in 1989, but dropped out shortly before opening night, blaming inadequacies in his singing voice.

He joined his friend Michael Caine in *Bullseye!* (1990), a pitiful Michael Winner comedy in which they played two characters apiece. He also appeared in *The Quest* (1996), directed by its star, the action hero Jean-Claude Van Damme, and in the Spice Girls' vehicle *Spice World* (1997). He had a supporting part in the two-hour pilot for a new series of *The Saint* (2013), but the show was not commissioned. In 2012, he undertook a highly successful UK stage tour of *An Evening with Roger Moore*, in which he reflected on his life and career.

Moore devoted much of his time to being a goodwill ambassador for UNICEF; it was for this humanitarian work that he was knighted in 2003. He had left Britain in the late 1970s to avoid what he considered the prohibitive tax rate for high earners, and took homes in countries including Switzerland and Monaco. Money continued to be much on his mind: his 2008 autobiography, *My Word Is My Bond*, is peppered with variations on the line 'a rather nice deal was agreed with my agent'.

Moore admitted to being a lifelong hypochondriac; among those to whom he expressed thanks in the acknowledgments of his autobiography are five GPs, four cardiologists, two dermatologists and a proctologist. He visibly enjoyed his time as Bond and expressed only occasional regrets about his career. 'I spent my life playing heroes because I looked like one,' he said. 'Practically everything I've been offered didn't require much beyond looking like me. I would have loved to play a real baddie.'

He is survived by his fourth wife, Kristina Tholstrup, whom he married in 2002, and by three children – Deborah, Geoffrey and Christian – from his third marriage, to the actor Luisa Mattioli, which ended in divorce.

23 MAY

From a balloon pop to a suicide bomb – witnesses in Manchester recount a night of horror

ELLE HUNT

For some it sounded muffled and far away, as though somewhere in the distance a big balloon had popped. For others the terror was all too immediately apparent.

The lights had just come on and Ariana Grande had left the stage after concluding an elaborate three-hour, four-part entertainment extravaganza with an encore performance of her latest single, 'Dangerous Woman'.

At 10.30pm following a sold-out show in the 21,000-capacity Manchester Arena, thousands of fans began to gather up their belongings and filter slowly out of four exits.

Then the bang.

For the first milliseconds minds did not immediately connect the sound with an explosion or a bomb.

'It sounded like a big balloon popping, but it was kind of muffled, like it wasn't in the stadium itself,' said a young Mancunian fan, identified as Sammy, in a video he recorded of his experience and posted on Periscope.

'There were a few screams, then there was silence. Then the whole arena literally split like the Red Sea – everyone was trampling over each other, sprinting to get to the nearest exit. It was like a scene out of a horror movie.'

In a short video posted to Twitter, where she had been counting down the days to the concert, Ellie Cheetham of Wigan captured the moment of the explosion, when fans milling around the arena were startled by a loud, muffled bang.

'The lights were already on so we knew it wasn't part of the show,' said Erin McDougle, 20, from Newcastle.

Then confusion gave way to bewilderment, which in turn gave way to chaos. Witnesses described thousands of people running for their nearest exit, trampling over others in their panic.

Majid Khan, 22, had been on his way out of the venue with his sister when the 'huge bomb-like bang' went off. He and others said it seemed to come from the tiered seating stage-right, near the Hunts Bank entrance and exit.

'Everyone from the other side of the arena, where the bang was heard from, suddenly came running towards us.'

Khan said there was a crush to get out of the Trinity Way exit, across the arena from the apparent source of the explosion, which was blocked: 'Everyone was just running to any exit they could find, as quickly as they could.

'Everyone was in a huge state of panic, calling each other ... it was just extremely disturbing for everyone there.'

Elizabeth Welsby, a 50-year-old teacher from Bolton, told Buzz-Feed the concourse of the arena was thick with smoke and the smell of explosive.

'All hell broke loose and everyone was running and screaming. We did run over two or three posters smeared with blood. Everyone was just screaming, lots of people were wondering what was going on.'

Those who had left the show before the encore was over, via either the Hunts Bank or City Room exits, were closer to the source of the explosion.

Ellie Ward, 17, said her 64-year-old grandfather was caught in the blast while waiting for her and her friend to emerge from the arena. He was hit by falling glass while standing by the merchandise stand in the corridors underneath the tiered seating.

Ward said he had severed an artery. 'He said he only realised what had happened when he felt the side of his head and it was bleeding ... We heard a massive shudder. We knew something was wrong.'

Oliver Jones, 17, was in the toilet when he heard the explosion echo around the foyer of the arena. 'I saw people running and screaming towards one direction and then many turning around to run back the other way.

'Security was running as well as the fans and concert-goers ... You see this on the news all the time and never expect it to happen to you.'

Abby Mullen, from the town of Airdrie in North Lanarkshire, Scotland, wrote on Facebook that she had left 'seconds' before the show finished in the hope of skipping the queue for a taxi. The blast went off metres in front of her.

Mullen posted graphic images of blood in her hair.

'That sound, the blood and those who were running around clueless with body parts and bits of skin missing will not be leaving my mind any time soon or the minds of those involved ...' she wrote.

'I understand these images might be upsetting however I feel as though people need to be shown just how cruel this world really is.'

Outside the arena, the scale of the emergency was becoming clear. The blast rocked the neighbourhood, with witnesses reporting smoke streaming from the arena entrance. Joe Gregory, parked outside the arena while waiting to pick up his girlfriend and her sister from the concert, captured its impact on his car's dashcam.

Suzy Mitchell, 26, said she heard the commotion from her bedroom at the back of an apartment block opposite the venue: 'Everyone was running away in big crowds.'

Police were alerted to the explosion at 10.33pm. As dozens of ambulances and police vans streamed into the area and a helicopter flew overhead, Greater Manchester police confirmed on Twitter shortly before 11pm they were responding to an 'incident' and asked people to stay away from the area.

Half an hour later, they said it was 'serious'.

Inside the stadium there continued to be widespread confusion and panic as fans struggled to get out. While some had been knocked off their feet by the explosion, many were unaware of the cause of the chaos as it unfolded around them.

Robert Tempkin, 22, from Middlesbrough told the BBC that people abandoned their possessions in their haste. 'Everyone was screaming and running, there were coats and people's phones on the floor. People just dropped everything.

'Some people were screaming they'd seen blood but other people were saying it was balloons bursting, or a speaker had been popped.'

Sammy, gathered with other fans at the backstage entrance where he'd run in the moments after the blast, said he was told by a member of the arena's security staff that the bang had been caused by a speaker falling over. He later realised that it was 'their way of calming people down'. 'There were many distraught children crying and having panic attacks at this point,' he told the *Guardian*.

Emerging from the stadium, Sammy found the street closed and full of police. A public address system repeated an alert for the area to be evacuated. 'There were people in the street saying it was a bomb. We didn't know what to believe.'

His father, waiting to pick him up near Victoria station, saw a steady stream of concert-goers covered in blood, said Sammy. 'One guy was carrying his daughter in his arms, begging for an ambulance.'

Many disoriented and distressed fans took refuge at the nearby Steven Charles snooker club, where a barman known as Tyler told the Press Association people had come in 'with panic attacks and in all kinds of disarray'.

He had seen people lying on the ground, covered in blood.

'We felt something but didn't know what it was – there was a sound like thunder. One girl had a panic attack and another had streaming tears, a woman had a heart attack just outside.'

Police later confirmed there had been 22 fatalities. The north-west ambulance service took 59 casualties from the arena to hospitals across the city, as well as treating 'a number of walking wounded' on scene.

As a police cordon was established around the arena, sealing off Victoria station, and armed and masked police filled the area, people continued to stream out of the venue, visibly shell-shocked, many injured.

Some were still holding the pink balloons that Grande had released before the concert started.

29 MAY

John Noakes was your beloved, daredevil uncle – we mourn the loss

LUCY MANGAN

There used to be just three television channels. There used to be a universally recognised teatime – five o'clock. And there used to be John Noakes. Now the last of these three poles around which childhood was slung has gone. John Noakes has died, aged 83.

He was – of course, of course – a *Blue Peter* presenter. He did his share of cooking spots, empty-washing-up-liquid-bottle-based 'makes' and announcements of the latest milk bottle top collection targets hit, but from 1965 to 1978 he was primarily the teatime magazine programme's action man.

Even if you were too young to have seen the originals, his most eye-catching feats have lived on in clip shows, repeats and anniversary programmes. The five-mile-high freefall with the RAF's Flying Falcons in 1973. Coming a spectacular cropper doing the Cresta Run a few years after that, and showing viewers his bruised (side)bottom a few weeks later in the studio. Enjoying the havoc created by the baby elephant who was unaware of the need to stay continent during a live broadcast in 1969. Amid numberless ascents of steeples and spinning poles, his ladder climb to the top of Nelson's Column in 1977 without a safety harness (or, according to him later, though denied by producer Biddy Baxter, insurance) still stands out.

If his co-presenters Peter Purves and Valerie Singleton stood in televisual loco parentis, Noakes was your beloved, daredevil uncle, with energy and enthusiasm to spare for the kind of spontaneous, crazy projects your parents could never quite bring themselves to get behind.

And like all the best uncles, he had a dog, Shep – the only one who could match him for energy and enthusiasm. Often, indeed, overmatching him; hence the emergence of Noakes's most common and famous utterance: 'Get down, Shep.'

My own most vivid memory of Noakes is not of him on *Blue Peter* or *Go with Noakes*, a series that ran for five years afterwards and of which I was an avid fan, but of him as a guest on another show in early 1987 being questioned about what Shep was doing now. He tearfully – though still with the underlying stoicism of the Yorkshireman, as he was – announced that Shep had died a few days before. It was the talk of school the next day, which – just as his own grief bore witness to the importance of that endlessly eager Border collie in his own life – was a testimony to the centrality of Shep and Noakes and *Blue Peter* to our own. Because there was only that trio of television channels at the time (and there was only television, and books if you could be bothered) and not much even on them that was dedicated to children, the little we had we all loved and bonded over. Television created unity that cut across cliques in a way that (whatever the other benefits brought by multimedia, multi-platform, multi-screen life) it does not – cannot – now.

There is still, despite the steady plundering and erosion of the concept by brands and hipsters, such a thing as genuine nostalgia; a sentimental longing for a past with which you have a personal connection. For thousands of us of a certain age, Noakes is that personal connection with a collective past and in the great outpouring of affection and sadness there has been online (and in what we tend to call, in these strange multi-screen times, real life instead of just life) we mourn the loss, perhaps, of both.

2 JUNE

It's Labour

EDITORIAL

For the fourth time in three years, Britain is once again at a moment of reckoning. Since 2014, powerful forces have threatened to pull us apart. Bonds of trust and respect have been damaged by a series of votes that have divided us from each other and the rest of the world. Next week, the British people have a chance to change that: to begin unwinding a political project of isolationist policies that with Brexit has seeded a fear of the future; to dispense with an economy where chief executives' pay races ahead while the poorer half of the population sees income fall; to jettison the Victorian idea that moral courage and enterprise could replace the state in securing people's freedom from want, ignorance and disease. The opportunity to reverse direction is the outcome of a series of votes that have shaken post-crash Britain. These started with SNP dominance in the wake of the Scottish independence referendum. The vote last year on Britain's membership of the European Union has also shrunk, for very different reasons, Ukip and the Liberal Democrats. The result is that, in England and Wales, we have the return of two-party politics and a straight choice between a Labour or a Conservative government.

These votes have shown an undoubted, if perhaps inchoate, wish for a different, fairer, better and more decent Britain – one that is less divided and more socially just; one that is more hopeful and less fearful. People are worn down by an economy that depends on stagnating pay to shore up employment and a hollowing out of civic life.

The Conservatives do not deserve our vote. Their claim that they will use the power of the state to help people and promise to raise the living wage, build affordable housing and deal with spiralling energy prices is a welcome development but one not matched by their policies. Their uncosted manifesto is a diversion from the consistently callous and negligent record in office. This has seen food banks become a feature of our communities, seen school budgets cut for the first time for 20 years and left patients waiting longer than ever in hospitals that are mired in deficits. Tory economics has created a new working class of people with

jobs but in poverty. Instead of being serious about rebuilding the
public finances without loading the costs on to the poor, the Tory
party wants to bring back foxhunting and ask new mothers who
have been raped for verification if they wish to claim benefits for
more than two children.

The Conservatives have also opted for an overtly hardline
approach on Brexit – driving their support with a false claim that
Britain is under attack by either internal or external enemies. It
ends up with the Tories promoting the worst possible outcome
for Brexit Britain: walking away from the EU without a deal and
an immigration policy that will undermine growth not create
it. This would be a disaster for all of us, cutting us off from our
biggest export market and neighbours with whom there are
bonds of common endeavour. It is the intertwining of austerity
with a hard Brexit that renders the Conservatives unfit for office.
The Tory plan to win the election was for it to be a presidential
contest, one centred on personalities rather than policies. The
idea was to present Theresa May as a strong leader who would
be better at getting a good deal for Britain from Brussels than
Labour's Jeremy Corbyn. She chose to hold an unnecessary election for which there was no appetite.

Her campaign has been grimly negative and entirely joyless.
Her jumpy U-turn on her social care proposals revealed Mrs May
to be a poor judge of campaign tactics. It was especially foolish
because it was presented as part of an intergenerational conflict
over shrinking resources. Mrs May is reluctant to risk much interaction with voters and is evasive with journalists. Her failure to
call out Donald Trump's destructive impulse over the climate
change accord speaks volumes. We should disregard the propaganda masquerading as news from the acolyte press: as Mrs May's
credibility on the campaign has withered, Mr Corbyn's has grown.
Mr Corbyn unquestionably has his flaws. Many see him as a fluke,

a fringe candidate who stole the Labour leadership while the rest of his party was asleep. In parliament he failed to reach beyond his faction. He is not fluent on the issues raised by a modern, sophisticated digital economy. His record of protest explains why some struggle to see him as prime minister.

But Labour's leader has had a good campaign. He has been energetic and effective on the stump, comfortable in his own skin and in the presence of others. He clearly likes people and is interested in them. He has generated an unfamiliar sense of the possible; once again, people are excited by politics. The campaign itself has been unexpectedly strategic, based on a manifesto adroitly pitched both at energising Labour's base and the under-35s, who have responded with rare enthusiasm. That manifesto quickened political pulses. It's not perfect – it over-emphasises the state and fails to tackle Tory benefit cuts – but it is a genuine attempt to address a failing social and economic model. In many ways, it is a painful reminder of how much of our collective sense of social justice and community spirit has been lost since 2010. Labour has set the terms of the political debate: most notably with a Keynesian response of increasing public investment, and increasing public spending financed by higher taxes, to stimulate the economy so that the country ends up wealthier than anything proposed under Tory plans.

If centre-left politicians want to regain support for their policies, they must find ways of engaging with provincial Britain – with its economic needs, its sense of place, and its estrangement from the corridors of power – as well as courting urban citadels. In talking about the big questions – about the inequality of wealth and power – in moral terms, of what is right and wrong, Mr Corbyn is on to something resonant, something common, something good. If he were to win, then he must respect all of the party's traditions, rebuild the Labour coalition in the Commons and recruit the party's best talents into government. Labour needs to find a convincing voice to conduct tricky Brexit talks. Mr Corbyn would need to stick to the manifesto: most important, given Labour's economic reputation, to show that his party can unlock growth through careful and prudent stewardship to pay for the public goods it wishes to deliver.

Our desire is for a Labour government, but our priority is to stop the Conservatives. All politics is local and there are unique dynamics in Britain's 650 constituencies. The electoral script in Scotland is now plainly different and we will consider the options there in a separate editorial. Similarly, Northern Ireland has its own narrative. There are many reasons to vote Lib Dem, not least their campaign for membership of the EU's single market and reform of the voting system. Likewise, the Green party – and the epoch-shaping concern over the environment – should not be dismissed. Our support for Labour does not mean a 'progressive alliance' of like-minded parties should be discarded. It should be embraced as an idea, but one whose time has not come. To limit the Tories by tactical voting makes sense.

Forecasts in politics are based on the premise 'if present trends continue' and it is in the nature of trends to change. That is what makes this election so interesting. We do not know what political groups are coalescing, what realignments are taking place. Politics is changing. What seems important today, history may well judge irrelevant. An election is a chance to snatch a cup from the stream of public opinion. While we stare into its depths, the river rushes on. Most pundits think the voters will repudiate Mr Corbyn's Labour party. They may do so. But Mr Corbyn has shown that the party might be the start of something big rather than the last gasp of something small. On 8 June, Labour deserves our vote.

3 June

Corbyn shows us there's a new way of doing politics

JOHN HARRIS

What strange times these are. Three weeks ago this election looked set to be a drab affair centred on a prime minister apparently unable to fulfil even the most basic requirements of campaigning, and the seemingly unstoppable prospect of a huge Conservative win.

'Awful and unpleasant' was the verdict of one journalist friend, and as I drove around the country trying to divine the national mood, it was hard to disagree. My personal low point was probably the council elections, in early May, when I watched a spirited and principled Labour candidate in a Lancashire village increase her party's vote share but still lose to the Tories, thanks to hundreds of former Ukip voters turning blue. The national contest felt locked down: what it seemed to say about the future was unimaginably grim.

To characterise what has happened since is hardly easy. Contradictions abound; everything comes with caveats. A lot of people still have what Labour MPs call a Corbyn problem. Despite no end of evidence that suggests otherwise – chiefly her U-turn on social care – many voters I have met remain convinced that Theresa May is as strong and resolute as she pretends to be: 'Thatcher, only a bit more gentle,' as a man in Tewkesbury said to me this week.

The details of Brexit are only just starting to intrude on the debate. And, contrary to the raptures rippling through the left-wing corners of the Twittersphere, a thoroughly undeserved

Conservative victory – and the prospect of truly foolish politicians handling the most fraught set of challenges for the UK since 1945 – still seems a racing certainty.

But here is the good news. As evidenced by the prime minister's travails, an entire way of doing politics – deadened, arrogant and often absurd – is dying in front of our eyes. Jeremy Corbyn's Labour party has revealed that the received wisdom of the past 15 years was wrong, and that talking in plain-spoken, moral, essentially socialist terms about the fundamental condition of the country need not entail political disaster.

Meanwhile, the idea that the opinions, instincts and prejudices of the British public can be reduced to polling data looks increasingly redundant. Voters are a fascinating, unpredictable lot – something that applies all the more in an age when the idea of tribal loyalties is increasingly a relic, and the accelerated way we communicate means that things can change at speed in completely unexpected ways.

Last Saturday five wildly divergent polls put the supposed Conservative lead over Labour at between six and 14 points. Three days later, YouGov published a seat-by-seat estimate – based on 'multi-level regression and post-stratification', apparently – and claimed we were heading for a hung parliament.

When *The Times* put this on its front page, it felt like we were in for a week of awful political coverage led by specious survey findings. On the whole, that has not happened, which may well reflect a new set of understandings: that dealing in anything more than vague predictions is a mug's game; and that to truly understand what's afoot, you have to go to different places and talk to people.

My own epiphany happened this week, during two hours spent with my *Guardian* film-making colleague John Domokos at a shopping parade in Wolverhampton South West, said to be the

Conservatives' No 10 target seat. The first person we met was a lifelong Labour voter who clearly thought Corbyn was a walking miracle. A few Tory supporters followed, with the opposite opinion of the Labour leader.

And then we encountered two people who embodied something altogether more interesting: a woman who said she tended to back the Tories, but after long conversations with one of her daughters and a rising sense that the country was in a mess, was now a Corbyn enthusiast. Similarly, a fortysomething woman told me that after a lifetime of voting Conservative, she was so concerned about schools, hospitals and poverty that she was switching to Labour.

I then stuck my head into the local barbershop, where the two young proprietors said that they mostly followed the election on Twitter, because they liked the 'jokes'. They then rattled through a few of their favourite Theresa May memes, largely centred on the idea she is the unthinking android Maybot.

This is part of the reason the Conservative campaign has unravelled. Before the advent of social media, politicians could teeter on the brink of absurdity and repeatedly fall the wrong way, safe in the knowledge that we all had to wait for the next helping of *Spitting Image* or edition of *Private Eye* for their bubble to be burst. Now it happens instantaneously. Moreover, for all its flaws, the Facebook age is egalitarian in spirit. Woe betide the politician who will not turn up to the debate, or who seems to have an aversion to meeting the public.

In the midst of all this, what can politicians do? Be yourself. Do not dissemble. Forget the old idea that if you endlessly parrot the same lines, you can be sure that most people will see the message only once or twice: the likelihood is that the parroting will be edited into a 20-second video clip, and you will be rendered absurd. Treat the orthodox media's rituals with a gentle mockery, which chimes with how most people feel about them.

This, clearly, is a big part of the Corbyn story. But so too is something much deeper, which will have profound and enduring consequences for his party. I do not know if Labour's manifesto is a practical programme for government. I do know that its headline proposals are perfectly suited to Corbyn's campaigning style, and have been received by many people as a pretty vivid diagnosis of what is wrong with their country – from food banks, through crisis-plagued hospitals, to profiteering train companies.

As a worldwide crisis unfolds for social democracy, that is some achievement, and it reflects something long known on the right. As Donald Trump and Nigel Farage could tell you, straight talking is everything, and it is imperative to talk in moral terms about right and wrong. In a world that looks ever more chaotic and confounding, one that is conveyed to people via the scrolling chaos of a newsfeed rather than the contextualised order of a newspaper, these are basic requirements.

As strange as it may sound, who will win this compelling, almost hallucinatory contest is only half the point. Its other stories have only just started to unfold, and most of the people charged with making sense of what is going on have barely begun to understand them.

5 JUNE

Why *Wonder Woman* is a masterpiece of subversive feminism

ZOE WILLIAMS

The chances are you will read a feminist takedown of *Wonder Woman* before you see the film. And you'll probably agree with it. Wonder Woman is a half-god, half-mortal super-creature; she is without peer even in superhero leagues. And yet, when she arrives in London to put a stop to the war to end all wars, she instinctively obeys a handsome meathead who has no skills apart from moderate decisiveness and pretty eyes. This is a patriarchal figment. Then, naturally, you begin to wonder why does she have to fight in knickers that look like a fancy letterbox made of leather? Does her appearance and its effect on the men around her really have to play such a big part in all her fight scenes? Even my son lodged a feminist critique: if she were half-god, he said, she would have recognised the god Ares immediately – unless he were a better god than her (being a male god).

I agree with all of that, but I still loved it. I didn't love it as a guilty pleasure. I loved it with my whole heart. Wonder Woman, or Diana Prince, as her civilian associates would know her, first appeared as a character in DC Comics in 1941, her creator supposedly inspired by the feminism of the time, and specifically the contraception pioneer Margaret Sanger. Being able to stop people getting pregnant would be a cool superpower, but, in fact, her skills were: bullet-pinging with bracelets; lassoing; basic

THE BEDSIDE GUARDIAN 2017

psychology; great strength and athleticism; and being half-god (the result of unholy congress between Zeus and Hippolyta). The 1970s TV version lost a lot of the poetry of that, and was just all-American cheesecake. Gal Gadot's Wonder Woman made her cinematic debut last year in *Batman v Superman*, and this first live-action incarnation makes good on the character's original premise, the classical-warrior element amped up and textured. Her might makes sense.

Yes, she is sort of naked a lot of the time, but this isn't objectification so much as a cultural reset: having thighs, actual thighs you can kick things with, not thighs that look like arms, is a feminist act. The whole Diana myth, women safeguarding the world from male violence not with nurture but with better violence, is a feminist act. Casting Robin Wright as Wonder Woman's aunt, reimagining the battle-axe as a battler, with an axe, is a feminist act. A female German chemist trying to destroy humans (in the shape of Dr Poison, a proto-Mengele before Nazism existed) might be the most feminist act of all.

Women are repeatedly erased from the history of classical music, art and medicine. It takes a radical mind to pick up that being erased from the history of evil is not great either. Wonder Woman's casual rebuttal of a sexual advance, her dress-up montage ('it's itchy', 'I can't fight in this', 'it's choking me') are also feminist acts. *Wonder Woman* is a bit like a BuzzFeed list: '23 Stupid Sexist Tropes in Cinema and How to Rectify Them'. I mean that as a compliment.

Yet *Wonder Woman* is not a film about empowerment so much as a checklist of all the clichés by which women are disempowered. So it leaves you feeling a bit baffled and deflated – how can we possibly be so towering a threat that Hollywood would strive so energetically, so rigorously, for our belittlement? At the same time, you are conflicted about what the fightback should look like. Because, as every reviewer has pointed out, *Wonder Woman* is by no means perfect.

The woman who can fight is not new; from Sigourney Weaver's Ripley in *Alien*, to Linda Hamilton's Sarah Connor in *The Terminator*, this idea has a long pedigree. Connor was a far-fetched feminist figure because her power was concentrated in her ambivalent maternal love – like a hypothetical tiger mother, which doesn't do a huge amount for female agency. She is still an accessory for male power, just on the other side of the mother/whore dichotomy. Ripley, being the same gender as her foe, recast action as a catfight, with all the sexist bullshit that entails (hot, sweaty woman saying 'bitch' a lot – a classic pornography trope).

But the underlying problem is that the male fighter is conceived as an ego ideal for a male audience, who would imagine themselves in the shirt of Bruce Willis or mankini of Superman and get the referred thrill of their heroism. If you are still making the film for a male gaze, the female warrior becomes a sex object, and her fighting curiously random, like pole dancing – movement that only makes sense as display, and even then, only just. That was always the great imponderable of Lara Croft (as she appeared in the video game, not the film): the listlessness of her combat, the slightly dreamlike quality of it. Even as it was happening, it was hard to remember why. When Angelina Jolie made her flesh, I thought she brought something subversive to the role; something deliberated, knowing and a bit scornful, as though looking into the teenage gamer's soul and saying: 'You don't know whether that was a dragon, a dinosaur or a large dog. You are just hypnotised by my buttocks.'

The fighter as sex symbol stirs up a snakepit of questions: are you getting off on the woman or the violence? An unbreakable female lead can be liberating to the violent misogynist tendency since the violence against her can get a lot more ultra, and nobody has to feel bad about it, because she'll win.

This is tackled head-on in *Wonder Woman*. The tension, meanwhile, between the thrill of the action, which is what combat is all about, and the objectification, which is what women are all about, is referenced when Wonder Woman hurls someone across a room and an onlooker says: 'I'm both frightened, and aroused.' A word on the fighting: there's a lot of hurling, tons of lassoing, much less traditional fighting, where people harm one another with punches. This is becoming a sub-genre in films: 'the kind of fighting that is ladylike'. It almost always involves bows and arrows, for which, as with so many things, we can thank Jennifer Lawrence in *The Hunger Games*. The way Lawrence fights is so outrageously adroit and natural that she makes it look as though women have been doing it all along, and men are only learning.

I find it impossible to imagine the feminist action-movie slam-dunk; the film in which every sexist Hollywood convention, every miniature slight, every outright slur, every incremental diss was slain by a lead who was omnipotent and vivid. That film would be long and would struggle for jokes. Just trying to picture it leaves you marvelling at the geological slowness of social progress in this industry, which finds it so hard to create female characters of real mettle, even when they abound in real life. Wonder Woman, with her 180 languages and her near-telepathic insights, would stand more chance of unpicking this baffler than Superman or Batman. But the answer, I suspect, lies in the intersection between the market and the culture; the more an art form costs, the less it will risk, until the most expensive of them – blockbusters – can't change at all. In an atmosphere of such in-built ossification, the courage of Wonder Woman is more stunning even than her lasso.

5 JUNE

I survived London Bridge and feel lucky. And angry. I cannot unsee what I saw

ANNA SERGI

Your team Juventus loses 4–1 in the Champions League final in Cardiff against Real Madrid. An awful match really, you think – you hate Ronaldo – as you walk down London Bridge at 9:45 on a Saturday night. It's so pretty that you stop for a photo. After eight years in this city, you still want to take pictures on London Bridge. It is 21:54 when you take the picture.

You get to Boro Bistro, a cute place with tables outdoors just underneath the bridge, in Borough Market. It's a warm night, even though it's just rained a bit. You sit down and complain with your friends, who are pro-Juventus too of course, but come on, you all agree, they truly played badly. Let's order whisky. You need something strong to drink after this utter failure. It's 22:01.

Then, choosing between a Jameson or a Lagavulin, you hear a bang. There is a canopy, like a tent, above your head, and a bike and a body bounce off it, the bike splitting in two, pieces of it scattering everywhere. A car has hit the bridge, and you sort of see what happens but mainly you can't. You grab your coat and your bag. People around you start moving quickly, you see someone coming towards the bar area, his white shirt half-red with blood, holding his neck with his hands. Did someone slash his throat? Then someone appears with a knife, chasing after him, chasing after whoever. You learn afterwards that this was about 22:08.

Then the insanity, people jumping on and off tables and chairs, yelling, screaming, get down in the restaurant basement, close the doors, it's so hot in here, no data service, and what the fuck happened anyway? A woman cries and cannot stop – you look at her and realise you are so very calm, you cannot believe how calm you are. You just hope they don't use the 'terror' word yet, because you don't have any signal and your family would be worried sick. There is loud music coming from outside. Was that a gunshot?

After an hour or so in the basement, some people make jokes about stealing some wine; others have lucid eyes; others cry. No one knows why we are being kept here: was that a car crash? And what about the stabbing? Are the two things connected? You just hope they don't call it terrorism, you hope it is not terrorism. But really you know it is anyway, this new type of terrorism we have here, who are you fooling? You are just worried that if someone says the word, people will panic even more, and in here it is so hot and closed, panic wouldn't be good at all. The criminologist in you remembers that terrorism is theatre. No one can handle that theatre right now.

They let you all out, police leading the way. The bar looks apocalyptic, the glass doors completely shattered, tables upside down, plates and glasses on the floor. Watch your step, if you can. You go outside. You see three corpses, covered with blankets. You see people in tears, some injured, while you are asked to move along, to abandon the scene as soon as possible. You are angry at whoever perpetrated this act, for whatever inconceivable reason, and whoever else might still be engaging in extremist acts. And, as a criminologist, you are also mad at Theresa May and her policies when she was home secretary – a prevention strategy that seemed to demonise Muslim communities while increasing surveillance money and cutting police funding. Your mind goes to the election, and how this could spin dangerously out of control.

Then you walk among the other zombie-like people. You check your phone, you answer concerned messages. You are safe, of course, thanks, you say – you don't know what happened. You just want to go home. Not in two hours. Now. You just want your bed.

But you stop for a whisky with your friends first. You cannot even talk. You all look at phones, updating Twitter to follow the news. The pub you end up at feels surreal – Lady Gaga is playing and there's a hen party with crazy people dancing and having fun. You float out of your body.

You take the train home, alone. You cry. Finally. You realise … if the Juventus match had gone on to extra time you would have been on the bridge at the exact moment of the attack, 22:08. If they had given you a more exposed table at the bistro, you wouldn't have been under the white canopy and things would have fallen directly on you – the body that flew off the canopy could have hit you. Or you could have been more exposed to one of the attackers. You learn that there were three of them, and that seven people died.

You feel lucky. And angry.

You spend the night in a state that feels like a half-awake coma – staring at the ceiling for about two hours when you get home. People call you, text, there are some truly wonderful messages. You feel lucky again.

But when you wake up you are still angry too. You have such a special relationship with Borough Market, with this difficult city in general. You think again that you are lucky, that people in the area have died, or been injured or probably saw much worse than you did. Lucky you. Really.

You are almost 32, and you have experienced a terror attack. You knew what to do: hide, run, tell, right? You cannot believe you are 32 and you know that when you hear a bang and commotion on London Bridge past 10pm on a Saturday night you are instantly prepared for a terror attack.

You mark yourself safe on Facebook, of course, as if you were really safe, whatever the hell safe means anyway. Sure, you won't be cowed. You will resume your life. You cannot give in to fear, as if it mattered really, whether you are scared or not. You cannot unsee what you saw.

Anna Sergi is a lecturer in criminology and deputy director at the Centre for Criminology, University of Essex.

8 JUNE

UK election: A night to remember (II)

LIVEBLOG

21.15   Here is a summary from yesterday of 15 of the most compelling election result predictions produced before the polls opened. The highest prediction for a Tory majority on that list is 122, but later Ian Warren, the elections specialist who runs the Election Data consultancy, topped that with a prediction of a Conservative majority of 124.

21.51   Kevin Maguire, associate editor, *Daily Mirror*: 'Mirror political writers predicting the Tory majority on the exit poll ranges from 35 to 100. I've gone for 70, with a heavy heart.'

21.53   Piers Morgan: 'As exit poll looms, I repeat my prediction: Conservatives to win by 90–100 seat majority.'

21.57 Steve Hawkes, deputy political editor of the *Sun*: 'Rumour Tories could be looking at 400 seats – we'll find out in a min.'

22.01 Exit poll suggests Britain is on course for a hung parliament.

22.13 Pound falls following exit poll. 'We're in for a long night,' says Jeremy Cook, the chief economist at World First. 'Currencies like governments with mandates – and doesn't like delays to Brexit.'

22.32 John McDonnell, the shadow chancellor, has just said he thinks Theresa May's position will now be untenable. He is probably right. What might save her temporarily – assuming she can form a government – would be the fact the Brexit talks are due to start a week on Monday.

22.48 Many politicians – for varying reasons – are not yet ready to respond, publicly at least, to the exit polls.

22:55 During the general election Theresa May repeatedly said that, if she lost just six seats, Jeremy Corbyn would become prime minister. Her claim was dismissed by factcheckers because losing only six seats would still leave the Conservatives, by far, the largest party. But Labour sources are now suggesting May's comment should be taken at face value.

23:54 We have had three results so far – all in the north-east. And here are the three swings: Newcastle upon Tyne Central – 2.1 per cent swing from Tories to Labour. Houghton and Sunderland South – 3.5 per cent swing from Labour to Tories. Sunderland Central – 2.3 per cent swing from Labour to Tories.

00:16 Some surprising predictions are afloat that Labour might take Kensington from the Conservatives.

00:19 Labour politicians were torn in the first hour after the exit poll about whether to believe the numbers. One candidate in a safe seat said turnout had soared in their constituency. 'People who never vote [are] coming out. If replicated means YouGov [were] right,' they said. 'Just depends if nationally it translates to local – or if vote has racked up in areas like this at expense of others.'

Another Labour hopeful in a marginal Midlands seat was far more sceptical. 'I don't believe it. This does not take account of postal votes. There is no way we have gained 34 seats,' they said. 'Look at the swing against in Sunderland. That could cost us seats in areas like mine.'

Two others in Labour–Tory marginals also privately voiced similar concerns.

00.31 The bookies have been sending press notices out about Boris Johnson's odds of becoming next Tory leader. Paddy Power have him on 2/1.

00.48 One of the less remarked upon elements of the early results, largely because it was widely expected, is the near-disappearance of Ukip, particularly in the north-east, the area where not so long ago the party liked to think it might supplant Labour. In the four early declarations from the region – two in Newcastle, two in and around Sunderland – the Ukip vote fell by anything from 9.4 per cent to 14.3 per cent. The highest proportion of the votes was 6.8 per cent in Washington and Sunderland West, where in 2015 Ukip came second, with almost 20 per cent of the vote.

Yes, this was anticipated. But it is nonetheless worth noting how a party that took almost 4 million votes – if only one seat – in 2015 had now been so quashed.

00.50 A Labour source played down speculation that the party was on the brink of a spectacular success in Kensington, suggesting the vote share might be up but the seat was 'probably not in play'.

01.13 Labour takes Rutherglen and Hamilton West from SNP.

01.47 A big result in north Wales with Labour retaking the Vale of Clwyd, which the Tories won in 2015.

02.03 Tory minister Jane Ellison, financial secretary to the Treasury, loses to Labour in Battersea.

02.13 Ealing Central and Acton was number two on the Tory target list. It's been retained by Labour's Rupa Huq with an increased majority – and a significant Conservative drop.

02.18 Angus Robertson loses in Moray. The SNP's Westminster leader has lost his seat to the Conservatives' Douglas Ross.

02.22 Senior Tories now accept the exit poll is broadly right.

02.26 Tories win Ochil and South Perthshire from SNP. Luke Graham has taken it from Tasmina Ahmed-Sheikh (who herself won the seat from Labour in 2015), with the Conservatives up 21 points – a 16 per cent swing.

02.27 SNP loses Midlothian to Labour.

02.31 The Labour party has spent the past six weeks fearing the worst in Hartlepool. With dire predictions of a Tory landslide, many felt this coastal town could be the first in the north east to fall like dominoes to the Conservatives. In the end, it wasn't even close. Labour beat the Conservatives by 6,500 votes – double the number that separated Labour from Ukip two years ago.

02.38 There were conciliatory words from Labour's Owen Smith, who stood against Jeremy Corbyn for the Labour leadership – and held on to his Pontypridd seat comfortably. 'He's definitely got something,' said Smith of Corbyn. 'He beat me fair and square and he's done very well in this election. He's to be congratulated for that.' Asked if he would hug Corbyn, he replied: 'For sure. He may not want to hug me but I would hug him.'

02.46 Nick Clegg loses in Sheffield Hallam. The former Liberal Democrat leader is out: losing by 19,756 to Labour's Jared O'Mara on 21,881.

03.19 Corbyn says May should go because she has lost seats, lost votes and lost confidence.

03.25 May says Conservatives will ensure stability. Theresa May is speaking now at the count in Maidenhead where she has just been re-elected. It is a huge honour being MP here, she says. Looking more widely, returns are still coming in, she says. But she says this country needs a period of stability. If the Conservative party has won the most seats and most votes, it will be incumbent on it to ensure that stability. She says she set out her priorities: getting the Brexit deal right, doing what is best for the country. She says her resolve is the same as before.

03.41 A recount is under way for Hastings and Rye, where the home secretary, Amber Rudd, is at risk of losing her seat to Labour.

04.05 Tory minister Gavin Barwell loses seat to Labour.

04.20 Alex Salmond loses Gordon to Conservatives.

04.35 In Northern Ireland the final results are in with Sinn Féin winning back the Fermanagh and South Tyrone constituency from the Ulster Unionists. The overall outcome is 10 seats for the DUP and seven for Sinn Féin, the latter party still boycotting Westminster. This leaves the DUP in a very strong position in terms of potentially helping to form the next government.

04.54 Amber Rudd wins in Hastings and Rye.

05.58 Hung parliament confirmed. The Conservatives will be the largest party but they cannot now win a majority.

06.48 Conservative MP Nigel Evans says: 'We didn't shoot ourselves in the foot, we shot ourselves in the head.'

07.01 Blame-game well underway: Conservative sources saying David Davis was cabinet minister who pushed hardest for snap poll. Senior Conservative tells me, of Davis, 'there are a lot of very, very pissed off people in cabinet – and with him in particular'.

07.39 The former cabinet secretary Lord O'Donnell says Theresa May will have to stay in post for now, but the result will make it very difficult for her to negotiate Brexit.

07.52 The pound has hit a five-month low against the euro, at €1.1322.

07.57 Things are close in Kensington – so close that the tired tellers have been told to go home for a rest and come back later.

08.20 Senior Conservatives have confirmed that Theresa May has no intention of resigning this morning. They plan instead to work on forming a government – most likely by making a pact with the DUP, which has 10 MPs in Northern Ireland and could deliver her a wafer-thin majority.

08.37 The shadow chancellor, John McDonnell, said Labour is 'ready to form a government', labelling any Conservative–DUP arrangement a 'coalition of chaos'.

08.51 The first evidence of turnout levels among younger voters is that it rose 12 points to 56 per cent of 18- to 34-year-olds since 2015, according to an 'exit poll' by the *NME/ The Stream*.

08.59 Jeremy Corbyn has declared his party the victors after addressing staff at Labour headquarters. 'We put forward our policies – strong and hopeful policies – and have gained an amazing response from the public. I think it's pretty clear who won this election,' he told the BBC. Asked if he hoped to form a government, he said: 'We're ready to serve the people who have given their trust to us.'

09.07 The DUP leader, Arlene Foster, has hinted she expects May to stand down. 'It will be difficult for her to survive given that she was presumed at the start of the campaign, which seems an awfully long time ago, to come back with maybe a hundred, maybe more, in terms of her majority,' she told BBC Radio Ulster.

09.30 The EU's chief Brexit negotiator, Michel Barnier, says the Brexit negotiations should start when the UK is ready, but that the (two-year) timetable and the EU's position are clear.

09.37 Groups campaigning for the rights of the 3.5 million EU citizens in Britain and 1.2 million UK nationals on the continent have said that with Brexit negotiations now likely to start with a hung parliament, it is even more vital that all political parties undertake to secure citizens' rights after Brexit.

09.46 The European council president, Donald Tusk, reminds the UK of the ticking clock on the Brexit negotiations.

10.14 Theresa May will go to the palace at 12.30 believing she can form a government.

13.18 The BBC is rowing back on its report that Labour has won Kensington as another recount is due to take place this evening.

14.07 The US leftist presidential candidate Bernie Sanders has congratulated Jeremy Corbyn on the campaign. In a Facebook post, the US senator said the result was a protest against inequality. 'I am delighted to see Labour do so well. All over the world, people are rising up against austerity and massive levels of income and wealth inequality. People in the UK, the US and elsewhere want governments that represent all the people, not just the 1 per cent. I congratulate Jeremy Corbyn for running a very effective campaign.'

14.57 Foster says DUP will talk to PM about how the two parties can 'bring stability' to the UK. 'The prime minister has spoken with me this morning and we will enter discussions with the Conservatives to explore how it may be possible to bring stability to our nation at this time of great challenge.'

21.04 Labour has taken the Kensington seat, the country's richest, from the Conservatives. Emma Dent Coad defeated Victoria Borwick, a former deputy mayor to Boris Johnson, by 20 votes. It is the last seat to return an MP and the announcement gives the final seats totals.

- Conservative: 318
- Labour: 262
- SNP: 35
- Lib Dem: 12
- DUP: 10
- Sinn Féin: 7 (not taken up)
- Plaid Cymru: 4
- Green: 1

9 JUNE

Jeremy Corbyn has caused a sensation – he would make a fine prime minister

OWEN JONES

This is one of the most sensational political upsets of our time. Theresa May – a wretched dishonest excuse of a politician, don't pity her – launched a general election with the sole purpose of crushing opposition in Britain. It was brazen opportunism, a naked power grab: privately, I'm told, her team wanted the precious 'bauble' of going down in history as the gravediggers of the British Labour party. Instead, she has destroyed herself. She is toast.

She has just usurped David Cameron as the 'worst ever prime minister on their own terms' (before Cameron, it had been a title held by Lord North since the 18th century). Look at the political capital she had: the phenomenal polling lead, almost the entire support of the British press, the most effective electoral machine on Earth behind her. Her allies presented the Labour opposition as an amusing, eccentric joke that could be squashed like a fly that had already had its wings ripped off. They genuinely believed they could get a 180-seat majority. She will leave No 10 soon, disgraced, entering the history books filed under 'hubris'.

But, before a false media narrative is set, let me put down a marker. Yes, the Tory campaign was a shambolic, insulting mess, notable only for its U-turns, a manifesto that swiftly disintegrated, robotically repeated mantras that achieved only ridicule. But don't let media commentators – hostile to Labour's vision – pretend that the May calamity is all down to self-inflicted Tory wounds.

This was the highest turnout since 1997, perhaps the biggest Labour percentage since the same year – far eclipsing Tony Blair's total in 2005. Young and previous non-voters came out in astonishing numbers, and not because they thought, 'Ooh, Theresa May doesn't stick to her promises, does she?' Neither can we reduce this to a remainer revolt. The Lib Dems threw everything at the despondent remainer demographic, with paltry returns. Many Ukip voters flocked to the Labour party.

No: this was about millions inspired by a radical manifesto that promised to transform Britain, to attack injustices, and challenge the vested interests holding the country back. Don't let them tell you otherwise. People believe the booming well-off should pay more, that we should invest that money in schools, hospitals, houses, police and public services, that all in work should have a genuine living wage, that young people should not be saddled with debt for aspiring to an education, that our utilities should be under the control of the people of this country. For years, many of us have argued that these policies – shunned, reviled even in the political and media elite – had the genuine support of millions. And today that argument was decisively vindicated and settled.

Don't let them get away with the claim that, 'Ah, this election just shows a better Labour leader could have won!' Risible rot. Do we really think that Corbyn's previous challengers to the leadership – and this is nothing personal – would have inspired millions of otherwise politically disengaged and alienated people to come out and vote, and drive Labour to its highest percentage since the famous Blair landslide? If the same old stale, technocratic centrism had been offered, Labour would have faced an absolute drubbing, just like its European sister parties did.

Labour is now permanently transformed. Its policy programme is unchallengeable. It is now the party's consensus. It cannot and will not be taken away. Those who claimed it could not win the support of millions were simply wrong. No, Labour didn't win, but from where it started, that was never going to happen. That policy programme enabled the party to achieve one of the biggest shifts in support in British history – yes, eclipsing Tony Blair's swing in 1997.

Social democracy is in crisis across the western world. British Labour is now one of the most successful centre-left parties, many of which have been reduced to pitiful rumps under rightwing leaderships. And indeed, other parties in Europe and the United States should learn lessons from this experience.

And what of our young? They have suffered disproportion-ately these past few years: student debt, a housing crisis, a lack of secure jobs, falling wages, cuts to social security – the list goes on. Young voters have been ignored, ridiculed, demonised even. They just don't care about politics, it's said, or they're just too lazy. 'Under-30s love Corbyn but they don't care enough to get off their lazy arses to vote for him!' one unnamed Tory MP told the Huffington Post's Owen Bennett. Those young voters did indeed get off their 'lazy arses', and they kicked several Tory MPs' arses out of the House of Commons.

And then there's the media onslaught. Even by the standards of our so-called free press – a stinking sewer at the best of times – its campaign against Corbyn and the Labour party was utterly nauseating. Smears of terrorism, extremism, you name it. They believed they could simply brainwash millions of Britons. But people in this country are cleverer than the press barons think, and millions rejected their bile.

But a note about Corbyn, and the leadership, too. I owe Corbyn, John McDonnell, Seumas Milne, his policy chief Andrew Fisher, and others, an unreserved, and heartfelt apology. I campaigned passionately for Corbyn the first time he stood, and I voted for him twice. A few weeks ago, a senior Labour MP denounced me as one of the chief gravediggers of the Labour party, and journalists have suggested I should be knighted by the Tory party for my efforts.

But I came to believe that, yes, indeed Labour was heading for a terrible defeat that would crush all the things I believed in. That's what all the polling, by-elections and the local elections seemed to say. I thought people had made their minds up about Corbyn, however unfairly, and their opinion just wouldn't shift. I wasn't a bit wrong, or slightly wrong, or mostly wrong, but totally wrong. Having one foot in the Labour movement and one in the mainstream media undoubtedly left me more susceptible to their groupthink. Never again. Corbyn stays and – if indeed the Tories are thrown into crisis as Brexit approaches – he has an undoubted chance of becoming prime minister, and a fine prime minister he would make too.

Now that I've said I'm wrong – perhaps one of the sweetest things I've had to write – so the rest of the mainstream commentariat, including in this newspaper, must confess they were wrong, too. They were wrong to vilify Corbyn supporters – from the day he stood – as delusional cultists. They were wrong to suggest Corbyn couldn't mobilise young people and previous non-voters. They were wrong to suggest he couldn't make inroads in Scotland. They were wrong to suggest a radical left programme was an automatic recipe for electoral catastrophe. No, Labour hasn't formed a government. But it is far closer than it has been for a very long time. The prospect of a socialist government that can build an economy run in the interests of working people – not the cartel of vested interests who have plunged us into repeated crisis – well, that may have been a prospect many of us thought would never happen in our lifetime. It is now much closer than it has ever been. So yes – to quote a much-ridiculed Jeremy Corbyn tweet: the real fight starts now.

16 JUNE

Theresa May was too scared to meet the Grenfell survivors: She's finished

POLLY TOYNBEE

That tomb in the sky will be forever Theresa May's monument. Grenfell marks the spot and her visit marks the moment the last vestiges of her career were finally rubbed out. She made it her own yesterday by that fateful 'visit' to a handful of senior fire officers, guarding her from any contaminating contact with the bereaved and newly homeless. Dead to emotion or empathy, she sealed her fate.

Precise blame comes later in the public inquiry: we are all overnight experts in cladding and sprinklers now. But political blame spreads right through the Conservative party, with no escape on offer. This goes far beyond the precise shockers – the Tory MPs who mockingly rejected housing regulation; the cuts to funding to councils responsible for retro-fitting fire suppressants; the disregard of coroner's instructions after the 2009 Lakanal House tragedy; and even the plan to opt out of EU safety regulations. Conservative Kensington and Chelsea council allegedly blocking its ears to tenants' well-founded anxiety is just the immediate scandal. But this event reaches far deeper, to the very sinews of its party's policy.

That tower is austerity in ruins. Symbolism is everything in politics and nothing better signifies the May–Cameron–Osborne era that stripped bare the state and its social and physical protection of citizens. The horror of poor people burned alive within feet of the country's grandest mansions, many of them empty, moth-balled investments, perfectly captures the politics of the last seven years. The Cameron, Osborne, Gove Notting Hill set live just up the road.

From the 40 per cent cuts to local councils, to the bedroom tax and the housing benefit cap banishing people hundreds of miles from family and schools, the people spilling out on to the street, sheltered by churches and mosques, are the unwilling emblems of deliberate Conservative attacks. Just remember how personally people have been abused by George Osborne – those idlers with the blinds down while hard workers set off at dawn. Or Iain Duncan Smith's: 'This is not an easy life any more, chum.' Together with their poisonous press, they hardened public hearts against those struggling and working hard on low incomes: how else could they make this April's £12bn benefit cuts politically palatable? Here's the moment public hearts soften and the idea of social security regains its meaning.

George W Bush was similarly exposed by his clueless reaction to Hurricane Katrina, leaving the poor vulnerable to the state's refusal to invest in flood defences. This government can't redeem itself, but it can limit the damage by quickly obeying its promise to rehouse every family nearby, one that was only dragged out of ministers reluctantly under fierce questioning by Labour MPs.

The government needs to pay the private rents to rehouse all these families locally. I know of at least one block of luxury flats in Kensington with the lights out permanently in most of them: the council should requisition the housing it needs, with plenty available. What of rehousing all the other tower block residents now horrified to find their homes too are potential firetraps?

The danger is that once this drama is over and news moves on, people get forgotten. Not this time. What a contrast was Jeremy

Corbyn's visit, hugging and embracing victims, promising to guarantee that never happens. No one could have devised a better parable to convey the difference between the two parties than those two leaders' visits. No doubt Grenfell residents would have shouted at the prime minister – but after her hermetically sealed election campaign, this confirms that a leader who dare never meet her people is truly done for.

23 JUNE

'Why did they wait for people to die?' Grenfell survivor tells of anger

AMELIA GENTLEMAN

In the streets around Grenfell Tower victims are instantly identifiable by coloured wristbands which allow them access to support services in a relief centre, located in a gym underneath the motorway. Khalid Ahmed, 20, who escaped from his eighth-floor home, has slipped his off and folded it into his pocket.

'Everyone can see it, and people were stopping me in the street, asking the same questions again and again. Where did you live? What floor were you on? How did you get out? It gets tiring,' he says.

Families who are still in shock and grieving are having to rebuild their lives from scratch. Some are organising funerals, and trying to work out how to get visas and flights for relatives travelling from abroad. But even for those who escaped without losing relatives, the list of immediate tasks is long: new clothes, new passports, Oyster cards, bank cards, driving licences have to be sourced, time off from work has to be agreed, and then there's the bigger question of arranging somewhere new to live.

Now that survivors have been rehoused in hotels across London, many say they feel isolated, too tired to travel to the residents' meetings that are being held in community centres around the tower. People are exhausted, disoriented and angry.

Ahmed is staying on the 16th floor of a hotel three miles from the tower; he is not thrilled to be so high up, but he doesn't feel inclined to make a fuss. His aunt, Amina Mohamed, is on the fourth floor. 'She refused to go any higher,' he says. They have already been offered a permanent home in a flat in neighbouring Westminster, but it is on an estate which has a bad record for gang crime, and she has refused it.

He remains in shock, watching the political fallout from the tragedy on a television in a victims' centre set up by local volunteers in a rugby club near the tower. He greets this week's declaration from Theresa May that governments 'simply haven't given enough attention to social housing' with scepticism and the news of cladding being removed from other blocks with some bitterness.

'At least we are learning, but it feels a bit too late. It took how many people to die for them to realise it wasn't safe? Putting flammable cladding on a 23-storey building, with one staircase, no alarms in the stairways, no sprinkler systems? Now they are ready to fix it, but before they were just unwilling to spend the money,' he says. 'Why did they wait for all these people to die just to do something simple? Victims are just demoralised.'

The noise of the cladding falling from the building is one of the memories that trouble him from the night of the fire. He hopes that those responsible will be pursued. 'As far as the cladding goes, and the way the fire was accelerated, someone should be held accountable.'

Ahmed, who has lived with his aunt since moving to London from Somalia when he was six, was awake playing on his PlayStation after midnight, listening to music with headphones on. 'My aunt is always telling me off for staying up late, telling me I'll get insomnia. I've been telling her: PlayStation saved your life,' he says.

When he smelled smoke at around 1am, he woke his aunt. As she got dressed, he went out to the deserted corridor, where he realised everyone else was asleep. He knocked on his neighbours' doors, and woke up the people in the other five flats. Over the past few days, when he bumps into them in the respite centre, they have been thanking him for alerting them and saving their lives. There was no smoke in the stairway as he came down with his neighbours, and there weren't many other people using the stairs at that time, around ten past one; he assumes that people upstairs were still unaware of what was happening. There was no noise of fire alarms until he got down to the fourth floor.

He spent hours outside the building, watching as the fire spread, looking after a young girl from Somalia, whom he hadn't met before and hasn't seen since, who was crying because her father was stuck in the building. 'That was very hard,' he says. Hundreds of residents stood watching the disaster, horrified by the flashes of mobile phone torches from people on the upper storeys, trying to signal to firefighters that they needed help.

'There was a man on the 16th floor, who kept on coming to the window, and you just watched as the fire connected, and then he was no longer there.'

While he feels grateful for an initial payment of £500 that he and his aunt have received to help cover the immediate costs of the tragedy, noting that it was hard in the first few days, with no money and no access to his bank account, he remains angry at the prime minister's slowness in coming forward to meet the victims.

'In any other neighbourhood Theresa May would have come straight away, sat with people, had tea in their homes. This is not really her area,' he says. The prime minister's subsequent efforts to express compassion for the victims have not satisfied residents, who feel let down by the chaotic response to the tragedy. 'People were thinking: you put us in this building and you don't care, and then you still don't care afterwards.'

Ahmed agrees to be interviewed in Avondale Park, which is a five-minute walk from the tower, but a place he has never previously been to, in the richer, leafier part of the borough. It is quiet, apart from the gentle pock-pock noise of a tennis game, somewhere out of sight, behind a hedge. Afterwards he walks to Holland Park tube station (because his usual station is still closed), a station he never uses. As he waits to get into the lift, a man in a grey top hat and suit comes out, wearing an Ascot badge. 'You don't get that in Latimer Road,' he says.

'You can clearly see the divide – different houses, different environment. I don't think that many people liked the tower block, and so-called poor people living in such a nice neighbourhood,' he says. He bridles at the way the block has been depicted as a centre of deprivation in the media, irritated at being cast as 'some lower status kind of person, with this portrayal of the tall block, a place that the government had got for poor people to live in squalid places. I wouldn't say it is poor. I wouldn't say it was high-end ... but people work – my aunt works, my neighbours work.'

Although the relief effort is improving, things remain muddled, he says. 'Everything is still all over the place. You get a call from someone who says: "I'm from housing," and then a few minutes later you get a call from someone else who says:

"I'm from housing." No one knows what they're doing.' He says he doesn't mind where he ends up living 'as long as it isn't a high-rise'.

Ahmed has lost all of his college coursework assignments, prepared as part of his entry application to study mechanical engineering at the University of Middlesex, but after going to his college in Uxbridge, he has been reassured that he will get special dispensation, and his place remains safe. He has lost all his documents, but he is trying not to complain. 'It doesn't feel good to be talking about losing my things, my passport, my work. Other people have lost children.'

26 JUNE

This shoddy DUP deal will cost Theresa May far more than £1 billion

MARTIN KETTLE

When Martin McGuinness arrived in 10 Downing Street for his first talks with Tony Blair in the build-up to what became the Good Friday agreement, he looked at the cabinet room table and remarked: 'So this is where all the damage was done.'

Blair and his aides thought McGuinness was referring to the IRA mortar attack on John Major and his cabinet in 1991. But he wasn't. McGuinness was mulling the whirligig of history that had brought him to the very place where Sinn Féin's Michael Collins signed the Anglo-Irish treaty in 1921 with David Lloyd George.

That treaty partitioned Ireland and triggered a civil war in the south, in which Collins himself would perish.

Today's agreement between Theresa May's Conservatives and Arlene Foster's Democratic Unionists will not have the bloody consequences of the 1921 treaty. Yet do not overlook the fact that this too is a Downing Street deal with massive implications for both parts of Ireland, as well as for British domestic politics.

On one level, it is possible to see the May–Foster deal as simply a piece of modern political pragmatism of a kind that is familiar in almost every parliamentary democracy in Europe. Government formation across Europe – from Germany to Greece, and from Scotland to Spain – operates in precisely this way.

In the Irish Republic itself, for example, the current Fine Gael minority government has exactly such a 'confidence and supply' deal with Fianna Fáil. It means that, in return for its support on crucial issues such as the budget or confidence motions, Fianna Fáil has some influence over government bills and policies.

May and Foster have now cut an essentially similar deal. May's Tories were eight seats short of a majority in the House of Commons after the election; the DUP has 10 MPs, giving May a majority of six.

Job done? May will certainly hope so. Everything that gives her the strength and stability she lost on 8 June helps to steady her ship and give her new government time to settle. Unless something goes very badly wrong on Thursday, the Queen's speech will now pass in the Commons.

But this deal shakes the pillars that uphold not just the politics of Britain but the politics of Ireland and Northern Ireland too. The price May has paid for it is hugely disruptive and potentially bankrupting – and will far exceed the £1bn price tag for the DUP's offer of support in yesterday's three-page agreement.

May now has to explain something tough and unpalatable not just to her party or her critics or to the devolved governments of Scotland and Wales, but to England, to NHS staff and to public service workers generally. She has to explain why the 1.8 million inhabitants of Northern Ireland, each of whom already receives more financial support from the British taxpayer than those in the rest of the UK, are entitled to another dollop of the extra public spending that has been so long denied to the other 63 million. In short, she has to explain why the millions who voted for change in Britain on 8 June are being denied the spending that those who voted for no change in Northern Ireland are receiving.

That's a very hard political sell, especially to a disenchanted public. It challenges the meaning of the union it purports to uphold. Yet May has just handed a genuine material grievance to every single voter in Britain. It suggests she has her own magic money tree growing in her back garden. If ever there was proof of May's potential for ineptitude, this is surely it. There is no guarantee that, with her popularity drained, her confidence blown, her rivals circling and her enemies closing in, she will get away with it.

Just as May's manifesto proposals on social care collapsed at the first whiff of grapeshot a month ago, so it also remains perfectly possible that this deal will not survive the realisation in Britain that Foster's voters are getting hospitals, schools, roads and farm spending that the rest of the country would also like a slice of. A public who are clearly fed up with austerity may simply not stand for it. It would be hard to argue that they should.

But the price of the deal could be even higher. The documents that were signed in Downing Street this morning go into considerable detail as to how the deal will work, what its aims are and where the DUP's ransom money will be spent. It is much more vague about the political consequences in Northern Ireland and for the power-sharing arrangements there.

Political common sense says that the Tories would surely not have done this trade with the DUP without ensuring that Northern Ireland nationalists were reconciled to the practical consequences in the province, and without ensuring that the Irish government's anxieties were dealt with too.

That same common sense would also say that, before parting with £1bn, the Tories would want bankable guarantees from the DUP that the devolved executive and assembly, which have been suspended since January, will now be up and running again in short order.

Yet May's recent record for political common sense is appalling. Why should it be any different this time? Assumptions that she will have squared things with nationalists and with Dublin don't sit with the slow downward spiral of mutual trust between the DUP and Sinn Féin that has left Northern Ireland without a government this year. It is hard to believe Sinn Féin will stroll back into the arrangements after such a visible illustration of the DUP's complicity with the Tories. What's in it for them? Dublin's cautious response today shows it is only too aware of all the pitfalls.

May never needed to do this deal. The DUP's 10 MPs were never going to bring a Tory government down, least of all to hand the keys to Jeremy Corbyn's Labour. Instead, May has given British voters a genuine grievance against Northern Ireland; given nationalists good reasons to mistrust power-sharing; undermined the UK's status as an honest broker; worried our nearest and closest neighbour; and landed the Tories with an embarrassing alliance with a socially conservative party that threatens to make a mockery of Tory modernisation.

No good will come of it, and none deserves to, as May and Foster will both surely soon discover.

28 JUNE

Michael Bond: Obituary

VERONICA HORWELL

Paddington station, as described in the opening chapter of Michael Bond's book *A Bear Called Paddington*, has the melancholy of a departed world. Some of its trains are still steam, whistling away to halts as yet unaxed. There are buns in the buffet. The Browns, waiting for their daughter to chug home from school for the holidays, find a creature from 'darkest Peru' who has stowed away on a boat to Britain. He is sitting on a small suitcase near the lost property office, wearing a hat and a label around his neck: 'Please look after this bear. Thank you.' The Brown family adopt him.

This did not seem a fantasy when it was written. Bond, who has died aged 91, was a BBC television cameraman who had nipped out to Oxford Street, London, late on Christmas Eve, 1956, for a stocking filler for his first wife, Brenda. Out of pity he bought a bear glove-puppet, rejected and alone on a shelf in Selfridges. Bond had been scribbling for over a decade – his first short story was completed in an army tent outside Cairo in 1946. He bashed out the bear opus in 10 days in the spring of 1957 on a typewriter in a tiny flat off Portobello Road.

He located the book in the shabby world around Paddington and Notting Hill, and created the bear out of his memories of evacuee children in the second world war, luggage-labelled against loss in transit; Paddington's friend Mr Gruber was based on Hungarian refugees he worked with at the BBC's monitoring service at Caversham Park, with their attaché cases packed with sad pasts, and their careful English. A generation later, the bear was interpreted as a sympathetic allegory of the Commonwealth immigrants of the 1950s: Bond initially wrote that Paddington came from 'darkest Africa', but his agent noted that the continent no longer had native bear species, so Bond amended it to Peru. In later life, Bond was touched by many letters from child immigrants who told him about their own fresh starts in England, just like Paddington's: many liked the way the bear politely challenged authority. By the time of the 2014 *Paddington* film, Bond's bear was a benign signifier of welcomed migration.

Seven publishers rejected the book, then Collins paid Bond £75, and brought it out in 1958: there were 13 sequels, though no later illustrators matched the original, Peggy Fortnum, who inked Paddington as stubborn, catastrophe-prone and kitted out in duffle coat (Bond had been wearing one, the government-surplus gear of an outside cameraman, when he found the original bear).

He began to bank serious writing money only in the 1970s, after Graham Clutterbuck and Ivor Wood (whose *Guardian* obituary Bond wrote) created a BBC TV series using an appealing animatronic bear – with a great hard stare – and simple, drawn backgrounds. The stories were narrated by Michael Hordern, who later remarked that his most challenging roles had been God, Lear and Paddington Bear.

That really began the cult. The books were translated into 40 languages, including Latin, and sold 35 million copies worldwide. The 2014 film, starring Hugh Bonneville and Nicole Kidman, used Ben Whishaw's voice, animatronics and CGI to bring the bear to life (Bond had a cameo as 'Kindly Gentleman'). The sequel is to be released later this year.

Bond based the good-hearted Brown family on his own father, Norman, who worked for the post office in Newbury, Berkshire, and the safe, warm house his mother, Frances, kept, smelling of

Brasso and Reckitt's bath cubes; the few events from his child-hood he cared to share with interviewers include his prize of a watch for winning a slow bicycle race and his father's occasional fall from the saddle while raising his hat to a lady.

Bond attended a strict Catholic school in Reading, Presenta-tion college, which he left as soon as he could, aged 14. He joined a solicitor's office, then followed his aptitude for building wire-less sets into transmitter engineering with the BBC. Despite his desire to be a wartime pilot, he so failed to cope in the air that he was grounded, then offered the choice of going down the mines or joining the army. After soldiering in the Middle East, Bond returned to the BBC in 1947 and got behind a camera in the improvisatory days of TV, shooting everything from *Dixon of Dock Green* to *Face to Face*: 'It was live ... everything was held together by string and there was always some disaster going on behind the scenes.' Writing radio plays for what was then Ceylon, and Hong Kong, and journalism for *Men Only*, *Lilliput* and the *Manchester Guardian*, was an extra, and Bond did not give up the day job until April Fool's Day, 1966.

Paddington was a rare British merchandising success, making £5m a year. The Paddington soft toy, freestanding in Dunlop wellies, was the mascot of the decade; the blue-rosetted beast Margaret Thatcher posed with at a Tory conference was a knock-off. (Long after, when David Cameron's arrival at a restaurant brought the number at table to 13, ministers drafted in a proper Paddington for luck.) The toy was joined by Aunt Lucy from 'the Home for Retired Bears, Lima', in the bowler hat of a native Peruvian. Auto-graph hunters began to arrive at the door of the Bonds' house in Haslemere, Surrey, and were kindly asked to stay.

However, the deals for more than 200 items, the prosecution of pirates, and the requests for more TV scripts pressured Bond into depression. There weren't enough hours in his day: he left

Haslemere before dawn and came home past dusk, then moved into a new Barbican flat in the City of London to be closer to work. For two years he was switched off by sleeping pills and on by whisky, but he said that his responsibility to Paddington got him through: 'There is something so upright about Paddington. I wouldn't want to let him down.' Bond spoke of the character easily (right through to his last story, published this April), as a more confident extension of his own shy self: 'Unless an author believes in his character, no one else is going to. He isn't me, but I wouldn't mind being him – he's never put down or deflated. He has the naivety of a child and the sophistication of an adult.'

Bond's first marriage disintegrated during those years (a relationship with one of his book editors produced his son, Anthony) and he took refuge in more work, writing 18 hours a day. He and Brenda divorced in 1981; he then married Susan Rogers, who was employed by his agent – he liked her telephone voice and, too nervous to ask her out to dinner, invited her to a Paddington play in Wimbledon. But he remained friends with Brenda, and they kept joint custody of the Christmas bear, always considered a member of the family: 'We ring each other and say, "He feels like coming to you now." I wouldn't go on holiday without him.'

The last *Paddington* TV shows were financed by the American Home Box Office channel in the 1980s: in *Paddington Bear Goes to the Movies*, the bear sploshed through 'Singin' in the Rain' with the amused permission of Gene Kelly himself.

Bond also devised and scripted another TV series, *The Herbs*, and many children's books set in a more contemporary world of pets on the patio, the most popular about the guinea pig Olga da Polga – a real Bond family pet, or rather, a sequence of pets.

The novels that Bond said he most enjoyed creating were whodunnits about Monsieur Pamplemousse, a former member of the Sûreté working undercover for *Le Guide*, the French directory of the highest cuisine. Travelling with his dog, Pommes Frites, Pamplemousse does a morsel of detecting among pages of descriptions of food and wine. Bond had begun his edible education with a daring 1948 trip across the Channel, continued it in the homes of those BBC refugees and the restaurants of Charlotte Street, and detoured on the annual road journey across France to the Cannes TV festival.

By *Paddington*'s golden jubilee, the middle-classness of the Browns, with the bear's bank account and foreign holidays, seemed ordinary to young readers. It was the changeless, sexless security of Paddington's home at 32 Windsor Gardens (based on Lansdowne Crescent), his food shopping with a basket on wheels at Portobello Market, that had come to be exotic.

In 1997 Bond wrote his own memoirs, *Bears and Forbears*, definitely not sexless. In all he wrote more than 150 books and was appointed OBE in 1997 and CBE in 2015 for services to literature. Yet he was reconciled to Paddington being his permanent achievement, with such cracking lines as '"Bears is sixpence extra," the taxi driver said gruffly. "Sticky bears is ninepence."' (Of course Stephen Fry read the audiobooks.)

Later editions decimalised the coinage and increased the pocket money, which was unwise: inflation no more affects the values of Paddington's universe than it might Pooh's Hundred Acre Wood. The animatronic bear, under a licence Bond did not directly control, appeared in 2007 ads for Marmite, substituted for marmalade in the sarnies: Bond apologised in a letter to *The Times*.

For the bear's 50th anniversary, Bond attempted a contemporary book, *Paddington Here and Now*, in which the bear was arrested (he is, after all, an illegal immigrant) when his trolley was clamped, and then doorstepped by the tabloids. His most recent Paddington story, *Paddington's Finest Hour*, was published in April.

At Paddington station concourse in 2000, the bear-shaped charity collection boxes and stuffed toys in glass cases (maintained by Bond, who kept having to turn out from his nearby Little Venice house to put the bears back on their feet) were superseded by a bronze statue of Paddington on platform one, one of the few memorials in London to inspire real affection. Passengers pose sitting on its plinth, eating sandwiches.

He is survived by Susan; his daughter by Brenda, Karen; his son, Anthony, and by four grandchildren.

Summer

David Cameron, why oh why are you still talking?

MARINA HYDE

In one sense, it was a surprise to find David Cameron saying arrogant and tin-eared things overseas this week: that's Liam Fox's job, and has been ever since he was restored to cabinet, in the greatest political comeback since Lazarus was found sharing a tomb with his self-styled adviser.

Yes, ever since the trade secretary took office and promptly stuck up a portrait of Cecil Rhodes in his office, Fox has been flying round the world in the service of pipe-dream traffickers. He's basically a bad ideas mule, a globetrotting repository for a hundred condoms stuffed with imperialist soundbites and meaningless generalities. The unpacking of them is never a pleasant operation. Something something 'post-geography world'; something something 'France needs high-quality, innovative British jams and marmalades.'

Fox was aiming his brain-cannon closer to home this week, alas, and we shall return to him shortly. On the world stage, it was Cameron's turn to lay it on thick. The former prime minister was one of the keynote speakers at the Asian Leadership Conference in Seoul. Amazingly, the title of his speech wasn't 'Just in Case Any of You Guys Are Thinking of Having a Referendum for Party-Political Reasons'. Nor was it 'I'm Sorry, I Was Looking for the Hot-Stone Spa and Seem to Have Exited the Lift on the Wrong Floor'.

But obviously, we ought not to delve too deeply into the oration's contents. These days, there is only ever one acceptable response to a David Cameron speech, and that is: 'Are you still talking? Wait – how is it that you are still talking? How is it possible that you seem to pop up several times a month, either in your guise of Captain Hindsight, or hawking yourself round the after-dinner-minted circuit?'

I mean, the one merciful thing you can usually say of pilot-error disasters is that they tend to claim the lives of those who made the cock-up. Yet seemingly every week, Cameron can be found on some lucrative platform or other, lecturing an audience too bored, blasé or beaten to call bullshit. For the rest of us, it's like hearing someone who ploughed an Airbus 380 into a music festival talk about what albums he's currently listening to.

According to Cameron's spokesman, the former PM 'never discusses' the size of his payment for this service. What he did discuss in Seoul was his austerity pay cap, explaining that those who criticised austerity were cavalier and 'selfish'. And as time goes by, I'm sure people will be ever more pleased to take lectures from him on the costs of recklessness, when his own party-political decision will be paid for by their schools and hospitals and whatnot.

In the meantime, it's one thing Cameron taking the enormous fee, presumably to make some auto-satirical point about the obscene rewards of failure. But it's quite another to imagine that, from that platform, you can pontificate about anything that so much as loosely pertains to the likes of nurses and firefighters. That, surely, is the point at which a lack of self-awareness tips over into sociopathy.

Struggling public servants, 'selfish'? Thanking you, Scary Antoinette. But from you, a period of wordlessness – if not headlessness – would now be most welcome. I don't mean that literally, of course. Come my magic-realist revolution, Cameron would be eternally imprisoned in a single Instagram shot of his own pedicure.

As for Liam Fox, the trade secretary this week decided to tag-team on some recent BBC bashing by Andrea Leadsom. Just don't call it a brains trust. According to Liam: 'It does appear that some elements of our media would rather see Britain fail than see Brexit succeed. I cannot recall a single time in recent times when I have seen good economic news that the BBC did not describe as "despite Brexit" ...' Player Two has entered the game.

No doubt we shall see more of this as the reality of Liam's task becomes slowly clearer to him – the excuse that Brexit would be marvellous if only various types of British people weren't so lacking in some way or other. We'd totally win Brexit if businessmen weren't so fat and golf-obsessed, or the BBC weren't so negative.

And yet, this is a level of sub-analysis that even most angry, one-eyed England football fans have outgrown in recent years. You no longer hear people explain that England would win the World Cup if only the media would 'get behind the team', or the side played with more 'passion'. Most people accept the reality that England are not very good, and appear to have some sort of psychological collapse every time they pull on the shirt.

Still, great British minds think alike, and it was only the other week that Andrea Leadsom was on *Newsnight* explaining: 'It would be helpful if broadcasters were willing to be a bit patriotic.' 'Sorry,' queried Emily Maitlis. 'Are you accusing me of being unpatriotic for questioning how negotiations are going?' Oh, Emily! You can't get into that one with Andrea. She's Brexit's little ray of sunshine. It would be like explaining quantum mechanics to Scrappy-Doo.

Even so, you may find yourself chillingly mesmerised by the fact that Andrea always smiles when she's delivering these assaults. She has that homicidally saccharine smile you normally see in customer services operatives who are administering a knockout financial blow. She'd be amazing on the Ryanair baggage desk.

Unfortunately, she seems to have her eye on another job with travel perks: to wit, foreign secretary. According to a report in *The Times* this week, Andrea declined Theresa May's attempt to demote her in the post-election reshuffle, instead demanding to be made home secretary. Though she'd settle for foreign. Ouch.

Having to listen to Brexit's Oxo mum tell you she wants to be foreign secretary and still not being able to sack her: Theresa May has now entered that phase of slow death that Gordon Brown once did, where the indignities are so excruciating that even sanguine observers slightly have to look away. I know she wanted to bring back bloodsports, but this is a bit much.

Still, with both Leadsom and Fox presumably mulling leadership bids, there is plenty more to come from the Tories in the months ahead. Don't ask how these selfless public servants will find time for Brexit. In fact, it is your patriotic duty not to even wonder.

8 JULY

I took my first antidepressant this week. The effects were frightening

DEBORAH ORR

Most people know about SSRIs, the antidepressant drugs that stop the brain from re-absorbing too much of the serotonin we produce, to regulate mood, anxiety and happiness. And a lot of people know about these drugs first hand, for the simple reason that they have used them. Last year, according to NHS Digital, no fewer than 64.7

million antidepressant prescriptions were given in England alone. In a decade, the number of prescriptions has doubled.

On Tuesday I joined the throng, and popped my first citalopram. It was quite a thing – not least because, like an idiot, I dropped my pill about 90 minutes before curtain up for the Royal Shakespeare Company's production of *The Tempest* at the Barbican. That's right. This isn't just mental illness: this is metropolitan-elite mental illness. It was a pretty overwhelming theatrical experience.

The first indication that something was up came as I approached my local tube station. I noticed that I was in a state of extreme dissociation, walking along looking as though I was entirely present in the world yet feeling completely detached from it. I had drifted into total mental autopilot.

Luckily, I was able to recognise my fugue. It's a symptom of my condition, which, as I've written before, is complex post-traumatic stress disorder. The drug-induced dissociation was more intense than I'm used to when it's happening naturally. I use the word advisedly. Much of what is thought of as illness is actually an extreme and sensible protective reaction to unbearable interventions from outside the self.

Because I've been in very good psychotherapy for about a year now, I've learned to identify times of dissociation, and 'ground' myself. Hitting myself in the centre of the chest works best for me, especially now that I've stopped wearing the necklace I used to thump into my breastbone. Of course, you look like a bit of a prat, striding about banging your chest, but there you are. The one thing that makes you feel normal is the one thing that alerts others to the fact that something weird's going on.

I've been resisting dissociation for pretty much every minute I've been on the drug since then. Being in good company helps most, and being in parks, fields, gardens and nature. You have to keep busy. The leaflet that came with the drug, which I read thoroughly before starting the course, does warn that in the first few days you might find that the symptoms you're trying to escape come back more strongly. Unfortunately, I tend to dissociate in order to avoid having panic attacks. So, as I get better at managing the dissociation, the panic attacks surge. It's like playing symptom whack-a-mole, except that you're whacking bits of your psyche, as well as your chest.

I spent pretty much all of Thursday in one long low-level panic attack – keeping busy, telling no one. I didn't want to mention it, because that would make it worse. At one point, in the park with my brother, he insisted, randomly, that I walk up the hill to the bus stop instead of down it, like I wanted to, in the heat. By the time I got to the bus stop, my legs were barely working, and I was in the grip of convulsive shudders.

I go along with things I don't want to do, things that ignore my wants and needs, then hate myself for my compliance. The little examples, such as this one, reawaken my feelings about the huge ones. I was bullied a lot as a child, and my parents were needlessly strict and deludedly all-knowing. It's grown into a major cognitive dissonance. I loathe being bullied or bossed about, yet at the same time it feels so familiar and comfortable that I'm complying before I even know it, eager to please people who can't be pleased.

Then I feel full of resentment and anger against the perpetrator of the control – so much so that it becomes overwhelming, and my mind and body rebel. I literally shake the feelings out. It's the reason why I recently began to seek NHS psychiatric help, on top of private psychotherapeutic help. A couple of interventions of epic proportions have recently been perpetrated against me. They have left me so poleaxed that I'm unable to assert myself enough to walk downhill.

A breakthrough occurred, though. I was able to tell my brother, calmly, what was happening to me and why. He kissed me on the cheek. He never does that.

Why am I writing this down for publication? Practically, it's because these powerful drugs arrived with so little guidance about what to expect. An NHS caseworker I'd been interviewed by once – not a doctor – called my GP's practice and arranged for a prescription to be written by a GP I'd had nothing to do with. I was told on the phone what the prescription was, and that it was waiting for me to pick up from the local pharmacy. I wasn't consulted about the drug I was being offered at all, although I had said that I wanted to try an antidepressant. I'll meet a different GP and the caseworker in two weeks' time.

The process has taken about five weeks, and has been circular. In crisis at the end of May, I asked my GP practice for help and was told to go to A&E instead. I didn't react well, and left upset and furious. Returning a few days later, I said that I would prefer a less dramatic referral to mental health services than A&E, which is how I met the caseworker. Then, back to the GP practice and that remotely dispatched prescription. Which is not to blame the practice. The whole system is itself in crisis mode all the time. Which is particularly bad, obviously, for people with mental health problems.

There is 'soaring demand' for NHS mental health services. Some 80 per cent of bosses of NHS trusts surveyed by the trade organisation, NHS Providers, have expressed worries that they have too little budget to provide 'timely, high-quality care'. That's so dangerous. I absolutely needed a year of psychotherapy before I started taking this drug. At the start of the therapy, I had become emotionally numb, unable even to weep. I wouldn't have had the insight to understand what this drug was doing to me, let alone control it or explain it to others when I couldn't.

I might never even have got the diagnosis that helps me so much to make sense of my entire life, because that took months. All I can do, apart from look after myself and my kids, is speak out about how complex is the task of managing a mental health condition. There's so very, very much more to it than popping pills.

13 JULY

Sugar is my poison.
My heart attack has finally
opened my eyes to the truth

GILES FRASER

I am now a member of the zipper club. I know, I thought it sounded rude too. But apparently it's the club name for those of us who have a scar right down the middle of our chest. I have one down my leg too, from groin to ankle. And as I spend time recovering from a heart bypass operation – mostly doing very little, watching the cricket, reading the paper – I have started to reflect on my condition. How did it come to this? How did the arteries of my heart become so clogged with gunk that I may have been just weeks from meeting my maker?

'Diabetic,' they said. 'Pah,' I thought. I don't feel any different. I just get up to pee a bit more at night. Some biochemical medical problem just seemed a bit too elusive, abstract, distant. I mean, when Diane Abbott blamed a bad interview on diabetes, who really took that seriously? Earlier this year, I was sent on a diabetes awareness day and spent the time looking out of the window, bored. They tried to explain it to me but I wasn't concentrating.

Well, now that someone has sliced through my breastbone as they might a Christmas turkey, the whole thing doesn't seem quite so distant. And suddenly – and unsurprisingly – I am concentrating. All ears to, and pretty evangelical about, the evils of sugar. Sorry to have doubted you, Diane.

Back in September 2016, the *Journal of the American Medical Association* published papers, discovered deep in the Harvard University archives, that demonstrated how the sugar industry has been manipulating research into heart disease for years. These papers revealed that the purveyors of this white poison – in behaviour straight out of the tobacco industry playbook – had been paying Harvard scientists throughout the 1960s to emphasise the link between fat and heart disease and ignore the connection with sugar. Since then, Coca-Cola has funded research into the link between sugar and obesity. And the confectionery industry has paid for research which 'demonstrated' that children who eat sweets are thinner than those who don't.

As I write, my son returns from the shops, perfectly on cue, laden with a chocolate bar, a full-fat Coke and a packet of lollipops. I want to tell him that Willy Wonka is a death-dealing drug dealer. But I bite my lip for now. He will think me a crank. Everything he likes has sugar in it. That's my fault – he got hooked on sugary breakfast cereals as a child. As Gary Taubes explained in his remarkable book *The Case Against Sugar*, published last year, it has 'assimilated itself into all aspects of our eating experience'. Advertisements have normalised the omnipresence of sugar as a part of a balanced diet. And my son's brain has become accustomed to the dopamine it releases. He has become an addict. Most of us are addicts.

In 1996, 1.4 million people in the UK had diabetes. Since then the figure has trebled to over 4 million. Diabetes now gobbles up more than 10 per cent of the NHS budget, with that percentage set to rise steeply in the coming years. The World Health Authority published a major report on global diabetes last year. Its figures show that the number of people with diabetes has gone up from 108 million in 1980 to 422 million in 2014. This is not just a matter of bad individual choices. You can't dismiss this as the aggregate of many millions of singular decisions, each one nothing more than a matter of weakness of will and responsible for itself alone. This has become a global epidemic.

For the last 30 years I have built a pretty effective protective shell against fat-shaming. I would probably have taken losing half a stone if offered, but I wasn't especially unhappy with my body shape. But now I see things differently. Now I see a multi-billion-dollar industry that makes its profits by keeping us obese and in the dark about why. After my operation, I cut out sugar and carbohydrates as best I could. I have lost 10 kilograms in the five weeks since. And I plan to lose a lot more. It's not a diet – I hate diets. It's a form of protest. The scales have fallen from my eyes. Beware the candyman.

13 JULY

Liu Xiaobo: Obituary

TANIA BRANIGAN

It was China's decision to jail Liu Xiaobo for 11 years over a call for peaceful democratic reform that spurred the Norwegian

Nobel committee to honour him with its peace prize in 2010 and propelled him to international renown. But his first nomination had come two decades earlier, after the Tiananmen Square pro-democracy protests of 1989, in which the author and intellectual played a key role, first as one of the prominent 'four gentlemen' who launched a hunger strike in support of the students; then by helping to broker a peaceful exit from the square for remaining demonstrators amid the bloody crackdown.

The events were the turning point in Liu's life. The writer, who has died aged 61 of cancer, was abroad when the movement erupted and he went home despite the risks. It brought jail, an end to his career as a brilliant young literary professor, and the ending of his first marriage to Tao Li; thereafter his contact with his son, Liu Tao, was limited. But the transformation was internal too. He never forgave himself for writing the confession that shortened his sentence. He believed he had not only sold out his dignity, but also the souls of the dead.

After 1989, many outspoken figures fled abroad or fell silent: 'Others can stop. I can't,' said Liu, believing that to abandon course would be a second betrayal. He dedicated his Nobel prize to the martyrs of Tiananmen Square.

Liu was born in Changchun, Jilin, in north-east China, to an intellectual family. His parents, Liu Ling and Zhang Suqin, were devoted to the party, but from his youth Liu struck an independent course. After studying Chinese literature at Jilin University, he began an MA in 1982 at Beijing Normal University, where he stayed on as a lecturer. His keen intelligence and razor tongue soon established his reputation: hundreds watched his dissertation defence, while students from other universities packed out his electrifying lectures. He was also a visiting lecturer at the universities of Oslo and Hawaii, and Columbia University in New York.

He made as many enemies as admirers in those years. He was as merciless in dissecting friends and apparent allies as political opponents. He was individualist to the core, his friend and biographer Yu Jie noted, and it cost him close friendships. Later on, he acknowledged that he had been preoccupied with ideals of justice and human rights, showing little concern for the people around him. While he let some down he was steadfast in his commitment to others, becoming especially close to Ding Zilin and Jiang Peikun, who had founded the Tiananmen Mothers pressure group in response to the killing of their 17-year-old son.

Friends noted that he was far less abrasive in maturity and, as co-founder and director of the Independent Chinese PEN centre, showed an unexpected talent for dialogue and compromise.

In 2008 he helped to draft and gather support for Charter 08, a bold call for peaceful political reform and an end to one-party rule, inspired by the Czechoslovakian dissidents who issued Charter 77 in 1977. Police detained him at his flat two days before its release and the following year he was given a punitive 11-year sentence for inciting subversion. He was adamant that this time no confession would shorten his sentence.

China censored discussion of Liu and his Nobel win domestically. But intermittently its media denigrated him as a shill for western governments, highlighting his support for the Iraq war and a remark in a 1980s interview that it would take '300 years of colonialism' for China to reach Hong Kong's level of development. Such comments were never contextualised, and though Liu saw western civilisation as a tool that was useful to reform China, he said it was utterly flawed and in need of critique itself. In any case, those comments bore no relation to his jailing.

Despite Liu's sometimes acid remarks he was anything but austere; and was warm and playful with those he knew well –

one letter to a fellow dissident, a serious discussion of political resistance, begins 'Dear Baldie, or is it Beardie?' He relished good red wine until hepatitis stopped him drinking. Friends teased him about his love of good food and voracious appetite, which he ascribed to the devastating famine of his youth, as well as to being one of five sons.

But even when notionally free, his life was shadowed by harassment, questioning, house arrest and surveillance. Asked why he continued – and why he made ambitious calls for fundamental reforms instead of targeting incremental improvements – he said his role was to push for changes that would benefit everyone.

It was in a labour camp, in 1996, that he married the poet Liu Xia. Her devotion sustained him and – painfully aware of his shortcomings in his first marriage – he was a very different husband the second time around. He took enormous pride in his wife's talents.

'Your love has been the sunlight that leaps over high walls and shines through iron bars,' he said in a statement at his trial in 2009. 'My love for you ... is so full of remorse and regret that it at times makes me stagger under its weight.'

They were planning for their life after his release. But late last month it emerged that Liu Xiaobo had been diagnosed with late-stage liver cancer, and he was transferred from prison to hospital, still under heavy guard.

'A calm and steady mind can look at a steel gate and see a road to freedom,' Liu once wrote of life as a prisoner. The gate remained locked and outside the political repression increased. Friends were bitter at the strikingly late diagnosis and the authorities' refusal to let the couple go abroad or release them fully. Yet the man who alienated so many in his youth had told his trial that he had no enemies, speaking kindly of the police, prosecutors and judges.

He insisted that love could dissipate hate, and that progress would be made. *No Enemies, No Hatred*, a selection of his essays and poems, was published in 2013.

Liu is survived by Liu Xia, who has been living under house arrest since 2010, and by Liu Tao.

21 JULY

Six months into America's nightmare, how likely is Trump's impeachment?

RICHARD WOLFFE

Donald Trump Jr is apparently feeling 'miserable' and wants 'these four years to be over', according to *People* magazine. We feel your pain, Don, we really do. At the six-month stage of your father's presidency, we all want these four years to be over. At least that's one way President Trump has brought us closer together.

Since we have to suffer through this purgatory together, we may as well tally up the toll of the last 180 days – and look forward to how the next 1,260 days will end. Like the long-term inmates of Alcatraz, we know that escape is a highly risky proposition that is the figment of our shared despair and the subject of some wonderful myth-making.

First, let's look at how far we've travelled together. President Trump started his term in office with approval ratings of 45 per cent and equal disapproval ratings. Since then, his approval rating has slumped eight points and his disapproval rating has hiked 12 points, in Gallup's presidential tracker.

Reporters have written endless stories about the loyalty of Trump voters to their president, but these narratives do not square with the numbers. It's very hard to get elected, or re-elected, with 37 per cent approval.

For some context, it's worth noting that Barack Obama was 22 points higher at this six-month stage of his presidency, in the middle of the worst recession in living memory. Gerald Ford was languishing at this level at the same stage of his presidency after he pardoned Richard Nixon, who left office in disgrace with 24 per cent approval. At his current pace, Donald Trump will hit Nixon's departure numbers in another 10 months. Just in time for the congressional elections.

But enough of the fake news. What about all those legislative accomplishments? Trump himself has told us that 'with the exception of FDR' no president has been as great as he. 'There's never been a president that's done more in this time,' he told reporters last month 'Who's passed more legislation, who's done more things than we've done.'

If you missed all these historic moments, you weren't alone. Among Trump's legislative record is the renaming of the veterans' outpatient clinic in Pago Pago, American Samoa. He also appointed three people to the board of regents at the Smithsonian.

Mere trifles? I think not.

Yes, we all know about the collapse of his big Obamacare repeal, despite the celebration of its passage through the halfway House of Representatives. OK, so there's been no infrastructure investment, or Mexican border wall, or tax reform. But Rome wasn't built in a day, and nor was the Trump hotel in Washington.

Presidential honeymoons come and go, along with congressional majorities. But the Trump legacy has already begun to write itself. Who else could have fundamentally realigned America's position in the world as quickly as the master builder himself? Global confidence in the US has plummeted 42 points since Trump moved into the Oval Office. Only one country has gained anything like that amount of confidence in Trump's America at the same time: Russia.

In his first six months, Trump has pulled out of the Paris climate agreement, alongside war-torn Syria and the noble state of Nicaragua. Having dismayed most of the world, Trump sent the only man he really trusts – Donald J Trump – on a one-man mission to make friends with the French. This he accomplished by travelling to Paris, shaking hands for a very long time with the French president and admiring his wife's physique out loud. In Paris, they say Trump's legacy is a fait accompli.

So what if he spooked his Nato allies and cosied up to Vladimir Putin over dinner at the G20 in Hamburg? Conventional politicians do conventional things like nurturing allies and isolating enemies. Trump was elected to blow up that model, if not the rest of the planet.

Trump himself has marked this auspicious six-month moment by hosting a panel investigating the fraudulent votes that he suspects undermined his own election. This is once again a presidential first: a sitting president who insists that his own victory was tainted. In fact, the vice-chair of his own panel admits that he doesn't know for sure if Trump's votes were above board.

Talking of tampering with elections, Trump capped his half-birthday in office with a doozy of an interview with the *New York Times* in which he dwelled at length on the Russia investigation that is already undermining his entire presidency.

In particular, Trump lamented appointing an attorney general who failed to stop the Russia investigation. Perhaps Jeff Sessions can ask James Comey how to sign a great book deal after getting iced by Trump. The former FBI director will surely have some friendly tips for his old boss.

What does the next chapter in the Trump Saga look like? There are only so many possible fates for our president: an early departure, defeat in his re-election bid or a second term. The first scenario hinges on the outcome of the congressional elections next year. The second and third depend entirely on what follows.

Early departure is not, like Nixon, going to happen voluntarily. Even in a coerced state, the president shows no sense of shame or expectation of defeat. Trump will need to be impeached and convicted at his impeachment trial, in order to leave office ahead of an election.

For impeachment to happen, Democrats need to win back at least the House. So far, the signs look promising: the generic congressional ballot gives Democrats a 14-point lead, which is pretty much what they were polling before they swept both sides of Congress at Bush's low point in 2006 and Obama's high point in 2008.

Let's assume the House under Nancy Pelosi cannot help itself with impeachment: there are just too many high crimes and misdemeanours to choose from – too many secret Russian meetings, too many dubious financial arrangements, and too much obstruction of justice.

What happens at Trump's trial in the Senate? Even with Democrats swiping back control of the Senate – against all the odds, given the seats up for election next year – they will never enjoy the two-thirds majority required to remove Trump from office.

If you think it was hard for Republicans to vote to repeal and replace Obamacare, you might ask yourself how hard it is for them to repeal and replace Donald Trump.

Under the constant attack of impeachment, and unable to pass any meaningful legislation, Trump will likely do what every other impotent president has done: focus on foreign affairs. He will also be sorely tempted to do what no other sane president has done: start a war to make himself look something other than impotent.

The provocations are not hard to find if you take Iran and North Korea at their word and ignore all the consequences of military action. Trump is especially expert at failing to see the consequences of his actions.

So after another three and a half years of a half-baked war, endless Russia revelations, unethical family business deals and a running Twitter commentary on all things *Fox and Friends*, President Trump will run for re-election with the national debate entirely focused on his specialist subject: Donald Trump.

Should he stay in office when the Senate could not force him out? Is he qualified to remain as president when he has compromised national security with the Russians so many times? Who but Trump could tackle the urgent challenge of the renaming of the main post office in Guam?

Anyone can talk about making America great again. Only one man can talk about making Trump great again. That may be his only mission for the next several years of our great national nightmare, but it is one he is uniquely qualified to accept.

For Democrats, the challenge is going to be to make the national conversation about something other than one loud, large man who is unhealthily obsessed with himself.

29 JULY

I take one last look around the house we've lived in for 24 years

TIM DOWLING

The packing takes two days. At the end of the first day, my office has been stripped of everything except the desk. I carry a kitchen chair up the stairs, and I sit there, pretending everything is normal.

That night, my wife, the oldest one and I go to the Thai restaurant over the road. The conversation is dominated by last things: nearby places we might not happen across for years to come; people we might see again as soon as next week, or as late as never. We over-order, just in case.

'I don't want to move,' my wife says.

'It was your idea,' I say.

'I know,' she says. 'I've changed my mind.'

'You talked the rest of us into this,' the oldest one says.

'I'm freaking out,' my wife says.

'It's exciting,' I say. 'I'm excited.'

'Shut up,' she says.

When we wake up the next morning in an empty bedroom, its former furniture indicated only by indentations in the carpet, the removal van is already outside.

'I'm not leaving,' my wife says.

'What you're going through is normal,' I say. 'Irritating, but normal.'

I have work to do, but no place to do it. I end up sitting on the floor of the youngest one's room, hunched over a keyboard, while he sleeps. When I next look up, he's gone, along with the bed.

As more stuff gets carted away, we gravitate to the kitchen, standing because there is nowhere to sit. The middle one bounces a tennis ball against the bare white wall, while the dog and the cat mill about anxiously. My wife and I are wearing rucksacks containing essentials, in my case an iPad, my diary, a phone charger, spare socks and a clean pair of pants. I was too late to rescue my toothbrush, which is in the van, somewhere.

The table goes. The enormous kitchen dresser I collected from Aldershot last week disappears while my back is turned. The men work around us, occasionally stopping to consult.

'Is this going or staying?' one says, pointing to a bookcase.

'Going,' I say.

'Staying,' my wife says.

Eventually, they come for the pots in the garden.

'These two are staying,' my wife says. 'That one can go. And the honeysuckle has to come. It's got my mother's ashes in it.'

At 3pm, we load the car with a few odds and ends, the dog, a cat in a cage and a tortoise in a box. It is my intention not to take one last look around the empty, dusty rooms of the house we've lived in for 24 years, but the removal men strongly recommend it, so I do. I pick up a few coins off the floor, and a pair of bent tweezers. My stomach feels as if I've just drunk something very cold.

Our three hulking sons wedge themselves into the back seat, their most important possessions stacked on their laps. My wife has the car in gear before I've got the passenger door shut.

'You'll have to be the one to come back at six and hand over the keys,' she says.

'OK,' I say.

'Once I've gone, I don't want to see this place again for a while,' she says.

'The future, please,' I say, pointing ahead. 'That way.'

The next morning, I wake up in a tiny room made of cardboard boxes. They surround the bed on three sides, stacked two high. Daylight streams in through a skylight. The dog is lying across my knees and the cat is asleep next to my head. Under the pillow, my right hand is cramped and partly numb. When I lift it up, I see that it's clutching my phone. According to the screen, it's 5.24am.

I sit up and look over at my wife, her face half concealed by the duvet. Eventually, she opens one eye and stares back.

'Pinch me,' I say. 'I think I'm in Acton.'

The eye rolls dismissively, and then closes. It's a fairly disappointing response to a line I've been saving for three weeks. I wonder if it's too early to wake up the youngest one, and try it on him.

13 AUGUST

Americans once carpet-bombed North Korea. It's time to remember that past

BRUCE CUMINGS

As they always do on the anniversary of the armistice, North Koreans celebrated their 'victory' in the Korean war on 27 July. A few days later, President Donald J Trump remarked that if the North Koreans made any more threats, they 'will be met with fire and fury, and frankly, power the likes of which the world has never seen'.

No American president has uttered words like this since Harry Truman warned the Japanese, between Hiroshima and Nagasaki, either to surrender or face 'a rain of ruin from the air, the likes of which has never been seen on this earth'. Trump's nuclear bluster, made off-the-cuff between golf rounds, was widely condemned, but a few days later he doubled down on it.

As a White House staffer told the *New York Times*, the president 'believes he has a better feel for Mr Kim [Jong-un] than his advisers do. He thinks of Mr Kim as someone pushing people around, and Mr Trump thinks he needs to show that he cannot be pushed.'

Trump is surrounded by people who echo his fantasies of ultimate power. Sebastian Gorka, a strange figure advising Trump (said to be a Trump 'favourite' and a dead ringer for a Bela Lugosi flunky in a *Dracula* movie), told Fox News that Trump's 'fire and fury' line meant 'don't test America and don't test Donald J Trump'.

We are not just a superpower, Gorka went on, 'we are now a hyper-power. Nobody in the world, especially not North Korea, comes close to challenging our military capabilities.' This has been a truism since the Soviet Union collapsed, but it doesn't explain how the US has failed to win four of the five major wars it has fought since 1945. One of those wars was in Korea, where rough peasant armies, North Korean and Chinese, fought the US to a standstill.

It was 64 years ago that North Koreans emerged from this war into a living nightmare, after three years of 'rain and ruin' by the US air force. Pyongyang had been razed to the ground, with the air force stating in official documents that the North's cities suffered greater damage than German and Japanese cities fire-bombed during the second world war .

Just as the Japan scholar Richard Minear termed Truman's atomic attacks 'exterminationist', the great French writer and film-maker Chris Marker wrote after a visit to the North in 1957: 'Extermination crossed this land.' It was an indelible experience still drilled into the heads of every North Korean.

On my first visit to Pyongyang in 1981, a guide quickly brought up the bombing and said it had killed several of his family members. Wall posters depicted a wizened old woman in the midst of the bombing, declaring 'American imperialists – wolves'.

The day after Trump's bluster, the DPRK government stated: 'The US once waged a tragic war that plunged this land into a sea of blood and fire, and has been leaving no stone unturned to obliterate the DPRK's ideology and system century after century.'

There are 25 million human beings living in North Korea. They bleed like we do, they live and die like we do, they love their kin like we do. Trump's callous and cavalier threat was perhaps the most irresponsible thing he has said since becoming president (which is really saying something), but most Americans will not know this because they know nothing about the carpet-bombing of North Korea.

What about the 50 million South Koreans, whose elders also suffered through this war? 'Trump doesn't seem to understand what an alliance is, and doesn't seem to consider his ally when he says those things,' Lee Byong-chul, a senior fellow at an institute in Seoul, told the *New York Times*.

'No American president has mentioned a military option so easily, so offhandedly as he has.' But here Trump has a precedent: Bill Clinton also didn't bother to consult the former South Korean president Kim Young-sam when drawing up plans for a pre-emptive strike in June 1994.

The next few weeks are critical to this deepening crisis, with annual 'Ulchi-Freedom Guardian' war games set to start up on 21 August, involving tens of thousands of American and South Korean troops.

North Korean generals have been preparing for moments like this for decades, gaming out war scenarios during several crises going back to January 1968 when they seized the US spy ship *Pueblo* and held the crew for 11 months.

Thus the North's statements in the current crisis (unlike Trump's) have a concrete, predictable nature: lots of bluster and bombast combined with quite specific plans, namely four medium-range missiles to be launched into waters near Guam on 15 August, if Kim Jong-un gives the go ahead.

Pyongyang always pursues tit-for-tat strategies: the US lifts B1-B nuclear-capable bombers from Guam for flyovers of South Korea – a constant not just under Trump but also during Obama's tenure – and the North chooses a scenario that will call attention to the nuclear blackmail that the US has pursued going back to the Korean war, and particularly during the decades from 1958 to 1990, when the US stationed hundreds of nukes in South Korea with standard plans to use them in the early stages of a North Korean invasion. Pyongyang also likes to choose dates that have historical resonance: 15 August is the anniversary of Korea's liberation from Japanese colonialism in 1945.

Upon the news of his wife's death, Shakespeare's Macbeth said, 'Out, out, brief candle! Life's but a walking shadow, a poor player that struts and frets his hour upon the stage and then is heard no more. It is a tale told by an idiot, full of sound and fury.' He famously added: 'signifying nothing'. Trump signified this: yet another American venture in extermination.

15 AUGUST

Condoms in Ambridge? Whatever next!

NANCY BANKS-SMITH

'There was a problem with the condom!' said Phoebe.

I felt like Eliza Doolittle's dying aunt, who came to so sudden she bit the bowl off the spoon. *The Archers* has been going for 66 years and this is the first time anyone has said condom. Phoebe had spent the night with Constantin, a long-lashed Latvian strawberry picker. This is not unheard of in Ambridge, but no one has been this specific before.

We got a candid crash course in contraception ('I usually have the injection but I forgot'), the morning-after pill ('You have to take it in 72 hours. If you vomit, it won't work') and venereal disease ('Young Constantin's been a busy boy this summer. You should get yourself checked out'). It certainly blew the cobwebs off my knowledge of contraception, albeit a bit belatedly. Go on, ask me anything! I may become an agony aunt.

So now we have to wait a couple of days for Phoebe's pregnancy test and a couple of weeks for the report from the sexual health clinic in Borchester. Hitherto sexual education in Ambridge has largely been in the hands of Joe and Bert doing their Rambling Syd Rumpo routine ('You ain't seen my marrow, Joe. Lovely and firm it is').

The hope is, obviously, to attract a sparky young audience to our grizzled and thinning ranks. Like Phoebe, we shall see. What with housing the homeless and feeding the hungry (Jill is barely sane on the subject of cauliflower cheese) *The Archers* has become quite painfully strident and socially aware recently.

So thank heavens for an old-fashioned wedding. Justin and Lilian – make a note in your diary – are getting married in December. 'Lower Loxley is the most magical place in winter,' said Lilian. Apart from the plummeting bodies, that is. 'Whatever you choose will be perfect,' said Justin, who, being a tycoon, hasn't watched a lot of soaps.

16 August

Why is the US still fighting the civil war?

JASON WILSON

In St Paul's memorial church in Charlottesville, Virginia, last Friday, just up the street from where white supremacists were gathering for a torchlight rally, Cornel West explained why African Americans saw the removal of Confederate monuments as so important.

On hearing that hundreds of white supremacists were gathered in a nearby park, the civil rights leader said, with a hint of weariness: 'These are chickens coming home to roost. We should have eliminated these statues a long time ago.'

'The idea that the American family has to embrace figures like [Confederate general] Robert E Lee, or Stonewall Jackson, who were fundamentally committed to enslaving black people in perpetuity ... These people are not heroes.'

But figures such as Lee and Jackson are heroes to some. Their admirers include Donald Trump. In a rowdy press conference on Tuesday, he compared them to celebrated figures in American history such as presidents George Washington and Thomas Jefferson. Their admirers also include the white nationalist movement, which is currently surging in the US. The foot soldiers of that movement terrorised Charlottesville last weekend. Trump downplayed their violent excesses, saying they were merely 'there to protest the taking down the statue of Robert E Lee'.

The day after the torchlight parade, a rally featuring hundreds of mostly young men in various states of paramilitary attire shut the city down. Hours later, one of their number allegedly murdered a counter-protester with his car. The next day, a planned memorial to the young woman who had been killed was shut down after 'credible threats' from white nationalists.

Their stated purpose in coming to the city for the 'unite the right' rally was to contest the removal of a statue of Lee from a downtown park. In the blizzard of online agitprop that 'alt-right' groups circulated before the event, the claim was often made that in rallying around the statue they were protecting 'white heritage'.

But how did monuments to the losing side in America's civil war become such an intense focus for a national white-supremacist movement? And what is the heritage they really represent?

Charlottesville's statue of Lee is one of about 1,500 such monuments to the Confederacy scattered throughout the US. Mostly, though not exclusively, those statues can be found in those southern states that broke from the union in 1861 over their desire to retain the system of slavery. In 1865, after the loss of more than 600,000 lives and the destruction of entire cities such as Atlanta, the southern Confederacy was defeated, and slavery was abolished.

But like most of the other monuments to the Confederacy's 'lost cause', the statue in Charlottesville was not built in the immediate aftermath of that war. Rather, it was commissioned more than half a century later in 1917, and erected in 1924.

It was part of a wave of statue-building in the south that took place between the late 1890s and 1920, according to research from the Southern Poverty Law Center. That wave crested in about 1911.

There was another, later, flurry of statue-building in the 50s, and around this time the Confederate battle flag became a popular symbol. In that decade and the next, some southern states, such as Florida, changed their flags to more closely resemble the standard of southern defeat.

According to Joseph Lowndes, a political scientist at the University of Oregon and author of two books on the US's racial politics and the south, the timing of these enthusiasms is not accidental. 'The statues go up in moments of racial reaction.'

The earlier craze was the moment when, Lowndes says, 'the Jim Crow order was really being built in the south'. So-called Jim Crow laws formally segregated public schools, public transport and public spaces generally in former Confederate states. Laws mandated that black people and white people use separate restaurants, toilets and drinking fountains.

According to Lowndes, the Jim Crow phenomenon was a reaction to the inroads made by the populist movement, which had fleetingly created political alliances of poor blacks and whites against the rich southern planter class.

Lowndes says that southern elites sought to 'take blacks out of the electorate and segregate public space' in order to 'redivide the black and white core' of the south's working class and small farmers. The monuments were also elements of this divide-and-rule strategy. They were ultimately built for a white audience, as 'elements of a culture that directed whites towards beliefs that aligned them with the planters', says Lowndes. 'It was a political project. Any political project requires symbols, and an imagery.'

One of the core beliefs at the heart of the Jim Crow project – and which these laws sought to implant – was that the civil war had not been an ignominious defeat, but a noble struggle. Leonard Zeskind, activist and author of *Blood and Politics*, a history of white nationalism in the US, says the purpose of the hundreds of statues erected around the turn of the century was 'to rewrite who won the war', in order to justify Jim Crow.

Lowndes says it was in part an effort to 'whitewash the civil war, and the reasons it was fought'. Eventually, Jim Crow was dealt a blow by the supreme court's 1954 finding, in Brown v Board of Education, that segregation in public schools was unconstitutional. From this time, a black-led civil rights movement fought to extend the implications of this decision into the full desegregation of the south, and carried the fight into other areas such as voting rights.

But many whites in the south, and their state and local governments, fought tooth and nail to preserve segregation. They were, in effect, fighting the civil war all over again. In Virginia, a strategy of 'massive resistance' devised by Senator Harry F Byrd Sr saw integrated schools defunded and schools closed, including in Charlottesville.

It was during this white resistance to civil rights that Confederate symbols and statues once again became popular, and were adopted both by ordinary people and whole states, as signifiers of the resilience of white supremacy. And it was during this time that there was another surge in the number of statues erected throughout the southern states.

Lowndes says: 'They are presented as being part of a continuous heritage, but the idea that these symbols have anything to do with anything but racial reaction is wrong.'

Not everyone agrees with this assessment – in particular, contemporary white Americans. According to the American Values Survey by not-for-profit polling organisation PRRI, around seven in 10 working-class whites believe that the flag is a symbol of 'southern pride' rather than 'racism'. Sixty per cent of whites of all classes feel this way, and so do 51 per cent of Americans as a whole – whereas 80 per cent of black Americans say it is a racist symbol, and it is African Americans fighting for racial justice who have been the foremost critics of Confederate symbols since they were erected.

The great African American intellectual WEB Du Bois wrote in 1931 of the grandiose inscriptions on recently erected monuments to the Confederacy that: 'Of course, the plain truth of the matter would be an inscription something like this: "Sacred to the memory of those who fought to Perpetuate Human Slavery."' Later, Zeskind says, 'the memorials started to get questioned in the 1960s in the fight against Jim Crow, and it's been pretty much going on ever since'.

Since the 2015 massacre of nine African American church-goers by Dylann Roof in Charleston, South Carolina, there has been a renewed focus on the persistence of Confederate monuments and symbols in southern cities from racial justice advocates, including the Black Lives Matter movement. In the wake of the Charleston murders, South Carolina's then governor, Nikki Haley, ordered the removal of the Confederate flag from the grounds of the state house in Columbia. But racial justice advocates want to go further by removing all Confederate relics from southern cities.

In Charlottesville on Friday, local Black Lives Matter chapter member Lisa Woolfork explained that for her and her fellow activists, 'these statues themselves are revisionist histories. They hide history. They tell a story from the 1920s of the "lost cause". It's a way of making the slave-holding south feel like they won.'

But while critics of the statues have been mobilising, white nationalists have been turning the statues into rallying points for resistance to multiculturalism, feminism and minority rights.

For them the fight never really stopped, and now it goes on as they rally around these symbols of the Confederacy.

Lowndes says that: 'These were largely regional sites as late as the 1990s,' of interest mostly to southern heritage groups, but also to more extremist 'neo-Confederate' groups such as the Council of Conservative Citizens, and the League of the South. (Neo-Confederates generally desire the restoration of segregation as a matter of law, and some, such as the League of the South, even want the old Confederacy to once again secede.) 'But they have now become national sites for a racist rightwing movement. They allow people to feel embattled. You can rally people to a last defence.'

Alexander Reid Ross is a lecturer at Portland State University, and author of *Against the Fascist Creep*, a broad historical survey of fascist movements to the present. He agrees that Confederate monuments have at once given the 'alt-right' a convenient set of symbols to organise around, and also swelled the constituency for radical neo-Confederate groups.

'Five or 10 years ago,' Ross says, 'there wasn't even a big regional constituency for neo-Confederates. But the increase in college-organising by the 'alt-right' and neo-Nazi groups has given them a new base.'

The alleged murderer in Charlottesville last Saturday, James Fields Jr, was himself a member of a group, Vanguard America, that explicitly targets college-age men in its recruiting, and hundreds of young men were active participants in the weekend's events. The spectacle in Charlottesville of the League of the South marching alongside neo-fascist and neo-Nazi organisations such as Vanguard America, the Traditionalist Workers Party and the National Socialist Movement demonstrates that, to some extent, their objectives have fused.

Ross says that Confederate monuments are attractive to these groups partly because they represent a period of unquestioned white supremacy. 'The civil war is seen as the last stand of a proper, gentlemanly white tradition.' But they also have value in terms of movement strategy. He compares their selection of the Lee monument in Charlottesville to the 'patriot movement'-inspired occupation of the Malheur national wildlife refuge in Oregon in 2016. 'You place an insurrectionary point somewhere and have people rally around it.'

George Hawley, a political scientist at the University of Alabama, and author of two books that examine dissident right-wing movements, says that national far-right movements have been attracted to the fight over Charlottesville's monument partly from 'opportunism, and a desire for controversy ... But it also comes from their sincere feeling that attacks on Confederate monuments are attacks on whiteness, per se.'

He says that the discussion around Confederate monuments is indicative of the growing estrangement between a resurgent radical right, and an embattled mainstream conservatism. In the past, he says, 'mainstream conservative media outlets were supportive of the maintenance of Confederate symbols', and did so under catchphrases such as 'heritage, not hate'. This changed after Roof's rampage in Charleston: establishment and so-called 'movement' conservatives 'stopped defending monuments'.

On the other hand, over the same two years, passionate defenders of Confederate symbols began 'echoing the progressive critique of the monuments', offering 'a more radical pushback against the idea that it wasn't about race'. From 'heritage not hate', then, some moved to the admission that their heritage was hate.

This was perfectly timed with the rise of the 'alt-right'. Like that broader white nationalist movement, they sought to leave behind the 'dog-whistling', coded talk about race that Republicans had been honing since Nixon realigned the south's politics with his 'southern strategy', and openly push white supremacy.

Southern politicians in communities polarised around disputes over monuments sometimes try to equivocate. During the debate over the statue of General Lee in Charlottesville, Mayor Mike Signer suggested that instead of removing such statues, they could be 'contextualised' with plaques or installations explaining the civil war and the reasons it was fought.

Woolfork, the Black Lives Matter activist, disagrees. 'There is no better context for these statues than the hundreds of white nationalists coming to defend them.' She says they need to go, because 'you cannot tell beautiful lies about ugly stories'.

There have been signs in the days since that the events in Charlottesville may have only accelerated the movement against Confederate statues. In Durham, North Carolina, a group of protesters pulled down a monument dedicated in 1924. On Tuesday night in Baltimore, hours after Trump's incendiary press conference, the city removed four Confederate memorials, including one of Robert E Lee and Stonewall Jackson. Other cities have committed to tearing statues down since the weekend.

For Cornel West, the sooner the better. As the white nationalist torchlight rally prepared to kick off not a mile away, he said that the heritage the statues speak for is not worth commemorating. 'The Confederacy is part of a tradition that's grounded in hatred, and is tied to one of the most vicious structures of domination in the modern world.'

After the weekend's events, it may be that more of the white Americans who consider these symbols a matter of 'pride' come to see his point.

22 AUGUST

Inside Conor McGregor's Dublin: the making of the fighter taking on Mayweather

DONALD McRAE

Patrick Hyland, a gentle and amusing former boxer who once called himself The Punisher, waits for the boys and girls he now trains at the gleaming Straight Blast Gym in Tallaght, Dublin 24. An empty ring sits in a far corner while, to his left, the MMA cage is also silent on a sleepy afternoon. It will be another hour before the chattering kids who dream of becoming boxers or UFC fighters tumble in to work with Hyland and the mixed martial arts trainers.

They all know that the distinct worlds of boxing and MMA collide in Las Vegas on Saturday night. It is a surreal boxing match which has little else but money wedged deep in its murky heart. Of course Hyland's tiny scrappers also know that Conor McGregor, from down the road in Crumlin, Dublin 12, will earn around $100m for his professional ring debut. McGregor, a brilliant showman and intelligent fighter who dominates the UFC, faces Floyd Mayweather, a masterly defensive boxer.

Mayweather is coming out of retirement for an even larger payday and the expectation that he will outclass a novice and lift his record above the great Rocky Marciano to a 50–0 mark – which would be perfect, but for the absurdity of an apparent mismatch.

The 33-year-old Hyland approaches the sporting melodrama differently by mixing humour and pathos. He met John Kavanagh, McGregor's coach, at a party in 2013. 'We were having a bit of a laugh, a few drinks, and we were yapping away and agreed that I'd spar with Conor.' The first session was a jokey MMA and boxing mishmash and when Hyland was kicked in the leg 'it felt like someone shot me with a big bazooka'. But then in 2015, he gave McGregor his first taste of elite-level boxing.

A friendship formed between two contrasting Dublin fighters and Hyland remembers how McGregor tried to console him after the death of his father. Patrick Hyland Sr killed himself in June 2015. He had always been in his son's corner and Patrick was devastated.

'Conor contacted me when my father died,' Hyland says, 'and I told him exactly what my dad thought of him. My dad always said: "McGregor's the new star" and that Conor reminds him so much of Bruce Lee. My dad was a Bruce Lee fan but he didn't like Conor's attitude. He was a boxing man and he said: "His attitude stinks. I'd say it to Conor's face if I see him." Conor laughed and said: "Listen, he's not wrong. Bless your dad. I'm sure he would have knocked me into shape." It was a good laugh.'

Hyland understands boxing far more intimately than most who, like me, have dismissed Saturday's event as a farce. Only last year, having lost only one contest in 32 fights, Hyland was good enough to challenge Gary Russell Jr for his WBC world featherweight title. Hyland tells some very funny stories about being knocked out by Russell but he is serious when assessing McGregor's boxing credentials.

'The second time I went down to spar Conor at his new gym [on Dublin's Naas Road in 2015] he was very good, very snappy. We sparred for 20 minutes and he held his own. He had a bit of weight on me but I was letting my punches go and he was taking them, moving, picking me with a jab, southpaw coming in with the left. He made me miss. He could box.'

Everyone in MMA extols the power of McGregor's left hand. Did he hurt the smaller Hyland? 'I've been boxing all my life so I'm used to taking shots. He had a bit of a pop. When it landed you felt it. I didn't mind it with a 16oz glove and headgear. But I don't want to be hit flush with an 8oz glove by Conor. So, just like in MMA, Conor should come straight out, no fear and have a go. But he needs to throw at least 100 punches a round to get Mayweather out of his comfort zone. How do you do that? But Conor is a genius so maybe he can. Everything he says, he does. It's amazing.'

Hyland smiles when I tell him about my lunch with McGregor's father. Rather than meeting in Crumlin, the working-class neighbourhood of Conor's childhood, or the more salubrious suburb of Lucan where the family moved when he was a teenager, Tony McGregor suggests lunch at the plush Westbury Hotel. McGregor Sr, dressed up to the nines, launches into a story about how he has just taken his son's lavish yacht on its maiden voyage across the Irish Sea.

'Conor's yacht has the Italian style, the polished veneer, the wood, the cream leather, the chrome,' McGregor Sr says. 'It really is fabulous.'

The yacht is called *The 188* – the amount in euros Conor received on welfare right up until the week of his first UFC fight in April 2013. McGregor Sr, who drove a Dublin taxi for 26 years, has just completed his 'skipper's course' so that he can sail *The 188* whenever he likes.

'I've had a few meaningless jobs over my time,' McGregor Sr says, explaining he was a hospital orderly when Conor was born 29 years ago. 'I'm 58 so I've chopped and changed. But I loved the taxi driving. I worked most nights and I had great fun with the people of Dublin.'

Beyond sailing, McGregor is planning to fill his retirement as a part-time celebrant who can marry couples in a civil ceremony.

So life has changed beyond recognition and McGregor surveys the Westbury in wonder: 'Look, apart from us, it's just ladies who lunch. Incredible.'

McGregor soon celebrates his favourite boxing photograph – in which a towering Muhammad Ali shouts 'Get up and fight, sucker!' over a stricken Sonny Liston in 1965. 'We still have a copy hanging in the utility room and it's quite possible Conor could be standing over Mayweather in a similar stance. Mayweather's evasiveness and defensive fighting will not stop Conor. His left hook has phenomenal power. People call this a mismatch but it's in our favour. Age, size, weight, power. We're 100 per cent confident. Conor is going to blow boxing to smithereens.'

That positive conviction did not feature when McGregor considered his son's future 10 years ago. There were raging arguments as Tony tried to persuade Conor his ambition of fighting in the UFC was a ludicrous fantasy. He needed a trade – and so Tony and his wife Margaret worked hard to find their wayward son a plumbing apprenticeship.

'That was me being a parent,' McGregor says. 'One of Conor's teachers told us he had the intelligence to be a lawyer but he didn't have the interest. I put a proposition to Conor. I'd give him €10,000 if he went to college. He didn't take the bait so I was concerned. I'd never heard of MMA before. I'd come in after hours and Conor would be watching UFC with his girlfriend Dee. I'd watch a few minutes while I was winding down after my night shift. But the two of them were engrossed in this combat sport.'

Conor McGregor once told me: 'I had no love for plumbing. But it's weird how society works. Rather than allowing you time to find the thing you love and can pursue with complete conviction, we're told: "You must work – no matter how much you dislike it."'

What are his father's memories of those plumbing days? 'It was very difficult to get him to the site in the foothills of the Dublin mountains. It was cold, wet, miserable. He would come home and it was obvious he had no interest. I'd throw him money, because as a taxi driver I had ready cash, trying to keep him motivated. We did this for a year and got him up every morning. I'll never forget one Monday morning I said: "Conor, it's time for work." He peered out from under the duvet and said: "Look, it's not for me." I closed the door and said to Margaret: "He's never going back." It was pointless.'

His son had immersed himself within the fighting camp run by Kavanagh – who still trains McGregor and will be in his corner against Mayweather. Kavanagh and a tight-knit community of MMA fighters – Owen Roddy, Aisling Daly, Paddy Holohan, Chris Fields, Cathal Pendred and Tom Egan – were eventually joined by McGregor, who left the Crumlin Boxing Club to explore his deeper interest in mixed martial arts.

Holohan, McGregor's friend and the magnificently bearded former UFC fighter who was forced to retire last year, runs his own Straight Blast Gym in Tallaght – a new centre, not far from Hyland's gym, specialising in MMA. After an hour-long lesson tutoring 60 teenage boys and girls, he remembers McGregor's arrival in 2007: 'I met Conor in Rathcoole at John's SBG. He had boxing shorts, a crazy haircut and a boxer's angry face. Most boxers have that face. Conor was there to compete, he wasn't there to join a family atmosphere. But after a spar or two, and some serious grappling, he realised we're helping each other.'

McGregor has always kept a small circle of trusted friends around him. Many from those earliest days remain, either at his side in Vegas or, like Holohan and Daly, in Dublin whenever he returns home. But, before that bond could be made, McGregor went out of his way to make a violent statement.

'He sparred Owen Roddy first,' Daly says as she pushes her glasses up the bridge of her nose and smiles at the memory of

McGregor's opening day. Daly was an early star of Kavanagh's gym and, as a woman, she was a pioneer and inspiration in Irish MMA. Her love of fighting, despite being so calm and thoughtful and having to retire earlier this year after a brain scan, is obvious. 'I remember Conor hit Owen really hard in the head and made him wobble. John was thinking: "Who is this guy? What does he think he's doing?"'

Kavanagh, trying to dilute the intensity, asked McGregor to spar Daly. She was used to fighting men and was not intimidated. 'Conor sparred really hard,' she says, 'and dropped me with a vicious body shot. It must have really been a tough shot for me to go down. John had seen enough. He was like: "Conor, get your MMA gloves on." John took Conor down straight away and dominated him on the ground. He didn't do anything horrible like hitting him in the head but he softened up his body – wiping the breadbasket with nasty little shots to show Conor what it meant. "You want to do MMA? Well, this is MMA."'

The next time Daly and McGregor sparred, she remembers, 'I could maul him. At that stage I probably was a purple belt training in jujitsu for four years and Conor was a new white belt. It was easy to control him. He was obviously tough and strong but I may have choked him.'

Daly laughs demurely when asked if she had taken offence to the way McGregor had hit her. 'Not at all. I was used to guys with egos because some of them think: "I'm not going to be shown up by a girl." Sometimes you had the opposite: "Oh, I can't touch you!" – like you were made of glass. Conor gave me more respect. He fought me like I was any other fighter.'

McGregor is a serious fighter who works obsessively hard to improve his skills. Daly and Holohan believe such discipline was forged in their camp from 2007 to 2013. 'Some people attribute their success to John, some people attribute it to the team,' Daly says. 'We all had the same driven goal and were very close – like a family in terms of we'd eat together, train together and socialise together. We were living and breathing MMA.'

Holohan and McGregor signed on while training six hours a day. Was Daly also claiming welfare? 'No. I worked part-time in a shoe shop in town. MMA doesn't have crazy early-morning starts so most of the time we wouldn't start training until 1pm. I was lucky with some morning shifts at work. People in the shoe shop would say: "Ais is a bit weird. It's crazy what she does." When things took off and UFC became a big deal it was like: "Oh, so that's what she was doing!"'

Daly was amused by McGregor. 'I grew up in Drimnagh, he grew up in Crumlin and so we're from similar areas. He was [six months] younger but there were girls I went to school with and hung around on my street that were Conor's age. He thought he was a smooth talker. There'd be stories of three girls in a group and Conor might be trying to chat up all three at the same time. "Did he say that to you too? He said that to me!" When girls talked they'd say: "Conor McGregor? You wouldn't go near him!"'

Daly and Holohan's memories are a credible antidote to the way in which 'Conor McGregor's Dublin' has been mythologised recently to an unrecognisable pulp. There has been much mirth in Dublin over *ESPN*'s cover feature on McGregor's past where Wright Thompson, usually an authoritative witness and a fine writer, seemed to have been suckered into melodrama. Some colourful talkers spun him a few old-fashioned yarns about drugs and gangs and how, according to Thompson, Dublin is a 'clannish, parochial place. Crossing the wrong street has traditionally been reason enough for an ass-whipping. Men have had to drop dates off at bus stops instead of walking them all the way home.'

Amid the wise-crackers who wish me the best of Irish luck as I head for 'the projects' of Crumlin, people seem to feel like Daly did towards *ESPN*'s exaggeration of Dublin's problems. 'I read a bit of the article and had to stop. It was not in touch with reality. But this will show you the impact of Conor. My mother's 61 and she was down at our local shops – which is like the Rovers Return and the centre of all gossip. She said: "I was talking to the women down the shops and they were telling me about this McGregor article being a load of rubbish."'

Holohan strokes his ginger beard sagely when I ask him if, beyond such bluster, Dublin has left its mark on McGregor. 'Yeah. Dublin really does form you. Dublin is a mean little city sometimes. Banter, as we call it, gets flung from an early age. If you don't know how to handle it you'll sink. You had to have a thick skin when we were growing up. There's a special thing in Dublin, in Ireland, and that wit leaves its mark on us. But I'm cool wherever I walk in Dublin. I'm down with the good people and the bad people. Both sides respect you just being yourself. I don't take no shit.'

He laughs with the warmth of a man who has just spent an extra 20 minutes helping his gym kids learn how to grapple once their allotted hour is up. It's also plain that Holohan had a harder upbringing in Tallaght than McGregor did in Crumlin. 'But if you asked me to go back again, I would,' he says, 'because it made me who I am. I grew up in a council estate 10 minutes from here. I had a single-parent household, but a lot of kids I grew up with are also tough little motherfuckers.'

In contrast, both McGregor's parents were much more actively involved in their son's life – especially after they rescued Conor in the wake of a humiliating early loss. In only his third fight, as a lowly-paid professional, McGregor was forced to submit after a minute by Lithuania's Artemij Sitenkov. The shock of the defeat was deepened by the embarrassment of losing in Crumlin – where McGregor was such a big talker.

'I was there,' Daly remembers. 'Sitenkov is super-tricky and renowned for his leg locks. It was a fight too soon for Conor and he was devastated. He was gone for the next six months.'

McGregor refused to go to the gym and, as he told me in 2015, he needed his mother to intervene. 'My mother rang John when I was drifting. John came to the house and got me back on track. My mother has done so much for me. I can't even put into words how much I love her. I miss her and my father dearly.'

He was talking in Las Vegas that day and on Wednesday his parents will fly to the same city to watch his $100m boxing debut. It seems hard to believe – even for Tony McGregor. 'We'd never seen that business acumen a few years ago – or the showbiz persona.'

Daly also sounds incredulous when remembering how quickly the McGregor juggernaut has moved since 2013. 'It's bizarre when you look back and realise I was far more famous than Conor. If you thought about MMA in Ireland then you'd say something like: "Oh yeah, that's the thing the girl with the pink hair does." Because, in Ireland, MMA meant Ais the Bash or whatever my name was. I did all those TV and radio shows and Setanta Sports made a documentary about me that was shown repeatedly for a year. I definitely felt at the beginning Conor would look up to me in terms of my experience and maybe ask a question or be super-supportive. I was the highest-graded jujitsu person on the team and he was intrigued by grappling.'

Those grappling skills will be redundant against Mayweather – and Daly is more measured than McGregor's family when assessing the fight. 'I really do feel Conor has a chance. He's 29, Mayweather is 40. Mayweather retired two years ago while Conor has been training and competing all that time. He has been working towards this fight since last year and he is much bigger than Mayweather – and hits much harder.'

Holohan is more strident. 'I think Conor will win. Conor is going to shock the whole world. I don't normally voice my opinion on his fights but this is different. This is going against people who say MMA is barbaric – that we're uneducated and stupid. Conor will shock them all.'

When I ask Holohan if any of them mind not making the kind of money their former training partner is earning, he shakes his head. 'At what price? If you asked me would I take Conor's life tomorrow, I'd tell you no. It's a hard life. I could not handle Conor's life. But he can. And he can handle Mayweather.'

The next day, on the way back to Tallaght to see Hyland, I drop by the Crumlin Boxing Club where McGregor first learned to fight. Paul Hayden, one of the trainers, leans out of the ring in cheery fashion. His 15-year-old son William, with whom he has been working, has just won gold at the European juniors in Croatia. Hayden is a big, tubby man who loves boxing – and he has misgivings about McGregor: 'I don't like the vulgar or arrogant things he says. Would I like my daughter to be going out with Conor McGregor? No! But he's a brilliant businessman and a product of Crumlin Boxing Club – so we have pride in him.'

Hayden grins and explains how, in the early hours of Sunday morning in the club, they will screen the fight: 'It's going to be packed.' Does he want McGregor to win? 'Well, I don't like Mayweather at all. So it'll be bittersweet whatever happens. If Mayweather loses it won't look good for boxing. And if he wins a part of me will be sorry. Conor is from Crumlin. He's one of us and what do we always tell the world? You can never beat the Irish!'

Hyland is emphatic. 'Of course boxing means so much to me, and it did to my dad, but I'd love Conor to win. I'm flying to New York and then the day of the fight we're driving down to New Jersey. We've rented a house on the beach so we have a load coming over from New York for a Conor McGregor party. Some people say he's not a role model because of the way he talks. But the kid was on social welfare and had nothing in life. He had a goal to be a millionaire and a UFC champion. Now he's a UFC double champion and making millions.'

Hyland is a boxing man to the core but, even more deeply, he and McGregor are from Dublin. He smiles helplessly – thinking of their sparring sessions and exchanges following the death of his dad. Hyland says a few more words just before the boxing boys and girls burst through the door. It sounds as if he's speaking for all of them and most of Dublin: 'Conor McGregor's just an Irish kid, a boy from Crumlin, and he's conquered the USA. He can inspire anybody. He's an absolute machine. How can we not want him to win?'

The Mayweather–McGregor fight took place on 26 August. It lasted 10 rounds, after which the referee declared Mayweather the victor.

27 AUGUST

Statues are not the issue. These are 'history wars', a battle over the past

DAVID OLUSOGA

As a teenager growing up in Newcastle, I played a small role in a long campaign of attrition waged by my generation against the city council. Our single objective was to ensure that by the end of each weekend the statues of central Newcastle all had a traffic cone on their heads, or had been made to look silly in some other way. As well as providing them with traffic cone hats (the classic), we balanced empty beer bottles on the outstretched hands of those statues striking heroic poses. If that didn't work, we'd try wedging cigarettes between their bronze lips.

Each week, the council would remove the traffic cones and clean up the monuments. Each weekend, we would pour out of pubs and clubs and, under the cover of darkness, climb up plinths again and put back the cones, bottles and cigarettes. The statue to the great railway engineer, George Stephenson, near the city's Central Station, and much lower than most of the others, demanded less drunken climbing and so became our favourite target.

It was not that we had any issue with George Stephenson, or with any of the other figures from the past whom the good people of the city had chosen to memorialise. It was just that we instinctively found these memorials pompous, kitsch and ripe for ridicule and we revelled in making them look preposterous. Youthful disrespect, perhaps, but we found it amusing. Statues don't seem so funny now.

In Charlottesville a young woman was killed while protesting against white supremacists who, alongside groups of neo-Nazis, neo-Confederates and the Ku Klux Klan, chose a statue of Confederate general Robert E Lee as the rallying point for their gathering.

In the US and the UK, drab, grey monuments that, just a few years ago, we might have paid little attention to are at the centre of heated and angry debates. More than 30 US cities are in the process of removing memorials to the Confederacy, or have already done so. Each removal is accompanied by a policing operation aimed at preventing violence. In Britain, serious violence has been avoided but tempers have frayed and divisions been exposed over the fates of statues to Cecil Rhodes and Edward Colston, the Bristol slave trader.

Despite the anger and the violence, little of this is really about statues. They're the focus, not the issue, which is probably why Donald Trump was so keen to talk about them rather than his refusal to denounce neo-Nazis. This, ultimately, is a battle of ideas. It is a new chapter in what the Australians call the 'history wars' – political struggles in which versions of the past that have long gone largely uncontested are exposed and challenged.

As statues, along with the names of streets, schools and other institutions, have been one of the ways in which certain versions of the past have been given literal solidity and the hint of official recognition, they have become physical targets in a conflict that is otherwise about what is less tangible – ideas and history.

The great untruth around which everything pivots is the idea that the defenders of these statues are the defenders of history and truth; while those who want to see them toppled or contextualised are the Huns at the gate, who would destroy national histories and bring down great men.

As a result of this positioning, we're yet to have a proper debate about the contention that statues always represent some form of historical truth. Instead, we've had a torrent of near-identical 'where do you draw the line', 'thin end of the wedge' arguments, the weakest of which are so formulaic that they could surely have been written by an algorithm. The faux innocence of the writers of such pieces is painfully disingenuous.

Yet something potentially positive and significant is emerging because, as the new history wars play out, the defenders of statues to slave traders and imperialists in Britain, and Confederate generals in the US, might prove their own worst enemies. By choosing to draw their lines and make their stands around the defence of statues, they are accidentally allowing histories that might otherwise have remained hidden to be revealed.

Here and in the US, the back stories of the statues, and the shadowy organisations and individuals who paid for them, are being revealed. As are details of the murderous careers of the men memorialised in marble and bronze. The very aspects of history that these monuments were intended to conceal are now circulating freely.

By attempting to brush aside Edward Colston's pivotal role in the early decades of British slave trading and directing all attention on to his philanthropy, his defenders have protested so much and for so long that more people know more about Colston and Bristol's role in the slave trade than ever. By keeping the debate going, Colston's defenders have achieved what historians like me never could. Had his statue been quietly removed years ago, the ugly details of his amoral life would never have become so widely broadcast. A bigger cat is out of the bag in the US, as millions are learning that many Confederate statues, around which the neo-Confederates and white supremacists are rallying, are not 19th century monuments, but cheap, mass-produced, cookie-cutter memorials erected in the 20th century. Many date not from the 1860s but the 1960s, and are therefore younger than some of the white supremacists determined to defend them.

The implication in much recent reporting has been that, by becoming totems around which those white supremacists are rallying, these statues are being co-opted and misused. The truth is that they are performing the function for which they were erected. Paid for and erected by southern lobby groups, rather than local people, they were intended to reinforce white supremacy and shore up a romanticised and profoundly distorted version of the civil war and its causes.

If the motivation to build monuments to the Confederacy had really been about southern heritage, why did it take 80 years for the programme of memorialisation to get properly started?

If history was the driver, surely the south would also be full of monuments dedicated to the slave system that made it the richest place on earth in the late 1850s? If this was about history rather than racism, why is it that the only Confederate general not to have been honoured with such a statue is General Judah Philip Benjamin, the only significant Jewish figure to have emerged from the Confederacy?

What about their locations? The four Confederate monuments that, until recently, loomed over Baltimore – a city that was never part of the Confederacy and in which African Americans make up 64 per cent of the population – were never intended to defend southern heritage but to assert power over black Americans. The defence of history argument is bunk. The fact that Donald Trump has regurgitated it should make that clear.

As the genesis stories behind these statues become more widely known, the myth that this is about history and heritage is beginning to collapse. These statues have a history all right, but one that has precious little to do with the civil war and everything to do with racism, and by defending them that history is being splashed across front pages. This was not the game plan.

What those who are fighting the history wars from behind these monuments have in their favour is that most of us, for understandable reasons, have an almost instinctual opposition to the removal of statues; we flinch at the idea of antiques of any sort being toppled or removed. The stones of the past have become almost fetishised – we are roused to anger when developers win permission to demolish Victorian buildings and moved to sorrow when fire or flood claim a slice of the past. Far more shocking are images of deliberate destruction – the dynamiting of the Bamiyan Buddhas by the zealots of the Taliban, the destruction of parts of ancient Palmyra by the thugs of Isis.

But we are growing more sophisticated as we come to understand that not all monuments were created equal and that some were erected for cynical reasons that have little to do with history or heritage. History, after all, is a process, not a position, and it is not best written in bronze and marble. It is complex, plastic and ever-changing; all things that heroic statues are not.

Historians spend their days engaged in the literally endless task of reshaping and expanding our view of the past, while statues are fixed and inflexible. Whatever we decide to do about them, here and in the US, we need to accept that statues are not delivery systems for the public understanding of history and that some were principally created to silence marginalised voices rather than commemorate events past.

28 AUGUST

I'm turning 40 without a partner, children or parents – and I'm free

STEVEN THRASHER

I turn 40 years old today. If I live about as long as my relatives have, this means my life is probably more than half over. There's nothing unusual about turning 40; people do it all the time. But unlike many of my friends, I 'lack' three things at this stage of my life: parents, a partner and children.

That my mom, dad and stepmother all died when I was in my twenties doesn't exactly make me a helpless orphan. Still, I was much younger than almost anyone I know to lose all of my parents. It still makes me a little weird even at 40 to be nobody's child. But I am certainly not unusual in being single; most adults in the US now are not married. And not having kids isn't so odd considering my sexual history as a gay man.

But it is highly unusual to lack parents and a partner and kids at my age.

Judging from Facebook, I am also 'lacking' a lot of other things people 40 years old are 'supposed' to have – most notably a home mortgage, a car loan and pictures of my kids' accomplishments. I have none of these things.

Having moved to New York City when I was 17, I have never owned a house or a car. Not having financial dependants, and not owning big things, makes me relatively financially unattached, though not rich. (As an unmarried person and as a renter, I pay higher taxes; and as most American households need two incomes to get by, I have to work both of those jobs myself.)

Yet 'lacking' all these things, I am not unhappy – far from it – even though not being attached to the financial and relational expectations so many have makes me suspect.

Leading my unusual life at 40 has its perks. My life is interesting. I travel the world. I read, write, teach and think for a living. I get to meet people in jails, at academic conferences and in classrooms. I've experienced the uprising and the teargas of the Black Lives Matter protests in Ferguson, Baltimore and New York. I went to the White House correspondents' dinner with Gary the dog and his human, Carrie Fisher. I've hiked the Rockies, the Alps and the Himalayas and have backpacked in pre-dawn darkness to watch the sun rise over Angkor Wat and the Taj Mahal.

I even got to start a PhD when I was 37, which has let me head into middle age as a college student – and to do so with all the knowledge I wish I'd had 20 years ago, during my first time on campus.

My life is often fun, but I'm aware of how transient it is. Everyone's life is fleeting, but I feel that I might be more aware of the liminal state of life than some of my more 'stable' peers.

Still, I am far from alone. I have beautiful, close friends. 'Lacking' certain relationships allows me to be flexible and available. I can show up for my friends when they need someone – especially when they are getting divorced and need a place to crash, or when they enter a hospice. (I've gone through hospice care with so many people now, the end of life doesn't frighten me.)

I have lovers, meeting men in far-flung reaches of the planet, wherever our paths intersect. Sometimes I know lovers only briefly, but sometimes there's a spark to an emotional or intellectual relationship which may last for the rest of our days.

I have great relationships with readers and with other writers – and with my teachers and students.

Friends confide in me – sometimes about things they can't discuss with their own spouses. And despite not having my own children, I have relationships with lots of kids. (Everyone is always having them, so there are always babies and young people around to befriend.) Sometimes these kids can talk to Uncle Steven about things they wouldn't mention to their parents.

I get to commune with my siblings, and I got to be with my sister Sharron (who did not have a parent, partner or children either) in her final weeks of life.

And I have gotten to be deeply involved with religious, intellectual, spiritual and intentional communities – including a monastic Christian commune in France, those dusty Burners in Nevada, an annual retreat of queer people of colour in California and the American Sociological Association.

The depth of many of these relationships wouldn't be possible if I were in more 'traditional' relationships. But many of the ways I relate to others aren't highly valued by society.

This is bizarre considering that, as we hit 40, many of my single friends seem much happier and more fulfilled than most of my married friends. Many (not all) of my married friends, gay and straight, seem like they are stuck in a script they had to follow. Many seem to feel regret or wonder about what might have been.

This isn't true for most of my single friends or for me. We are largely still seeking and exploring (and often improvising) what the story of the script is. Opportunity still feels before us. We get to discover new authors and look at new art. And when Occupy Wall Street or Black Lives Matter or Hurricane Sandy relief or the Trump resistance need our help, we have more space to dedicate to loving one another, ourselves and our community than many of my married friends.

This freedom can create a sense of being unmoored, but it contains great potential. We get to dream big, radical political dreams and work towards making them real without worrying about a mortgage. We get to risk loving in many ways, getting hurt and loving again.

I do miss my parents and wish they were still around, though I am lucky that I get to write about them often. But since I can't wish them back, I celebrate the freedom I have.

I love that there will be new first kisses, and that I'll get to experience the thrill of touching someone's hand (or waking up next to them) for the first time. I love that I am radically free to spend time with friends in the hospital, and that I'll perhaps get to reunite with old lovers as friends or lovers once more.

And this is what I am trying to embrace at 40 – this sense of being radically free.

29 AUGUST

In Houston's Fort Bend County a furniture showroom becomes an unlikely refuge from the storm

TOM DART

Fort Bend County is a part of the new Texas: fast-growing, pros-perous, diverse and dynamic where it segues into suburban Houston – rural and traditional in its outer reaches. Hindu temples and Indian restaurants coexist with gun stores and ranchers in cowboy hats.

Now it is the scene of an unfurling disaster as levees are stretched beyond their limits, water spills from creeks and rivers rise from relentless rain. The area's population of 750,000 has either evacuated, stayed in place in subdivisions that are now islands or decamped for shelters that fill up almost as soon as they open.

While central Houston was hammered by tropical storm Harvey over the weekend, fresh visions of calamity emerged on Monday in the sprawling suburbs to the city's west and south-west, where housing developments and strip malls have ravenously consumed what once was absorbent prairie land.

Their proximity to the area's many lakes and streams was a selling point. On Monday it was an existential threat.

A northern section is imperilled by rain and controlled water releases from dams managed by the US army corps of engineers as they seek to dictate the flow into the Buffalo bayou and protect central Houston.

To the west and south, as far as 50 miles away – for this is Texas, and Texas is vast – mandatory and voluntary evacuation orders grew for Fort Bend County residents within range of the Brazos and San Bernard rivers. By Monday afternoon the list included over 200 neighbourhoods, many with blandly idyllic names – Pecan Grove, Avalon, Majestic Point.

Much of the Houston region's flood planning is designed for so-called 100-year events, which have a 1 per cent chance of occurring in any given year. 'A flood of this magnitude is an 800-year event and it exceeds the design specifications of our levees, and is potentially dangerous for a good portion of Fort Bend County. A 59ft-river level threatens to overtop many of the levees in our area,' Robert Hebert, a senior county administrator, said in a statement on Monday. The Brazos may not crest until Wednesday.

So where did hundreds of people go? To the store. Just off Highway 99 there is an immense outpost of Gallery Furniture, a Houston-based enterprise owned by Jim McIngvale, a local celebrity dubbed 'Mattress Mack' who has a penchant for promotional flair.

On Monday, it provided the discordant scene of the bedraggled and frightened fleeing an American nightmare and being cared for in a place that is a shrine to the concept of American exceptionalism.

It was at capacity and two dozen people and pets waited outside for space to become available. In the showroom, kids caromed off mattresses set up as a bouncy castle while flooded or pre-flooded adults lounged anxiously on reasonably priced settees.

Patriotic images of soldiers and battlegrounds flashed up on screens. Rain pattered on the glass roof of a vast central atrium reached by a meandering route between American-made furnishings, with motivational quotes painted on the walls. Beneath rows of American flags and a model of a spacecraft, men dragged mattresses into cubicles decorated with pictures of eagles, skyscrapers, rolling countryside and oil derricks.

Books, toys and food were set up next to cages containing a squawking keel-billed toucan and a hyacinth macaw, a few feet from a long pond where colourful fish swam beneath a green carpet of lily pads.

As workers directed logistics and handed out supplies, Gallery Furniture was less a symbol of American excess than a stirring example of the abundance of American compassion in the face of tragedy.

Charline Jackson sat on a mattress with her daughter and granddaughter. 'We were rescued walking in water up to our waist,' she said. 'I was born here close to 70 years ago and I have never seen anything like this in my life. Never ever.'

First they were taken away from home by truck, then they got on to a boat. 'Once we got to higher ground it was no longer higher ground,' she said. 'I forgot it was a street.'

Across the room, Don and Karla Biasiolli, married for 25 years, settled in for what might be a long stay away from Pecan Grove. 'Soon as we were told to evacuate, my wife said, "We're going,"' Don said. They live in a single-storey home that had not yet taken in water, but an inundation seemed likely and they feared being stuck there without electricity for weeks. 'Only three roads out of the neighbourhood and they're all about to be flooded,' Karla said.

Outside, Veronica Torres, her 13-year-old twins, Lou and Victoria, her sister, Carmen, and their German shepherd, Charlie, sat patiently – if a little uneasily in Charlie's case. 'I don't know if this is going to be one day, a few days or a week,' Veronica said, resting on a comforter provided by the store. 'We'll just wait it out.'

The family left their house as a precautionary measure and Veronica felt uncomfortable driving on ponded roads so decided against travelling far. 'I really didn't know where to go other than here,' she said.

Their home, 10 minutes' drive away, is 'right by the Brazos river. The only thing keeping us from the river is a levee [by] soccer fields.'

They took precious possessions upstairs, raised a piano on bricks, blocked a door with blankets and bags of mulch and disassembled a sofa.

'The water drains very quickly but I don't think it can drain that fast if you've got a river flowing into the neighbourhood. We just pray God will protect us.'

29 AUGUST

Why are the crucial questions about Hurricane Harvey not being asked?

GEORGE MONBIOT

It is not only Donald Trump's government that censors the discussion of climate change; it is the entire body of polite opinion. This is why, though the links are clear and obvious, most reports on Hurricane Harvey have made no mention of the human contribution to it.

In 2016 the US elected a president who believes that human-driven global warming is a hoax. It was the hottest year on record, in which the US was hammered by a series of climate-related disasters. Yet the total combined coverage for the entire year on the evening and Sunday news programmes on ABC, CBS,

NBC and Fox News amounted to 50 minutes. Our greatest predicament, the issue that will define our lives, has been blotted from the public's mind.

This is not an accident. But nor (with the exception of Fox News) is it likely to be a matter of policy. It reflects a deeply ingrained and scarcely conscious self-censorship. Reporters and editors ignore the subject because they have an instinct for avoiding trouble. To talk about climate breakdown (which in my view is a better term than the curiously bland labels we attach to this crisis) is to question not only Trump, not only current environmental policy, not only current economic policy – but the entire political and economic system.

It is to expose a programme that relies on robbing the future to fuel the present, that demands perpetual growth on a finite planet. It is to challenge the very basis of capitalism; to inform us that our lives are dominated by a system that cannot be sustained – a system that is destined, if it is not replaced, to destroy everything.

To claim there is no link between climate breakdown and the severity of Hurricane Harvey is like claiming there is no link between the warm summer we have experienced and the end of the last ice age. Every aspect of our weather is affected by the fact that global temperatures rose by about 4°C between the ice age and the 19th century. And every aspect of our weather is affected by the 1°C of global warming caused by human activities. While no weather event can be blamed solely on human-driven warming, none is unaffected by it.

We know that the severity and impact of hurricanes on coastal cities is exacerbated by at least two factors: higher sea levels, caused primarily by the thermal expansion of seawater; and greater storm intensity, caused by higher sea temperatures and the ability of warm air to hold more water than cold air.

Before it reached the Gulf of Mexico, Harvey had been demoted from a tropical storm to a tropical wave. But as it reached the Gulf, where temperatures this month have been far above average, it was upgraded first to a tropical depression, then to a category one hurricane. It might have been expected to weaken as it approached the coast, as hurricanes churn the sea, bringing cooler waters to the surface. But the water it brought up from 100 metres and more was also unusually warm. By the time it reached land, Harvey had intensified to a category four hurricane.

We were warned about this. In June, for instance, Robert Kopp, a professor of Earth sciences, predicted: 'In the absence of major efforts to reduce emissions and strengthen resilience, the Gulf Coast will take a massive hit. Its exposure to sea-level rise – made worse by potentially stronger hurricanes – poses a major risk to its communities.'

To raise this issue, I've been told on social media, is to politicise Hurricane Harvey. It is an insult to the victims and a distraction from their urgent need. The proper time to discuss it is when people have rebuilt their homes, and scientists have been able to conduct an analysis of just how great the contribution from climate breakdown might have been. In other words, talk about it only when it's out of the news. When researchers determined, nine years on, that human activity had made a significant contribution to Hurricane Katrina, the information scarcely registered.

I believe it is the silence that's political. To report the storm as if it were an entirely natural phenomenon, like last week's eclipse of the sun, is to take a position. By failing to make the obvious link and talk about climate breakdown, media organisations ensure our greatest challenge goes unanswered. They help push the world towards catastrophe.

Hurricane Harvey offers a glimpse of a likely global future; a future whose average temperatures are as different from ours as ours are from those of the last ice age. It is a future in which emergency becomes the norm, and no state has the capacity to respond. It is a future in which, as a paper in the journal *Environmental Research Letters* notes, disasters like Houston's occur in some cities several times a year. It is a future that, for people in countries such as Bangladesh, has already arrived, almost unremarked on by the rich world's media. It is the act of not talking that makes this nightmare likely to materialise.

In Texas, the connection could scarcely be more apparent. The storm ripped through the oil fields, forcing rigs and refineries to shut down, including those owned by some of the 25 companies that have produced more than half the greenhouse gas emissions humans have released since the start of the Industrial Revolution. Hurricane Harvey has devastated a place in which climate breakdown is generated, and in which the policies that prevent it from being addressed are formulated.

Like Trump, who denies human-driven global warming but who wants to build a wall around his golf resort in Ireland to protect it from the rising seas, these companies, some of which have spent millions sponsoring climate deniers, have progressively raised the height of their platforms in the Gulf of Mexico, in response to warnings about higher seas and stronger storms. They have grown from 40ft above sea level in 1940, to 70ft in the 1990s, to 91ft today.

This is not, however, a story of mortal justice. In Houston, as everywhere else, it is generally the poorer communities, least responsible for the problem, who are hit first and hit worst. But the connection between cause and effect should appeal to even the slowest minds.

The problem is not confined to the US. Across the world, the issue that hangs over every aspect of our lives is marginalised, except on the rare occasions where world leaders gather to discuss it in sombre tones (then sombrely agree to do almost nothing), whereupon the instinct to follow the machinations of power overrides the instinct to avoid a troubling subject. When they do cover the issue, they tend to mangle it.

In the UK, the BBC this month again invited the climate-change denier Nigel Lawson on to the *Today* programme, in the mistaken belief that impartiality requires a balance between correct facts and false ones. The broadcaster seldom makes such a mess of other topics, because it takes them more seriously.

When Trump's enforcers instruct officials and scientists to purge any mention of climate change from their publications, we are scandalised. But when the media does it, without the need for a memo, we let it pass. This censorship is invisible even to the perpetrators, woven into the fabric of organisations that are constitutionally destined to leave the major questions of our times unasked. To acknowledge this issue is to challenge everything. To challenge everything is to become an outcast.

2 SEPTEMBER

How a German river marks a cultural divide between east and west

PHILIP OLTERMANN

'Imagine Europe as a pair of lungs,' says Reiner Haseloff, the state premier of Saxony-Anhalt, as he stares from the top deck of a river cruiser at the winding waterways below. 'The Elbe is where the two lungs meet.'

The river that cuts a roughly diagonal line from the North Sea to the Polish–Czech border has been more than just a waterway for at least 21 centuries.

As historian James Hawes traces in a recent book, Roman emperors dared not venture beyond the Elbe and in the middle ages it formed the eastern border of Charlemagne's empire.

The Nazi party made its breakthrough in the conservatively minded lands of East Elbia and the Iron Curtain, which placed the river predominantly in the communist east, merely added a military dimension to a century-old cultural divide between the largely Protestant, eastward-looking Germany of the Elbe, and the more Catholic, west-facing Germany of the Rhine.

The country's federal elections on 24 September are likely to serve up a reminder that, almost 30 years since the fall of the Berlin Wall, the waters of the Elbe still run deep. 'The geographical centre of Europe lies east of the Elbe,' says Haseloff, a politician in Angela Merkel's Christian Democratic Union. 'Underestimating that fact is a problem that runs through all democratic parties in Germany, including mine.'

If Alternative für Deutschland becomes the first overtly nationalist party to enter the German parliament since 1961, it will be largely due to its success in the east. Averaging around 7 per cent in the old west in the latest polls, the party stands to gain between 11 per cent and 22 per cent in all eastern states apart from Berlin. Already in second place in Mecklenburg-Vorpommern, Saxony and Thuringia, the AfD has realistic hopes of replacing the leftwing Die Linke as eastern Germany's main voice of protest.

East of the Elbe, where the chancellor has scheduled a disproportionately high number of campaign rallies this month, is also where her decisions at the height of the refugee crisis have found their fiercest criticism.

A survey from April 2017 suggests social attitudes to the issue in the former East German states remain more in line with eastern European countries, such as Hungary, than with the western part of the country.

A ferry trip across the Elbe between Lower Saxony and Mecklenburg-Vorpommern illustrates the divide. In Hitzacker, a 16th-century spa town on the western banks of the river, the roads into the centre are lined with posters for the Christian Democrats and the Greens.

Straight across the river in Dömitz, however, every other lamp-post is clad in the blue and red of the AfD's election posters. The party, which campaigns for tighter border controls and wants to copy Switzerland's referenda-based model of direct democracy, managed to grab 20 per cent of the population's vote in state elections last year.

Hitzacker's social mix is unusually diverse for the country's most sparsely populated region: many middle-class urbanites who protested against a nuclear waste disposal site in nearby Gorleben in the 1970s later retired here among farmers and older landed gentry. Half-timbered buildings on the town square house an organic greengrocer, a homeopathic therapist and a shop selling ceramic flower vases that cyclists can attach to their handlebars.

Gerhard Harder, a former teacher from Hamburg, says that during the 2015 refugee crisis 'everyone mucked in. Some older ladies were literally fighting over who could take in individual refugees.' The only regret is that many asylum seekers have since moved away to bigger cities.

Such views are harder to find in Dömitz, which used to be the biggest port between Hamburg and Magdeburg.

The mayor, Helmut Bode, a CDU member and part-time driving instructor, says the East German state actively discouraged the social mix that marks out Hitzacker. 'The SED [East Germany's governing party] had no interest in making the border zones attractive to live in. The last thing it wanted was to have intelligent or creative people living so close to the west.'

Economic restructuring after 1989 left many of the town's buildings in the hands of owners who lived elsewhere and were reluctant to invest in their maintenance. One of the two factories closed down; the other downsized. In the last three decades, Dömitz's population has fallen by a third. A large shopping centre in the heart of the town lies empty and the museum has had to close earlier this year due to disrepair.

In 2015, Dömitz took in 30 refugees. 'Some of them were very educated too,' says Bode. 'But in the end they moved on because they couldn't find any work.'

Yet economics only goes some way to explaining the new cultural divide. Die Linke dedicates three full pages of its election manifesto to how it would bring about 'equal living standards in east and west'. Meanwhile, the AfD, which threatens to usurp it, calls for abolishing inheritance tax, one of the mechanisms for bridging the wealth gap between east and west.

Members of the party's eastern faction tend to emphasise a period in which the east used to dictate terms to the Germany of the Rhine. Thuringia's leader, Björn Höcke, has called for a revival of 'Prussian values', while the party's joint election candidate Alexander Gauland has suggested that Germany's policy towards Russia should be inspired by Otto von Bismarck, the Prussian statesman and first chancellor of Germany, who was born on the banks of the Elbe.

André Poggenburg, who heads up the AfD in Saxony-Anhalt, calls for a centralised education system focused on 'classic Prussian virtues such as straightforwardness, a sense for justice, honesty, discipline, punctuality, orderliness, hard work and dutifulness'. He told the *Guardian*: 'Let me make this clear: the AfD doesn't want a revolution, but we want a thorough reform to make Germany more suitable to the mentality of the east and the impulses that are set here.'

Opposition to such ideas, Poggenburg says, has to do with 'the strong leftwing movement', which 'wants to prevent anything that unifies and strengthens Germany'.

Asked what economic policies his party offers to bridge the divide between east and west, Poggenburg proposed that money currently invested in what he considers 'unnecessary projects', such as integration courses for asylum seekers, should instead be used to fund a new apprenticeship scheme for medium-sized businesses.

For Merkel – who was born on the Elbe but in Hamburg, the old west – one of the biggest domestic challenges in her fourth term will be to win back the trust of eastern Germans alienated by how she steered the country through the refugee crisis, including those in her own party. Haseloff, like Merkel a former scientist raised in the east, and once regarded as one of her close allies, has a line on immigration which is not always easy to distinguish from that of the AfD.

'If we care about preserving Europe's inner coherence, then we need to find a solution to the migration problem that guarantees a certain cultural homogeneity and doesn't overstrain the native population,' he says.

'And above all we need patience. The Bible says: God visits the iniquities of the fathers on the children, to the third and the fourth generation. Europe and Germany will need until the end of this century to eliminate the last vestiges of the old Iron Curtain.'

4 SEPTEMBER

Munroe Bergdorf on the L'Oréal racism row: 'It puzzles me that my views are extreme'

NOSHEEN IQBAL

By 8.12pm on Sunday, Munroe Bergdorf is done in. It is a week since she was announced by L'Oréal as the face of True Match, a campaign that marries makeup to social justice, and three days since she was sacked unceremoniously. A BBC2 producer is on the phone, talking to her about an interview with Victoria Derbyshire the next morning. 'It has been the worst week of my life,' she tells him, trying to deflate the tension with a laugh. Prompted to explain why it has been so bad, she reels off 'the death threats, threats of rape, threats of assault, people telling me to kill myself, the general bombardment and fear that something else will happen'. She pauses, then sighs. She hasn't left her flat in days. 'The most ridiculous thing is that you call out racism and they respond with more racism. It just doesn't make any sense.'

Bergdorf, a 30-year-old, black, queer, trans woman who models and DJs, is no stranger to abuse and ridicule. Her very existence is subversive and threatening enough to the mainstream that a trickle of racist, homophobic and transphobic bile has become par for the course in her daily life on and offline – but now it has become a torrent.

As the *Daily Mail* reported it on Friday, 'with a dizzying fanfare, she was brought in as the "face of modern diversity". But days after she was announced as L'Oréal's first transgender model,

Munroe Bergdorf launched an extraordinary rant declaring all white people racist.' The story went viral, reported everywhere from Al-Jazeera to the *New York Times*.

'I'm trying to think of the best ways to get across what I actually said,' she tells me, over a picnic of French fries and apple Tango at her kitchen table.

She explains that, the morning after the rally in Charlottesville, Virginia, where an anti-racist protester was killed by a white supremacist, she wrote a Facebook post in response to that event. 'It was an epic three-parter about how racism is a social structure and how, if this is the case, what can you do to combat racism?' She says the post was deleted by Facebook for breaching its terms on hate speech; the racist, transphobic comments made about Bergdorf, however, were left up. (A Facebook representative said: 'We haven't yet got to the bottom of what happened to Munroe's post', but 'we are looking into it'.) The post was then filleted for its most incendiary lines: 'Most of ya'll don't even realise or refuse to acknowledge that your existence, privilege and success as a race is built on the backs, blood and death of people of colour,' she wrote. 'Your entire existence is drenched in racism. From micro-aggressions to terrorism, you built the blueprint for this shit. Come see me when you realise racism isn't learned, it's inherited and consciously or unconsciously passed down through privilege. Once white people begin to admit their race is the most violent and oppressive force of nature on Earth ... then we can talk.'

Unsurprisingly, Bergdorf made some people uncomfortable, made some people cheer and pissed off many others, including her mother, who is white and reads the *Daily Mail*. 'That was an awful conversation. I'm half-white. My mum thought I was lumping her in with everyone, but this isn't about individuals. To understand my point, you have to take yourself out of the conversation – it's not about you – and truly think about society, structurally, economically, as a whole.'

But isn't that the trouble? Lots of people won't and don't understand. Not everyone reads Frantz Fanon and Patricia Hill Collins for kicks – academic theory will only go so far in convincing the average person on an average street that institutionalised, systemic racism is just as damaging as a violent, racist attack.

'I don't regret what I said,' she says, calmly. 'I'm an activist. Being an activist means calling people out, not just saying what everyone else is saying and what everyone else wants to think and upholding the common consensus. L'Oréal knew that when they hired me.'

This isn't provocation for provocation's sake; Bergdorf knows there is no time to pussyfoot until everyone else catches up.

'I can wholeheartedly say that the dictionary definition of racism was written a very long time ago and not by a person of colour. It doesn't allow us to have a conversation about modern-day racism. If you're not aware of it, then make yourself aware of it. Racism isn't just calling someone something, it's a whole system. If you think we live in an equal society, you're living in a daydream. You need to recognise that there is such a thing as white privilege and you can be homeless and still have white privilege, because you can still have a better chance of getting out of homelessness than a person of colour in the same position.'

Isn't the problem that the language is outmoded? It's hard to get people on board when 'racist' is a loaded catch-all umbrella to describe everything from unconscious biases in the workplace to US neo-Nazis.

'We do have the language,' she says, 'but it needs to be out there: unlearning, micro-aggressions, being complicit, unconscious bias, privilege – these need to be taught, we need to address why syllabuses only teach white history, we need to speak about slavery and the brutality of colonialism.'

Bergdorf's speaking voice is an even-handed murmur; she pauses occasionally, apologising for what feel like rocks in her throat. Someone she knew from university, she says, sold the story to the *Daily Mail* and bragged about it.

She deliberately hasn't seen friends or family since the story broke because 'I need to deal with it without being told constantly "It's going to be OK", when who knows if it will be.' Her flatmate has been around and friends have rallied, but, for the most part, she has been managing alone, without an agent or a PR. She has four upcoming campaigns this year; three of her clients have yet to call her to confirm that is still the case. It is irrelevant, she says, because her principles will always come first.

'My body has always been political – the way people respond to my body has always been political, whether or not it was about gender or race,' she says. 'I grew up in a white-majority area on the borders of Hertfordshire and Essex ... but I'm mindful of my parents and giving too much away; they're really worried.' She had a solidly middle-class upbringing, with one younger brother who is 'straight and super-woke and the first person I called'. Her dad is Jamaican and her mum is white English. 'Dad was tough on me growing up as a very effeminate boy, but we're very close now. Mum is feisty and super-successful, heading up PR for a financial company.'

Bergdorf was horribly bullied at her all-boys school and beaten up. She says the loneliness she felt through her teenage years was intense. 'I lived in my own head and in make-believe. I was obsessed with Cyndi Lauper – I still am. She gave me a lot of strength: that quote "On my darkest days I wear my brightest clothes" is still true for me.' We laugh – today she is wearing sombre, black tights and a grey marl top; understandably, she is not ready for dressing up. 'The mornings have been the worst, as my anxiety has been super-high and it's difficult to get up.' She shows me pages of abusive social media screenshots. 'I didn't get out of bed till 1pm today.' Isn't it a form of self-harm, to put herself through it? 'No, I need to know what's going on so I can feel in control. And I'm resilient: I worked hard at it.'

Bergdorf studied English at the University of Brighton. 'I guess I was genderqueer, but there weren't really the words to express my identity – I just started wearing makeup and heels.' A three-year career in fashion PR followed university before she 'crashed and burned'. When she decided to transition at 24, she also learned how to DJ so 'I could be myself, self-care and make money. Needing that time and space to yourself is why a lot of trans girls fall into sex work, because the process is expensive and the money is reliable.' She sighs. 'Trans women of colour are being killed at an alarming rate.' When she was transitioning, she says the average life expectancy for a trans woman like her was 30. 'At the time, I thought: "That's only a few years. I should be speaking about this."'

Bergdorf was raped during the period she was transitioning; she reported it to the police, but the attacker was never found. She took even more strongly to activism. 'It wasn't just standing up for rights that were my own,' she explains. 'Islamophobia, antisemitism, anything I saw that I didn't think was right, I would protest or post. I think that's the stance everyone should take: if white people protested and worked to dismantle racism ... I would have loved to have seen the reaction around Brexit from liberals with racism. If people rallied around issues that don't affect them as well as ones that do, we'd be getting shit done.'

Bergdorf built an audience – and influence – within the LGBT community, partially through DJing. 'It was the best investment. I was 25, got loads of gigs and it felt like it was what I was always meant to do. I had a lot of fun. I was a complete wild child and went off the rails and did all that rock star shit.'

Despite cabin fever, and stressful breaks to deal with her buzzing phone, Bergdorf is warm, smart and charming; on meeting her, you can understand how she has made the connections that have built her career. A shoot for a couture Lebanese Muslim collection was her first modelling gig; campaigns with Illamasqua and Boy London followed.

She was shopping on Thursday afternoon when L'Oréal called her about the story the *Daily Mail* said it was going to publish. 'I kept explaining the context and the full post and they wouldn't listen. They said not to go out and not to talk to anyone.' In a statement, L'Oréal said, without irony, that it 'supports diversity and tolerance towards all people irrespective of their race, background, gender and religion ... we are proud of the diversity of the ambassadors who represent this campaign. We believe that the recent comments by ... Munroe Bergdorf are at odds with those values and as such we have taken the decision to end the partnership with her.'

L'Oréal's key ambassador, Cheryl Cole, was found guilty of assault for beating up a black nightclub toilet attendant, but evidently that doesn't conflict with the company's policies. (Cole was cleared of racially aggravated assault.) Clara Amfo, a Radio 1 DJ and a L'Oréal True Match ambassador, quit the campaign in solidarity with Bergdorf, partially in protest at the hypocrisy of the situation.

'It puzzles me that my views are considered out of touch and extreme,' says Bergdorf. But it is an argument from which she can't run. 'I said no three times to *Good Morning Britain*,' she says. 'But then I thought: "This is what you're meant to be doing and this is a conversation that needs to be had. A lot of people are relying on you."' On Monday morning, her conversation with Piers Morgan goes as we discussed it would the evening before:

Morgan asks if he is racist, says he is offended at being considered racist or sexist and shuts down Bergdorf. 'The split between support and hatred has been about 50/50,' she says later that day. 'On the one hand, it's amazing, but it is horrible and awful to think that people hate me.'

25 SEPTEMBER

German election has redefined narrative of European party politics

JON HENLEY

After the Brexit vote in Britain and Donald Trump's rise to power in the US, pundits predicted that a wind of populist, anxious, resentful, anti-politics-as-usual change would sweep across Europe. Like a series of dominoes, the governments of the Netherlands and France – and possibly, if rather more implausibly, even Germany – would fall to the Eurosceptic forces of Geert Wilders, Marine Le Pen and Frauke Petry.

The heavy defeats of Wilders' Freedom party and Le Pen's Front National (now in deep crisis) in elections this year ended that narrative and swung the momentum the other way: in Europe, or at least western Europe, populism was dead.

The 13 per cent share and third-place finish of the far-right Alternative für Deutschland (AfD) in Germany's federal elections are a reminder that both narratives are flawed. Populism in Europe is here to stay – but evidently can be beaten.

Even Germany, with the weight of its history, is not immune. The context of its vote was, though, particular: it took place barely two years after chancellor Angela Merkel's humane but politically risky decision to open the country's borders to more than a million refugees and migrants. Nearly 90 per cent of AfD voters, who came from all of Germany's established parties and none (35 per cent did not vote in the 2013 election), said they wanted stronger borders and felt Merkel's migrant policy ignored people's concerns.

One of a string of populist parties across the European Union claiming to be 'the voice of the people' abandoned by a supposedly corrupt, unaccountable elite, the AfD would have struggled to clear 5 per cent in national polls without that decision. But populist parties have successfully harnessed the broader fears and resentments of discontented voters across the EU, and are generally performing better in elections now than at any time since the second world war. There is no reason to think they will go away any time soon.

The illiberal governments of Poland and Hungary, with their attacks on the independence of the media and judiciary and steady erosion of democratic checks and balances, show what happens when populists run the country. In Norway, the populist, anti-immigration Progress party is a junior coalition partner again after elections in which it won with just over 15 per cent of the vote. Populist parties are also in governments in Finland, Hungary and Slovakia.

Austria's populist Freedom party is polling at 24 per cent before elections on 15 October, on course to join a government led by the centre-right People's party – successfully rebranded the New People's party by its 31-year-old leader, Sebastian Kurz.

But as events in the Netherlands, France and Germany showed, populist parties – even when they have polled at or near

20 per cent, as the PVV, Front National and AfD did during their respective campaigns – can be beaten back. All ended up winning around 13 per cent of the vote. And even if, like the AfD, they make a significant electoral breakthrough, they are not predestined for government. If your support is based mainly on opposition, it has a ceiling. Populist parties also collapse more readily than others into infighting and factionalism – as the AfD appears already to be doing.

Nonetheless, as the Dutch political scientist and expert on populism Cas Mudde remarks, in an electoral landscape increasingly fragmented by the decline of traditional mainstream parties and the rise of new alternatives, populist parties, even if they win 10–15 per cent of the vote, can still wield considerable influence. In recent years populist parties have won an average of 20 per cent of the vote, often split between two or more parties, in elections in many European countries, Mudde notes: unprecedented since the war, but far from being a majority.

'Populists tend to ask the right questions but give the wrong answers,' Mudde says. 'They force issues on to the agenda that mainstream parties have ignored.' Liberal parties will have to start treating them like regular parties, he says.

'You fight populists not by ignoring them, demonising them or adopting their agendas, but by clearly addressing all the issues – including the ones they care about – on the basis of your own ideology. By making a positive, clear and convincing ideological case.'

Index